Pavan K. Varma was born   with
honours in history from St Stephen's College, Delhi, and then took
a degree in law from Delhi University. President of his college
debating society, he also won the Sir C.P. Ramaswamy Aiyar
Memorial English Essay Prize (1973).

A member of the Indian Foreign Service, he has been posted in
Bulgaria, Romania and in New York, at the Indian Mission to the
United Nations. He has been Press Secretary to the President of
India and the official spokesperson for the Foreign Office. He is
currently the Director General of the Indian Council for Cultural
Relations.

Besides *The Great Indian Middle Class*, *Being Indian*, *The Book of
Krishna*, *Krishna: The Playful Divine*, *Maximize Your Life*,
Yudhishtar and Draupadi, *Selected Poems by Kaifi Azmi* (tr. by
Pavan K. Varma) and *Ghalib*, all published by Penguin Books
India, he has authored *Mansions at Dusk: The Havelis of Old Delhi*
and *Delhi* (with Raghu Rai).

Pavan Varma is married and has two daughters and a son.

Also by Pavan K. Varma

~

Being Indian: Why the Twentieth Century will be India's
Selected Poems by Kaifi Azmi (tr. by Pavan K. Varma)
The Book of Krishna
Maximize Your Life
Ghalib: The Man, The Times
Krishna: The Playful Divine
Yudhishtar and Draupadi
Mansions at Dusk: The Havelis of Old Delhi (with Raghu Rai)
Delhi (with Raghu Rai)

The Great Indian
Middle Class

PAVAN K. VARMA

PENGUIN BOOKS

PENGUIN BOOKS
Published by the Penguin Group
Penguin Books India Pvt. Ltd, 11 Community Centre, Panchsheel Park,
New Delhi 110 017, India
Penguin Group (USA) Inc., 375 Hudson Street, New York, New York 10014, USA
Penguin Group (Canada), 90 Eglinton Avenue East, Suite 700, Toronto, Ontario, Canada
M4P 2Y3 (a division of Pearson Penguin Canada Inc.)
Penguin Books Ltd, 80 Strand, London WC2R 0RL, England
Penguin Ireland, 25 St Stephen's Green, Dublin 2, Ireland (a division of Penguin Books Ltd)
Penguin Group (Australia), 250 Camberwell Road, Camberwell, Victoria 3124, Australia
(a division of Pearson Australia Group Pty Ltd)
Penguin Group (NZ), 67 Apollo Drive, Rosedale, North Shore 0632, New Zealand (a
division of Pearson New Zealand Ltd)
Penguin Group (South Africa) (Pty) Ltd, 24 Sturdee Avenue, Rosebank, Johannesburg
2196, South Africa

Penguin Books Ltd, Registered Offices: 80 Strand, London WC2R 0RL, England

First published in Viking by Penguin Books India 1998
Published in Penguin Books 1999
This revised edition published in Penguin Books 2007

ISBN-13: 978-0-14310-325-7   ISBN-10: 0-14310-325-3

Typeset in Garamond by Mantra Virtual Services, New Delhi
Printed at Rashtriya Printers, New Delhi

For
SS, in friendship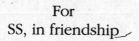

Vatan ki fikr kar nadaan
musibat aane wali hai
teri barbadiyon ke mashvarein hain aasmaanon mein.
Na samjhoge to mit jaaoge Ai Hindostan walon
tumhari daastan bhi na hogi daastanon mein

~

O unheedful,
think of your country,
calamity stares you in the face.
The signs of your destruction resound in the skies,
O people of Hindustan!
Understand, for if you do not, you will cease to be.
In the annals of history there will be of you
not even a trace

—Iqbal

Contents

Acknowledgements

As with my previous books, I have greatly enjoyed the process of research and writing. But there were some important differences. This was my first book on a contemporary subject. This not only presented its own challenges in terms of the source material and the need for objectivity, it also forced me to think seriously about some of my own views on a kind of life that was unfolding all around me. Secondly, unlike my earlier books, which were written as and when I found time from my preoccupations as a diplomat, this had an inflexible deadline, for Penguin had commissioned it as one of their publications for the fiftieth year of India's independence and now I have revised it for the sixtieth anniversary of independence celebrations.

Given the constraint of time, this then was the only book where I took advantage of some leave to write full-time for a couple of months. My study became my office. My wife, but for whose faith I would not have written anything at all, resigned herself to having a house-husband. My children took time to recover from having a father at home who had lunch with them when they came back from school. And my mother said that she missed the feeling that I was somewhere around when I went back to work. Needless to say, there was a general sense of relief in the Varma home when I did go back to work. But for me, when I look back now, it was a truly wonderful period, when the day had a rhythm of my making, and my pleasures had a simplicity and an autonomy so difficult to achieve in the humdrum preoccupations of office.

I owe a debt of gratitude to Lena, Nina and Girish who worked with me in Moscow. I am grateful, as always, to the Library of the India International Centre, and to those who run it, for invaluable help and support. To David Davidar, the presiding deity at Penguin India, who initiated the idea of this project, what more can I say than, as always, thank you. My thanks are due also to Ravi Singh of Penguin who worked with the manuscript in his quietly efficient manner. I have benefitted greatly from the many distinguished people, too innumerable to mention, who so graciously shared their views on the subject. Throughout its writing, my constant companion in my study was my dog Sultan, and I can never adequately repay his stoic loyalty.

Preface

When, in 1991, India embarked on a process of economic reform, opening up its economy and inviting foreign investment, the Indian middle class came into new prominence. There was much debate about its actual size, its consumption patterns, and the pace of its growth in the years to come. But in the general euphoria of change and anticipation, what seemed to have been overlooked was that the class in question was not conjured up overnight; it had a past and a history, which preceded its great discovery as a consumerist predator.

The purpose of this book is to try and understand this class; not only to map what it buys or would like to own, but to study how it has grown and evolved over the years. The work, thus, analyses the growth of the middle class during the pre-independence years; its progress in the first decades after 1947, when the memory of the freedom movement was still vivid and the Gandhi-Nehru legacy held many of its members in thrall; and its transformation in the years after 1964 (the year Nehru died) when, in tandem with the evolution of the Indian state, this class lost its innocence and changed in size and character. It is a study also of the inner landscape of its thinking and its behavioural patterns, of what it likes to believe about itself and what the truth really is. In such a study there is, naturally, a process of selection. It was not my intention to make a mechanical compilation of all aspects of the middle class, but to subordinate the choice of information to an analytical framework.

I believe the most important aspect of this book is the questions it raises about the future. Can India prosper in the long run in an enduring manner if the privileged sections of its society refuse to see any interest or priority beyond their narrow self-interest? The idea here is not to invoke some unattainable idealism, or argue the case for an unrealistic altruism, but to stress that it is in the long-term interest of the middle class itself to pause and think, and to try and develop a vision which can occasionally rise above the simplistic level of material pursuits. The argument is that to do so is, ultimately, a pre-condition for the well-being of the middle class itself, for no nation can prosper if its more well-to-do citizens actually think that the best way to counter the unspeakable squalor and poverty and disease and illiteracy of the vast majority is to take as little notice of them as possible.

It is also the argument of this book that this is, perhaps, the most important project that modern India must undertake. For all the achievements of the Indian State in the last sixty years, there is, for its middle and elite classes, a crippling ideological barenness which threatens to convert India into a vastly unethical and insensitive aggregation of wants. Moreover, the democratic process will continue to empower enough of the unwashed masses to make the secession of the successful unworkable. If the secession of the successful is not possible, then they must learn to so engage with the needs of the 'other' India, right outside their narrow little worlds, so as to make India as a whole a better place to live and prosper in.

In the course of this work I have deliberately avoided the not uncommon obsession with computing the exact size of the middle class and its precise income and consumption parameters. Such an exercise is better handled, as indeed it has been done, by market surveys commissioned by those who wish to sell or to buy.

The endeavour in this book is to overarch isms. The nation, and, indeed, the middle class, itself is tired of the deceit of ideology. The project here is the seemingly minimalist but profoundly significant one of the resurrection of social sensitivity and the arousal of social concern in the long-term interests of this class. No policy can succeed in India if this basic transformation is not attempted, and if the current withdrawal of the most influential segment of the nation from any commitment to community and social welfare is not arrested.

The project will not be easy to implement. But the difficulties cannot become an excuse to allow the present cynical drift to continue. There is too much at stake, including the very credibility of the Indian State. Small beginnings will have to be made. New role models will have to be found. A new ideology will have to bring together a coalition of the concerned. And, above all, unrealistic and uncompromising options will have to be scrupulously eschewed. What India needs is a pragmatic revolution, one which widens the middle ground between the mostly inimitable social activism of Mahatma Gandhi and the complete insensitivity to any social concerns which is the dominant trend of the middle class today.

Introduction

This book was first published ten years ago when India was celebrating the fiftieth anniversary of its independence. Now, when we are in the sixtieth year as a free nation, it is perhaps time to refocus our attention on a class that has continued to play a pivotal role in the making of modern India. India is evolving; it is a nation in transition, emerging from the shadows of the past to the possibilities of the future. There is a great degree of tumult and jostling as a country of a billion people and great complexities makes this transition. The middle class has been a key player in this process. Some of its defining characteristics are still the same. Yet, in tandem with changing India, there is evidence of change too. What are these changes? Are they significant enough to warrant a reassessment of the essential character of the Indian middle class? Or, are they merely a continuation of the attributes identified earlier? And, if in some way the class is reinventing itself, will its new avatar endure?

There is little doubt that the middle class has grown numerically in the last decade. The economic reforms of 1991, and the higher growth rates they heralded, benefited the middle class more than those below it. As the size of the economic cake grew, so did the jobs and business opportunities for middle-class Indians. The IT boom at the turn of the millennium was a sponge for the thousands of technically trained graduates produced by the expanding network of higher education institutions. This network, both in the public and private domain, had, of course, come up in the previous decades in response to middle class needs, in spite of the lip service paid by policy makers to the primacy of primary education.

Although the middle class has grown in the last ten years, it is difficult to give an exact figure about its size. To my mind, in the Indian context, anybody who has a home to live in and can afford three meals a day, and has access to basic health care, public transport and schooling, with some disposable income to buy such basics as a fan or watch or cycle, has already climbed on to the middle class bandwagon. By these parameters, the middle class could well be upwards of four hundred million: below the two percent of the very rich, and above the three hundred million consisting of

those below the poverty line plus the two hundred million or so who may not be destitute but are still very poor.

The heterogeneity of such a large swathe of people hardly needs reiteration. In 1947, the middle class, a creation largely of the colonial interaction with the British, was a small and exclusive club. This began to change in the 1960s and 70s, and more dramatically after 1991. Today the few members of the original club who survive would be shocked to find that those whom they thought to be far below their 'status' consider themselves to be their equals. Among the new entrants are the 'bullock capitalists' from the countryside, who husbanded their landed resources carefully and benefited both from state subsidies for agriculture and the Mandal reservations. Others include millions of shopkeepers, small time entrepreneurs, property agents, semi-skilled industrial and service workers, and lower level salaried households where the combined income of husband and wife generates a disposable income substantially greater than the pensions of the old guard.

But this heterogeneity, mirroring the expanding canvas of the economy, has also an easily identifiable underlying homogeneity. Almost every member of the middle class is a traveler on the same highway of upward mobility and aspiration. In 1997, the average middle class person was just about emerging from the shadows of the socialist era, and beginning to revel in the new consumerism that the reforms of 1991 gave both legitimacy to and opportunity for. In those early days after liberalization, his self assertive materialism was spontaneous but tentative. There was still a reticence in completely disowning the ideological imperatives of the past. The middle class could sense that its time had come, but was not quite sure whether it should say so emphatically. Today, that hesitation in pursuing the good things of life has been completely shed. Consumerism is no longer a dirty word, and any notions of Gandhian austerity and Nehruvian socialism have been definitively disowned.

To bolster this ideological shift, there is both more money and more of the things that money can buy. The country is united as never before by advertisements for an ever-increasing spectrum of objects of desire. The old notion of living within your means has been buried under an avalanche of plastic—the number of Indians carrying credit cards has quadrupled since 2001. According to an estimate done by MasterCard, by 2015 'the growing affluent class of Indians will spend $14.4 billion on shopping ($5.6 billion in 2005), $8 billion on dining and entertainment ($5.3 in 2005), $13.6 billion on travel and leisure ($3.3 billion in 2005), $8.9 billion on automobiles, personal computers, mobile phones, etc ($2.8 billion in 2005) and $6.4 billion on health and medicine ($1.8 billion in 2005). That makes it a total of $51.3 billion.

And as they shop they fuel the cycle of consumption, investment and job creation.'[1] With the economy expected to grow by nearly nine per cent this year, job creation could touch a new high in the years to come. Jobs in the manufacturing sector alone are set to double by 2010 from the existing 41.5 million; the IT sector, notching a 35 per cent revenue growth rate last year, will create over 150,000 jobs; and salaries in the corporate sector, already at unimaginably high levels for new entrants, will increase by an average of 14 percent, the highest in the Asia-Pacific region in 2007.

According to a recent study done by the McKinsey Global Institute, by 2025 the middle class would have expanded to 583 million people with incomes increasing by eleven times over what they are today. Arguably this could be a conservative estimate, because the Institute does not count as part of the middle class a group it calls the 'aspirers', even though it concedes that such people could spend as much as half of their income on purchases above the basic necessities. It characterizes two groups of consumers a notch above the 'aspirers'—the 'seekers' and the 'strivers' who, it says, will constitute the new Indian middle class. However the sub categories are defined, the sheer size of this burgeoning class is set to make India one of the largest consumer markets in the world. 'Within a generation', writes the Newsweek magazine, 'the country will become a nation of upwardly mobile middle-class households, consuming goods ranging from high-end cars to designer clothing. In two decades the country will surpass Germany as the world's fifth largest consumer market.'[2]

A great deal of compressed energy—far more than ever before—is a very visible attribute of the class today. At the core of this energy is a talent for entrepreneurship and ability for hard work that must have few parallels anywhere. Indians love the spiritual halo ascribed to them by foreigners, but are in truth among the world's most ingenious and resilient entrepreneurs, with their feet on the ground and their eyes on the balance sheet. Indeed, in the world view of Hinduism, Artha, the acquisition of wealth is among the four highest *purusharthas* or goals of life, along with *Dharma*, the obedience of the Shastras, *Kama*, the pursuit of desire, and *Moksha*, the path to salvation. There is no biblical injunction in Hinduism to the effect that it is more difficult for a rich man to reach heaven than it is for a camel to go through the eye of a needle. On the contrary, Lakshmi, the goddess of wealth and prosperity, is a ubiquitous presence in homes across the country. Not surprisingly, entrepreneurship in the service of material gain is an irrepressible Indian trait, and adversity and competition have only honed this talent further. The middle class always knew that India guaranteed the survival only of the fittest; the opportunities were few, the level playing fields fewer, and the people seeking the same breakthroughs many. In a world harsh to losers, the winning formula required an ability to anticipate opportunity, flexibility of tactic, a canniness to judge human needs and an ability to make the circumstances fit the need. A scarcity economy and shortage of capital had trained this class to be inventive about improvising on inputs and reducing costs. To this was added an ability to be incredibly focused on the results, often, if not mostly, without worrying about the means. The phenomenal growth of the Small Scale Industries in the 1960s and 70s, in spite of the asphyxiating regulatory controls and the depredations of a shamelessly extortionist bureaucracy, are proof of this entrepreneurial energy.

The remarkable thing is that this entrepreneurial feistiness manifests itself in a milieu where almost no coordinate can be taken for granted. The organized sector of the economy—

private, public and corporate—employs less than 5 per cent of the workforce. The overwhelming majority is self-employed, squeezing out an income in conditions of work that can hardly be imagined by a businessman in the developed world. In Europe, 90 per cent of the people work in the formal sector; they are productive in controlled environments where the predictability quotient is high and the safety net is visible. By contrast the 'footpath businessman' of India works on a razor's edge where everyday is a new challenge. The increased space for enterprise that 1991 opened up showed anew what middle class Indians can do if allowed to pursue their natural talent for making money. Many of them were first generation entrepreneurs, and most did not belong to the traditional trading classes—further proof, if any, of the commercial acumen of Indians as a people. The pioneers were risk takers. They had a sense of vision, a belief in themselves, and were exceptionally nimble in seizing the right business opportunity. In any assessment of the middle class today, tribute must be paid to the innovativeness, drive, determination, adaptability and risk taking abilities of a great many of its members.

Education was something the middle class always valued, but its importance has only grown in these last years. Traditionally, the feudal gentry had the insulation of landed wealth and the hereditary rich had money; for the average middle class person, however, education was the only means to move upwards, and maintain, if not widen the distance from those at the bottom of the ladder eking out a living from menial labour. Educational avenues had been increasing ever since 1947, but job opportunities multiplied manifold after the economic reforms of 1991, and the advent a little later of information technology. The current ferment of middle class India is testimony to this. Rigidly stratified societies generate intense pressures for upward mobility. When these pressures collide with opportunity, the release is explosive. At the turn of the new millennium, computer firms began to sprout almost overnight, and for once the government too was quick on its feet, investing in computer schools and training institutions and introducing and upgrading IT-related courses. Sensing the monetary possibilities, private training institutes began to proliferate. Overall today there are well over a thousand engineering colleges and as many institutes providing a Master of Computer Application degree. The country's nearly 300 universities and their affiliated colleges produce more than two million degree holders a year. Of these, close to 150,000 are engineering graduates, and the figure goes far beyond a million if the products of polytechnics are taken into account.

The middle class has put in a great deal of hard work to be a part of—and benefit from—this unfolding educational boom. For every seat in a technology institute there are thousands of aspirants. In 2007, nearly 300,000 students sat for the combined entrance exams for admissions to the IITs; only around 2000 were selected, less than one per cent of those who tried. This kind of competition could be daunting; it could lead to resignation, an acceptance of the improbability of success, a withdrawal from the arena of battle. Not so for middle class Indians. On the contrary, the competition has only accentuated the desire to succeed. Parents begin to groom their children from an early age for the struggle ahead. Families with modest budgets spend extravagant amounts on private tuition. Children prepare for entrance exams with single minded determination, and often the effort is nothing short of heroic. In my recent book *Being Indian*, I quote two examples, which bear repetition. Shatrunjay Verma, the 16 year old who was at the top of the two million candidates who sat for the school-leaving exam of Uttar Pradesh in 2003, came from a village, Bagula Nagla, which did not have electricity; he used a kerosene lamp to study and cycled 10 kilometres daily to school. The other example is that of Patwatoli village in Bihar, home to the backward Patwa (weaver) community. The hamlet is impoverished, and could be expected to breed Naxalites rather than engineering graduates. Yet, by the year 2002, 22 boys of Patwatoli, driven by the middle class dream, had passed the entrance exam to the IITs, and today five times as many have found placement in engineering institutes. The boys came from poor families. They lacked the money to join expensive preparation classes and were only able to afford books by giving tuitions during the day while studying all night for the exams. Lack of proficiency in English was a handicap, but one of the students confessed to going to sleep with a dictionary to add to his vocabulary! In 2007, Anupam Kumar, the son of a rickshaw-wala qualified for the IIT; his younger brother, Abhishek, is now preparing to follow in his footsteps. Santosh Kumar, the son of a landless farmer from Bihar, has also made it, and his younger brother, Saurabh, is planning to do the same. Santosh took tuitions in a nearby institution housed nondescriptly under a thatched hut but named grandiosely after the famous Indian mathematician Srinivas Ramanujan. It is run by a local maths teacher, Anand Kumar, who too qualified for the IIT but could not finance his higher education when admitted to Cambridge. Last year 28 of the 30 students trained by Anand qualified; this year he expects all thirty to do so

Not surprisingly, middle class heroes are self-made, successful people. Probably the most popular of them is Narayana Murthy, who qualified for the IIT in 1962 but could not join because his father, a government servant earning

Rs 500 a month, did not have Rs 150 a month for the hostel. In spite of this, Murthy went on to found Infosys, and is today one of the richest men in India. The middle class likes these rags to riches stories; it is appreciative of the hard work, determination and dedication of such people and covets the lifestyle of the rich; but it has little time for those who remain in rags. This, of course, connotes a serious limitation in its vision, given that in India almost one-third of the population is still very much in rags. The propensity to not see anything beyond its own interests, except to eye the perquisites of the very rich above, was the critique of this class when I wrote ten years ago. And not much, to my mind, has changed since then.

Why is this so? Why are most Indians so insular in their interface with society? Why are notions like community and the larger well being not wired into their psyche? In 1997, I was still an optimist. I believed that the middle class, which is so sensitive to its own self-interest, would precisely for this reason, realize that it needs to be more inclusive in its vision. The need for it to do so is self-evident. The question is whether it will. Some of this doubt is based on personal experience. When this book was first published, it created considerable discussion and debate, and I had a great many speaking engagements across the country. Everywhere the audience was attentive to the need for greater social involvement in a country where poverty and illiteracy and malnourishment were unacceptably high. But the same people who seemed to agree in theory, did very little to change themselves in practice. It was as if their personas were divided into two watertight compartments: one, at the level of theory, where they appeared to be malleable, the other at the level of action, where their behaviour seemed to be unalterable, as though carved in stone. One question that was asked very often was whether one person's effort would make any difference if everything else remained the same. My answer, that each individual matters, and that change is an incremental process, cut little ice.

Along with journalist Renuka Narayanan, I then published a book, *Maximize your Life: An Action Plan for the Middle Class* (2000), which we hoped would provide concrete and practical guidelines for socially relevant middle class behaviour. My argument was that ordinary middle class people did not have to become Mahatma Gandhi; his idealism and social sensitivity were of such a high order that it was difficult, if not impossible, for the average person to emulate him. The danger was that not being able to be like him, most middle class Indians had swung to the other extreme, where notions of public good played no role whatsoever in their lives. The challenge was to find a modus vivendi, a middle ground between these two polarities. Ordinary people, who had not opted out of society, or were not oblivious to the temptations of the good life, could also do much to qualify to be citizens and not merely residents of where they lived. To illustrate that this was possible I began to write a fortnightly column for the Hindustan Times, profiling individuals and organizations, who occupied this middle ground, so that they could provide role models for at least some in the middle class who wanted to do more but did not know where to begin. The columns, titled *People Like Us*, were later compiled into a book.

Maximize your Life did not set the cash registers ringing. In fact, of all my books, it sold the least. *People Like Us*, had a following, but was discontinued after a year. Gradually, but surely, I came to the conclusion that an active concern for the deprived and the suffering is not a prominent feature of the Indian personality. The rich in India have always lived a life quite uncaring of the ocean of poverty around them. In a country with one of the largest concentrations of the absolutely poor, the aspiration for affluence, as an insular goal unto itself, is universal; the poor are deprived but not different from the rich in this respect. They want to be rich—and why not—but once they clamber onto the middle class bandwagon or higher, they display exactly the same insensitivity as the rich to those left behind. The lush growth of consumerism that sprouted after 1991 was not only a middle class phenomenon—although this class provided its most visible expression—but was, in general, entirely in keeping with Indian inclinations as a whole. Though identified with a larger social grouping—kin, caste or community—Indians are generally incredibly self-obsessed, wrapped up in their personal world of loss and gain to the exclusion of anything else. It is accepted that people are born to their own destiny, and suffer or prosper in accordance with their previous karmas. Life is a continuing saga, and the possibility of redemption from want and hunger that the poor seek can await a next birth, with no need for human intervention. It is such an attitude that nurtures an inherent suspicion of collective altruism, and sustains the conviction that personal profit has ideological primacy over public good. Hierarchy is accepted as an essential feature of society; those below are ordained to be deprived, and those at the top are entitled (not without envy) to what they have. If the opportunity arises to break out of a preordained slot, it must be seized against the opposition of others, through individual effort, and for personal gain.

Given such a world view, the project of social sensitivity, whatever the sermons in its favour, seems to me to be seriously crippled ab initio. Prime Minister Manmohan Singh's recent call for greater social responsibility and the need to curb conspicuous consumption, received a predictably cynical reception. Some critics felt that the PM should have first given attention to the profligacy of the government and its ministers and minions before appealing to the corporate world, and they were not entirely wrong. But essentially, Gandhiji's original idea of trusteeship, where he believed that the rich could be motivated to voluntarily forsake some of their wealth for the poor, was, in India, a typical case of the messiah of the poor blinded to the real world by the intensity of his own idealism. The proclivity to pursue personal well-being with little thought for any other social priority is an Indian trait, and the middle class cannot but mirror it. In terms of realistic policy formulation the choice is thus very narrow. Socialism, or even a widely spread out welfare state, was always doomed to failure. And the only kind of capitalism that can succeed seems to be condemned to be socially insensitive.

In such a situation, the real curb to the middle class' callous insularity, is not the well-intentioned lectures of politicians, but the democratic empowerment of the poor. Six decades of the working of democracy has given voice and power to the unwashed masses; but for this, the successful would have seceded long ago in India to form their own republic. Reluctantly, and against its own wishes, the middle class is beginning to understand that in the India of today, priorities other than its own have acquired clout. For a class that has since 1947 played—disproportionate to its size—an exceptionally influential role, this is a new phenomenon.

Of course, the class is still powerful, but it realizes now that in order to get what it wants it has to compete with other erstwhile more quiescent constituencies. It is this realization that is forcing some of its more percipient members to begin to engage with society in their own self interest. The newfound activism of some Resident Welfare Associations in the metropolitan cities is a good example of this development. Some other areas of middle class activism are also in evidence. When a Trial Court judge acquitted Manu Sharma, the spoilt son of an influential politician, who in a fit of inebriated rage on the night of 29 April 1999 pumped a fatal bullet into the head of young and attractive Jessica Lal in the presence of countless people merely because she had denied him a drink, the middle class—perhaps for the first time in such an intense and pervasive manner—gave public expression to its outrage. The communications revolution proved to be a valuable ally in conveying its anger. Almost every member of the middle class has a mobile phone, or plans to acquire one soon enough. SMS-ing has become a very potent tool in galvanizing this class into collective action. The exponential increase in the reach of the media, and in particular the electronic media where the fight for TRP ratings can make one single issue appear to be the most important event in the destiny of the nation, is also a significant factor. For weeks on end television channels conducted 'public' polls on what the people thought of the acquittal; committees were formed to ensure that Jessica was not denied justice; candle light vigils were held in public places. Finally, the case was appealed in the High Court and the two-judge bench set aside the verdict of the Trial Court and served Manu Sharma with a sentence of imprisonment for life on 20 December 2006. The middle class had, undoubtedly, scored an important victory.

However, it is important not to lose a sense of perspective. Although the Jessica Lal case could perhaps symbolize the first glimmering of hope that educated Indians can break from their individualistic insularity towards conscious and collective action in the public sphere, it was still, in essence, a case of the middle class responding to an issue which belonged to its world and to its own well-being. Jessica was a middle class girl whose brutal murder sent a chill down the spine of all urban middle class Indians. The blatancy of the attempt to whitewash the culprit became a matter of personal concern, and it was willing to come together to oppose it. This was a positive development, but sobriety demands that we do not take a quantum leap in wishful thinking into believing that middle class Indians will react similarly to the dozens of rapes and murders and acts of collusion among the powerful that go unreported or happen to people who are not from its ranks. Even today, for every one Jessica Lal for whom the middle class so laudably organized itself into action, there are thousands of smaller acts of injustice, corruption and unethical behaviour to which it is a party, and mostly a beneficiary. In fact, where corruption is concerned, the middle class proclivity to express moral outrage about its existence in 'high' places, and be a party to its practice in its own world, continues unchanged. Here again, I have reluctantly come to the conclusion that Indians in general do not consider corruption to be categorically wrong. It is considered to be another instrumentality to achieve a desired goal, wrong if practiced by someone else and right if useful for oneself. There is a pragmatic acceptance of its necessity, and a benign tolerance of its practice, notwithstanding the hypocritical outpourings on the need to eradicate it. The only antidote to this scourge in our country, is, therefore, the neutral intervention of technology, and associated policy reforms that take away, to the extent possible, the role of human discretion.

One area where the middle class does seem to have changed is in its response to communal provocation. When the agitation against the Babri Masjid was at its peak in the early 1990s, a great many middle class Indians were effortless recruits to communal forces. Secularism was the official credo, but under its rhetoric was a great deal of angst against the perceived appeasement of the minorities, and this made for a great deal of private belligerence. Today, Gujarat notwithstanding, this class seems to have largely seen through the use or religion by political parties. Most of its members want to swim away from the islands of religious exclusiveness towards the dividends of the secular mainstream, and just get on with their lives. The difference in the way the middle class reacted in Mumbai to the bomb blasts in 1993 and in 2003 illustrates my point. In 1993 the explosions militantly polarized the two communities, and violence continued for days afterwards; in 2003, both Hindu and Muslim organizations strongly—and immediately— condemned the dastardly provocations, and Hindus and Muslims could be seen standing in line together to donate blood for the injured. Mumbai was back on its feet the very next day. The truth is that less middle class Indians are joining the RSS or the Bajrang Dal; and more Muslims at the conservative Darul Uloom at Deoband are studying computers and English, than ever before. Instability caused by religious strife militates against the middle classes' unwavering focus on upward mobility. Political parties have been forced to contest the secular ground to woo middle class Indians, and this is all for the good.

In fact, the expansion of the secular arena has spawned a pan-Indianess that has the entire middle class in its embrace. A great many factors have over the decades contributed to this: educational opportunities, job mobility, radio (including the new entrant FM) and television (including cable TV, of which there are millions of subscribers in the countryside), films (as many as a thousand a year, and, as importantly, the associated music industry), the growth of the market, advertising and consumerism, the growing circulation of newspapers (a national readership of close to 200 million), domestic tourism (over 200 million Indians are traveling around the country on holiday), instant connectivity over telephone and mobiles, and an assertive popular culture that alone can explain why Daler Mehndi's Punjabi pop albums sold a record number of copies in Kerala where most people had no idea of what he was saying. Consequently, most middle class Indians today wear the same clothes, eat the same fast food, hum the same film song after watching the same film, long for the same objects of desire, speak the same Hinglish, aspire for the same jobs, agonize over the same sitcoms, and, in general, have quite unknowingly become more like each other in an overt way than ever before.

This overarching alikeness—for lack of a better word— has diluted primeval loyalties but not displaced them. For instance, caste still retains its fealty but is no longer as asphyxiating. Matrimonial ads spanning several pages in most leading dailies continue to be arranged according to caste. But a greater number than before mention that it is not an insuperable barrier provided other factors (read money and position) compensate. Certainly, many more inter-caste marriages take place, especially in the bigger cities, and caste is much less a factor in employment. In the gradual conversion of India's salad bowl into the melting pot that it has become today, the middle class has undoubtedly been in the vanguard.

And yet, no one can be entirely sure what is cooking in this melting pot below what is visible on the surface. Signs of needed change are as quickly confronted by conventional immobility. The kaleidoscope is full of colours, but the pace is so fast that a definitive pattern is difficult to trace. In an urban scenario, where new townships with giant malls and offices come up almost overnight, and youngsters tired of imitating western accents stagger out at dawn from call-centres spread across the country, the personal world of the middle class is in a phase of transition where the past and the present coalesce in strange and unpredictable ways. If films and the media are one indicator, there is a much greater acceptance of sexual permissiveness; yet life-styles are still conservative and the tolerance of hypocrisy commensurately greater. Recently a provincial government sought to ban the use of vibrating condoms manufactured by a state owned company as being 'against Indian culture', but the leading dailies have columns of ads on massage parlours that guarantee anything a customer wants in the caring hands of Russian, Spanish and Indian women. Public display of intimacy is not an uncommon metropolitan phenomenon, yet rightist groups on occasion still make a fool of themselves trying to intimidate cuddling couples. More middle class women are going to college and taking up jobs, yet traditional gender stereotypes prevail, even among those who claim to be emancipated. Bright engineers in modern organizations like Infosys in Bangalore deny the existence of traditional hierarchies on campus, and accept them at home in dealing with their parents, wives or servants. A great many educated men denounce dowry in public and acquiesce with their parents in perpetuating it in private. Tradition and change continue to happily coexist in India, and the average middle class person is, in more ways than one, a good example of a harmonious schizophrenic. In fact, as I have argued more than once, the Indian mind is not a cupboard, but a chest of drawers: pull out one drawer and it could have a key board with a 21st century person's fingers on it; pull out another and it could be a ring for the same person by a quack claiming to be an expert on horoscopes.

Betwixt this change and stasis, a new barrenness is becoming a part of the middle class landscape. Old structures, like the joint family, are disintegrating, and new reservoirs of belonging and assurance are yet to emerge. Nuclear families living in the crevices of rapidly expanding and anonymous cities are still learning to cope with the sought after yet unfamiliar pressures of new jobs and lifestyles. There is the palpable excitement of new possibilities, but also a subterranean sense of alienation and ennui. A nostalgia for the predictable and less frenzied coordinates of the past often seems to constrict the surge of adrenaline needed to cope with the competitive opportunities of the present. This probably explains why in spite of the loosening hold of organized religion and ritual, there is a mushroom growth of modern day religious gurus competing to provide a salve to middle class anxieties. Several television channels are dedicated to their sermons, and the yoga guru, Baba Ramdev, has now acquired near iconic status. A frenetic entertainment industry is seeking too to fill the void, and the home grown imitation of American Idol—to cite but one example—had great swathes of the middle class glued to the idiot box for evenings on end. For families going through the more remunerative yet increasingly humdrum chore of earning a living, the world of glamour has also acquired—with more than a little nudging by the media—a seduction of its own. In all of this there is a great deal of cultural rootlessness and mimicry—witness the huge popularity of Valentine's day when almost all the teenagers I asked could not give a line by line translation of the national anthem—that seriously threatens to make the world of the middle class a derivative photo copy of the dominant paradigms of western culture.

As India appears to be finally emerging as a global power, one overriding sentiment that infuses the middle classes' world view is a new sense of pride. As the chief beneficiary of the economic changes since 1991, it is convinced that India's destiny is about to change, and that the country is at last set to get its due in the international arena. Unfortunately, this euphoria often tends to make it even less concerned about the plight of the poor and the deprived. The suicides of farmers or the squalor of the slums, the unsightly sight of malnutritioned children or the large numbers of those who still cannot read and write, have no presence in the neon lights of oversize malls and the glitter of new job opportunities. For this class what matters is that the economy is growing at a pace never seen before, that in many areas India's achievements command a new respect in world forums, that so many Indians have done so well abroad, and that the country is a nuclear power. To be fair, the middle class believes that is has contributed its share in India's turnaround, and deserves to celebrate. The average middle class person has, indeed, slogged to move up the ladder in circumstances where nothing can be taken for granted: schooling, water, electricity, medical care, higher education, housing—everything is a struggle. In New Delhi, for instance, uninterrupted electricity is a luxury reserved only for the very privileged. People consider themselves lucky on the nights there is only a short power cut! The next morning they wake up with a spring in their step, ignore the garbage around them, and get on with their lives. The city is short of drinking water by 150 million gallons a day, but continues to grow and prosper regardless. Three-fourths of its households own a TV; 50 per cent of the people operate a bank account; and there are more cars and scooters on its roads than all the metros put together. The miracle is that most people seem to be somehow getting by, and, in fact, planning for more as if nothing is wrong. Those with a fan think of buying a 'cooler';

those with a cycle dream of a scooter; those with a small car hope for a bigger one; those who have done less well live to make their children do better. In this unending cycle of rising expectations, adversity is taken in stride. The tribulations of today are tolerated for the rewards of tomorrow. The obstacles of the world are par for the course. And, the average middle class person, cocooned in the preoccupation of his or her world, deals with them with an insouciance and resilience and stoicism that is best summed up in a scrawl I once saw written behind a three wheeler in Delhi. The words of wisdom, remarkable for their brevity, simply said: 'Hota Hai: It Happens'.

Pavan K. Varma
25 June 2007

The Relevance of Beginnings

It was the night of 14 August 1947, hot, muggy and full of the dense moistness that comes with the rains at this time in New Delhi. It was not an ordinary night. For, at the stroke of midnight, India was to become a free country, putting an end to two centuries of British rule. All over the country, through its vast and sprawling plains, its verdant coastlines, and in the towns and villages nestled amidst its mountain ranges, ordinary people, largely illiterate, ill-clad, and mostly malnourished, waited with a sense of heightened anticipation for the fruition of an event long fought for and awaited. In the bigger cities, specially the capital, Delhi, animated crowds milled around, hugely excited by the imminent event. Again, these were ordinary people, aware of the momentousness of the event, but still a little fuzzy about what it would mean for them in real terms in the years to come. They were there to celebrate, and to hear their beloved leader Jawaharlal Nehru speak to them. And, at the stroke of the midnight hour, Nehru spoke. In English.

'Long years ago we made a tryst with destiny,' Nehru said. 'And now the time has come to redeem our pledge . . .' He spoke with passion and feeling and a transparent sense of destiny. He was heard in rapt silence by the representatives of the Indian people who had assembled for this historic occasion in the plush chamber of the imposing red-sandstone Parliament House built by the British. Unfortunately, the elegance of his prose and the content of his speech inspired only a minuscule number of Indians, mostly from the middle classes, who had access to a radio and, more importantly, could understand English. For, to the overwhelming majority of Indians, despite years of British rule, English and the way of life of which it was both a symbol and an instrument were incomprehensible and alien.

The question that arises then, quite logically, is why Nehru, who had spent a lifetime struggling against British colonialism, and who had, indeed, acquired the stature of an icon in the Indian freedom movement even in the estimation of the masses, choose to speak to them on such a momentous occasion in a language they did not comprehend?

The answer to this question provides the key to understanding the nature of the impact of British colonialism on India, the genesis and content of the Indian national movement, and the emergence, as a result of the interaction of both these processes in the decades leading up to 1947, of the Indian middle class.

The creation of a native elite in its own image was the most spectacular and enduring achievement of British colonialism in India. The intention to do so was stated without the slightest ambivalence by Lord Macaulay as far back as 1835. In his Minute on Indian Education, Macaulay said: 'We must at present do our best to form a class who may be interpreters between us and the millions we govern; a class of persons, *Indian in blood and colour, but English in taste, in opinions, in morals, and in intellect* [emphasis mine].' In a country whose culture and civilization was thousands of years old, this was an audacious enunciation of policy. But there were objective reasons why the policy succeeded beyond the wildest hopes of Macaulay. First, the British were ideologically convinced about the superiority of their own race, religion and culture. The civilization and culture of India may have been respected by the very early colonizers, but this respect did not last very long. It was soon replaced by the crusading zeal of a new British generation, weaned on the evangelical fervour of Charles Grant and William Wilberforce and the utilitarian credo of the Mills brothers. In the eyes of this generation, very much entrenched by the end of the nineteenth century, India was the dark land of heathens wallowing in a corrosive moral evil, hopelessly burdened by prejudice and superstition and rendered effete by its own social contradictions. British rule, informed by enlightened Christian values, was the only panacea for this benighted land. It was in the interests of the Indians themselves.

Such an appraisal was only to be expected in an imperial power, but significantly, and this is the second reason for the success of Macaulay's policy, the Hindu revivalist movements of the nineteenth century, led by English-educated Hindus from the middle and upper classes recently exposed to the New Learning of the West and genuinely appreciative of its emphasis on humanism and science, internalized this unrelentingly critical appraisal as valid. The prime movers of this Hindu social renaissance were motivated by noble intentions: to cleanse their religious and social institutions of the many corruptions that had crept into them over the centuries. But in so doing they essentially sought to gain 'respectability' in the eyes of the British and 'raise' themselves to better absorb the new ideas of science and rationality of which the latter claimed to be the harbingers. The most important of such revivalist movements were the Brahmo

Samaj and the Arya Samaj. Raja Ram Mohan Roy, who founded the Brahmo Samaj in 1830, was himself a great protagonist of English education. The Arya Samaj was less anglicized overtly, but even its more militant assertion of the Vedas as the sole repository of wisdom and authority sought to win the 'respect' of the feringhees by emulating 'the ideological and the organizational characteristics of Christianity'.[1]

Thirdly, unlike other colonial powers such as the French and the Dutch, the British followed a much more liberal policy of giving English-educated Indians access to posts in the administration. If it was essential to have a knowledge of Persian to get a job in the administration of the Mughal and princely courts, now it was necessary to know English to be employed by the Angrezi Sarkar. English was also a passport to enter the legal profession which offered promising opportunities to young men in the traditional service communities. Earlier the judiciary was dominated by British barristers; but soon a second tier of Indian lawyers, called pleaders or vakils, emerged, many of whom found both money and recognition by mastering the judicial intricacies of Privy Council pronouncements. 'The volume of litigation was rising sharply . . . owing to the new property relations which the British Government had established after 1857, and there was a great flow of legal briefs from the rural districts to the courts in the city.'[2]

The social segment from which these new beneficiaries came represented largely a continuity: middle-class Indians from an educated background, whose families had traditionally found employment in the government departments of revenue, police or justice. It is owing to this historical memory that the Webster's Dictionary even today defines a 'baboo' as 'a native clerk who writes English'. Relative to the people at large, who remained illiterate (not the least because of the conscious British policy of neglecting primary education in the vernaculars in preference for higher education in English), the number of baboos was small. But they were still a sufficiently noticeable feature on the landscape of the new dispensation for Bankim Chandra Chatterji to write caustically in 1873: 'The baboos will be indefatigable in talk, experts in a particular foreign language, and hostile to their mother tongue . . . Some highly intelligent baboos will be born who will be unable to converse in their mother tongue . . . Like Vishnu they will have ten incarnations, namely clerk, teacher, Brahmo, accountant, doctor, lawyer, magistrate, landlord, editor and unemployed . . . Baboos will consume water at home, alcohol at friends', abuses at the prostitutes' and humiliation at the employers'.'[3]

The important point to note, however, is that the members of the nascent Indian middle class of the nineteenth century did not feel a sense of humiliation in collaborating with the agencies of British rule. Indeed, it would not be inaccurate to say that they had acquired a stake in the perpetuation of British rule. They sought access to the employment opportunities it provided; they were appreciative of the civilizational values it stood for and envious of its material achievements; they hankered for social acceptance within the paternalistic framework it promised and were unashamedly emulative of the lifestyle of those sent to govern them. This is not to say that they did not feel the occasional sense of resentment at the British flaunting their assumption of racial superiority. They felt hurt when the British sahebs overtly persisted in maintaining their distance and separateness from their native emulators. Compartments in trains were reserved for Englishmen, and however anglicized an Indian may have been in deportment and demeanour, he was rarely allowed entry, even if there was no place in the rest of the train. Chairs and benches in public parks were also reserved for Europeans. But these were pinpricks, in the nature of things, to be tolerated, and in some instances politely opposed; they were not part of a larger social or political awakening which questioned the legitimacy of British rule.

And yet it is essential that we do not allow our analysis at this stage to become subjective or critical with the advantage of historical hindsight. The educated Indians of this period seeking to prosper under British patronage must be judged by the choices and options available to them in the circumstances prevailing then. Many of their reactions were in keeping with those of elites in subjugated countries, distanced from their own peoples, who are newly exposed to the political domination of an alien civilization that seeks to judge their behaviour by its own standards and values. It has insightfully been argued that the behaviour of such people is both imitative of and hostile to the colonial model before it. It is imitative because it accepts the superiority of the civilizational values of the alien culture. But it is also hostile because it incorporates a rejection, 'in fact, two rejections, both of them ambivalent: rejection of the alien intruder and dominator who is nevertheless to be imitated and surpassed by his own standards, and rejection of ancestral ways which are seen as obstacles to progress and yet also cherished as marks of identity.'[4]

This psychological penumbra between rejection and acceptance was lived by many members of this class, and the example of Motilal Nehru is an illustrative one. Motilal's early education was confined entirely to Persian and Arabic; within the home his adolescence was moulded by the milieu of a Kashmiri pandit family. He began to learn English only in his teens. The transition from one educational paradigm to another must not have been easy, for he never distinguished himself in his studies, and in fact never completed his graduation. However, he did exceptionally well in the High Court Vakil's examinations. (At this point of time Motilal was just another aspirant from a middle-class Indian family—the affluence and political prominence which would place him above this category would come later.) As a young lawyer Motilal made no secret of his rejection of many elements of his own heritage. 'He did not look back to a revival in India of ancient times. He had no sympathy or understanding 'of them and utterly disliked many old social customs, caste and the like, which he considered reactionary.'[5] On his return from Europe, for instance, he refused to undergo the customary prayaschit or purification ceremony and created quite an uproar in the conservative Kashmiri community by his aggressive and rather disdainful attitude to such ceremonies. At the same time, 'he was attracted to Western dress and other Western ways at a time when it was uncommon for Indians to take to them except in big cities like Calcutta and Bombay . . . He had a feeling that his own countrymen had fallen low and almost deserved what they got . . . He looked to the West and felt greatly attracted by Western progress, and thought that this could come through an association with England.'[6]

The formation of the Indian National Congress in 1885 took place in this context. The theory that it was set up by an Englishman, Hume, as part of a conscious British policy to provide a 'safety valve' to the rising discontent among Indians is perhaps untenable. It is also true that it did create for the first time an all-India platform to give voice to the opinions of Indians. Yet it was essentially an upper- and middle-class affair that did not seek to challenge British rule but to create a forum which could facilitate a dialogue with the British on such matters as the increasing participation by members of this class in the legislative councils set up by the British Government and the progressive Indianization of the civil services and the army. The method to achieve these goals was to be within the framework of the law, through constitutional agitation and the presentation of petitions and appeals. Jawaharlal Nehru has written about this phase with appealing candour in his autobiography: 'My politics had been those of my class, the bourgeoisie. Indeed all vocal politics then (and to a great extent even now) were those of the middle classes, and Moderate and Extremist alike represented them and, in different keys, sought their betterment. The Moderate represented especially the handful of the upper middle class who had on the whole prospered under British rule and wanted no sudden changes which might endanger their position and interests. They had close relations with the British Government and the big landlord class. The Extremist represented also the lower ranks of the middle class.'[7] Lawyers, as the most prominent group, but also those from the landed gentry, and some journalists and educationists from professions newly adopted by the educated middle classes, constituted in the main the leadership of the Congress; its support base was largely confined to the middle and lower middle classes in the cities and towns. The content and style of the meetings of the Congress was of a piece with the social background and motivations of the participants. Nehru attended the Bankipore session of the Congress in 1912 and recalled: 'It was very much an English-knowing upper-class affair where morning coats and well-pressed trousers were greatly in evidence. Essentially it was a social gathering with no political excitement or tension.'[8]

Outside the 'politics' of the Congress, the dominant theme was the opportunities of service and employment in the infrastructure of the sarkar. For those who found employment, particularly in the slightly elevated echelons, a noticeable feature was the manner in which they tried to model themselves on their English superiors. It is once again Nehru who hits the nail on the head: 'This official and Service atmosphere invaded and set the tone for almost all Indian middle-class life, especially the English-knowing intelligentsia . . . Professional men, lawyers, doctors and others, succumbed to it, and even the academic halls of the semi-official universities were full of it. All these people lived in a world apart, cut off from the masses and even the lower middle class.'[9]

The political emergence of Gandhi in 1920 gave, for the first time, a mass character to the national movement. Of seminal importance to our study is to analyse how this development influenced the existing hegemony of the middle class, its control of the content and formulation of policy, and the character and content it gave to national aspiration and politics. Hitherto, as we have seen, the involvement of the segments below the intelligentsia and the middle class, namely, the industrial workers and the peasantry—the vast majority of the population—was minimal. The Swadeshi movement launched in 1903, with its emphasis on traditional popular festivals and melas such as the Ganapati and Shivaji festivals and the use of folk theatre forms such as the jatras in Bengal, had taken its message beyond the frontiers of drawing room parlours. Yet its impact could not be sustained or go beyond the lower middle classes in the cities. The Home Rule League movement, led by Annie Besant, had also acquired popularity, but largely among the educated. The phase of revolutionary terrorism, from 1908 to 1918, was no doubt contributory to the growth of nationalist feeling, but this too was essentially a middle- and lower-middle-class movement and had spent itself out for the lack of a mass base. It was Gandhi's personal lifestyle, his identification with the poorest and the deprived, and the Indian ethos he conjured up for the articulation of his goals and ideals, which combined to win for him and the freedom movement, for the first time and on a generally sustained basis, the involvement of the masses. This mass involvement was more than evident during the non-cooperation movements of the 1920s and 1930s and in the Quit India movement of 1942. It was equally identifiable in the support Gandhi received for the charkha and swadeshi movements and for his policies of socio-economic reform.

Yet this populist transformation was achieved largely without any change in the entrenched social structure or the economic inequities in society. It thus involved the masses without empowering them. Through their participation the struggle for freedom acquired the profile of a mass movement; but essentially the focus of power and the control of policy remained where they had always been—with the dominant elites. This peculiar paradox of a powerful political movement against an external force and the absence of radical, transforming change in the internal domain is perhaps explained by the organizational strategy of mass mobilization adopted by the Congress to capitalize on Gandhi's wider appeal. In every area and locality the natural interlocutors for the Congress leadership were the 'dominant men and powerful social groups'; and it 'utilized their power, their influence and their commitment to nationalism to recruit new social classes and broaden the base of the struggle. Such a modus vivendi for the aggregation of an anti-imperialist alliance was productive of the most spectacular results so far as the mobilization of the popular classes in the cities and villages were concerned.'[10] However, 'such access to mass constituencies through the mediation of dominant interests' placed the initiative in the privileged and economically powerful. Hence, Professor Ravinder Kumar, the eminent historian, concludes: 'Indeed, there is reason to believe that by the 1930s, upper and middle class interests had crystallized within the national movement in a manner which ensured that the lowly classes, urban and rural, participated in nationalist agitations only under the hegemony of the propertied classes.'[11]

An entire genre of recent academic work, labelled as subaltern studies, which seeks to examine historical developments not from the standpoint of the elites who played an overtly dominant role in their unfolding, but in terms of the impact these developments had on the 'unseen' players, the masses, in the context of their own consciousness, only reinforces this conclusion. The largely city-based, educated, middle-class leadership of the Congress was self-consciously aware of the goals of the freedom struggle and its own ordained role in that process. The masses, particularly after the advent of Gandhi, were enthused by the concept of freedom from the feringhees. But within this broad area of congruence the motivations that animated the masses, and their perceptions of events and leaders, were often at considerable variance with the grand and heroic version commonly accepted of Indian nationalism. This distinction between 'elite nationalism' and the 'hinterland culture' is vividly brought out, for instance, in Shahid Amin's painstakingly researched study of Gandhi's visit to Gorakhpur in 1921. For the common workers and peasants of Gorakhpur district Gandhi had indeed become an iconic figure, but within the framework of faith, tradition and mythology. He was perceived as an avatara, an exalted soul in the Hindu tradition, whose darshan was an elevating end in itself and who could, in the tradition of mahatmas, even perform miracles. 'To behold the Mahatma in person and become his devotees were the only roles assigned to them, while it was for the urban intelligentsia and full-time party activists to convert this groundswell of popular feeling into an organized movement.'[12] This dramatic dichotomy in the level of participation was often transparently mirrored in the difference, in tone and content, between the editorializing of the English-language daily Pioneer of Lucknow and the stories surfacing in the local Hindi daily of Gorakhpur, the Swadesh. The significant point is that 'even in the relationship between peasant devotees and their Mahatma there was room for political mediation by the economically better off and socially more powerful followers'. By the same token, there was little room 'for the "deified" Mahatma inspiring popular attitudes and actions independent of elite manipulation and control'.[13]

Gandhi's most revolutionary contribution to the methodology of struggle against a more powerful enemy was his creed of non-violence. An instrument of action linked to a larger and deeper philosophical vision and espoused with the most unwavering conviction, it captured the imagination of the Indian people and on more than one occasion left the British groping for an effective response. As a legacy, it gave to the Indian freedom movement a moral high ground that has become its chief distinguishing characteristic. However, ironically, this strategy of struggle which succeeded so spectacularly in uprooting the world's most powerful colonial power was not the most effective in bringing about enduring changes in the existing socio-economic structures in India. This is not to imply that both Gandhi and his political heir, Nehru, did not seek to change the glaring inequities in the Indian social fabric. Their intentions in this regard are beyond a shadow of doubt. Yet the fact of the matter is that non-violent non-cooperation against the external enemy turned out to be non-violent moral persuasion against the vested interests blocking the desired change internally. And moral persuasion alone has rarely, if ever, succeeded in bringing about the restructuring of societies. Gandhi brought about the participation of the masses in the freedom struggle; but he did not seek, as a consequence of this, to dislodge the middle- and upper-class leadership of the Congress. His way was to try and transform, through the force of his personal example and the moral pressure that was its luminous corollary, the relations within the existing social structure; he did not wish to change the structure itself. His path-breaking struggle for the upliftment of the harijans has to be seen from this reference point; it is this same approach which renders explicable his concept of the rich holding their wealth as trustees for the poor.

It can also be argued that Gandhi was an astute pragmatist. His goal was the freedom of India and the end of British rule; uncontrolled social turmoil could have become a hindrance in the achievement of that goal. But, given his consistent emphasis on the definition of freedom being more than merely the absence of the British, this does not appear entirely plausible. The truth is that Gandhi was a reformer, not a revolutionary. It is not the purpose of this book to debate the merits of either of these stances. There are many societies which have benefitted from the violent social churning associated with revolutionary change, and there are others which have not. For the purpose of this study it is sufficient to note that Gandhi's approach to social transformation, profoundly moving in its moral sensitivity to the conditions of the less privileged and containing within itself the potential for far-reaching social metamorphosis, did little violence to the entrenched upper- and middle-class leadership of the Congress.

Even in an inevitably adversarial position vis-á-vis the

Congress, the British were, it must be noted, far more comfortable in dealing with the English-knowing, urban-centric middle-class constituents in the Congress than with the unwashed masses. In any case, the latter had no independent platform of their own. They were in the greater part both impoverished and illiterate and overwhelmingly subordinate in the social hierarchy—hardly in a position to be interlocutors of the British. As a colonial power the primary aim of the British was the perpetuation of their rule. To this end, they had in the past shown both acumen and agility. For instance, after the revolt of 1857 they had expertly shifted their patronage away from some of their erstwhile partners in the Muslim feudal nobility to certain elements in the socially inferior but politically more reliable mercantile classes. Conceivably, several decades later, they could have similarly overarched the Congress leadership to form alliances with segments of the sadharan janta, the common people. It would appear that they did not do this because they preferred to deal with the offspring of Macaulay's legacy. Here they were on familiar ground: these were people in their own mould, who spoke their language and were well versed in the niceties of British constitutional history. As a conservative colonial power the British had an abhorrence of uncontrolled social turbulence. The memories of the carnage of 1857 could never be obliterated from their minds. This dread—and the British realized this—was equally shared by the bulk of middle-class Indians, who, while believing in the liberal doctrines recently fashionable in the West, wanted change at a pace they could control. Constitutional protest, interspersed with the occasional phases of more radical agitation, always non-violent and led by their own ilk, was an acceptable strategy of political agitation, for it worked towards desired goals without the social upheaval that could erode the middle class' hegemony over events.

Gandhi was unpredictable; his methods and social concerns, his appeal to the masses, his alternative vision for India's development, even his sartorial preferences, were things which the British often found difficult to comprehend or deal with. But even he had his redeeming features; after all, he was well educated, had studied British law in England, wrote the Queen's English: he was somebody they could talk to in their own language. Moreover, his potential for political inflammability was circumscribed by his own choice of non-violent agitation. Of course, the British were themselves the first to recognize its effectiveness as a political weapon. But it was still preferable to the political violence and turmoil—as witnessed at Chauri Chaura, or as espoused by the fringe element of terrorists—that could result should the reins of the freedom movement fall away from his hands and those of his lieutenants.

If there was one person who was a consistent and perceptive critic of the upper- and middle-class orientation of the Congress, it was Nehru. We have seen his frank admission of his own class background and his dismissive characterization of the drawing-room politics of the English-speaking leadership of the Congress before the advent of Gandhi. But he had some basic problems even with the politics of Gandhi: 'For years I have puzzled over this problem: why with all his love and solicitude for the underdog he yet supports a system which inevitably produces it and crushes it; why with all his passion for non-violence he is in favour of a political and social structure which is wholly based on violence and coercion? Perhaps it is not correct to say that he is in favour of such a system . . . but . . . *he accepts the present order* [emphasis mine].'[14] And given that the social order did not change, Nehru could categorically state, as late as 1935:

'Most of those who have shaped Congress policy during the last seventeen years have come from the middle classes. Liberal or Congressmen, they have come from the same class and have grown up in the same environment. Their social life and contacts and friendships have been similar, and there was little difference to begin with between the two varieties of bourgeois ideals that they professed.'[15] Nehru concedes the entry of a large number of people from the lower middle classes, but his conclusion remains unchanged: 'Even so, the upper middle class was strongly represented in the Congress, though in numbers the little bourgeoisie was predominant.'[16]

If Gandhi, through the idiom of his politics, brought about the involvement of the masses, Nehru, at a theoretical level, was far ahead of his colleagues in emphasizing the need for the Congress to associate itself with workers and peasants and represent their interests in its working. He became acquainted with the plight of the poor peasantry quite early in his political life. Even then he could not but note how totally ignorant the city-dwellers were about agrarian conditions; newspapers had hardly a line on the developments in rural areas, and when they did it was more to voice the interests of the landlord classes. In his autobiography, Nehru writes about the travails of the exploited peasantry with a genuine sense of revelation. Being fresh out of England, there is, of course, the slightest trace of pardonable condescension towards the honest toiling masses. But his concern is transparent, and, specially after his exposure to the developments in the Soviet Union, this was transformed into a theoretical conviction in the relevance of socialism and the need for the Congress to give a more radical socio-economic content to its agenda. He saw with commendable clarity that national movements frequently claim a unity of purpose that seemingly transcends class divides. 'It had often been stated,' he wrote, 'that the Congress represented the nation, including every group and interest in it, from prince to pauper . . . But the claim is on the face of it untenable . . . It is true that a nationalist anti-imperialist movement offers a wide basis for agreement, *as it does not touch the social conflicts* [emphasis mine].'[17]

Nehru wrote and spoke, with embarrassing regularity for some of his colleagues, about the vested interests seeking to preserve the upper- and middle-class bias of the Congress at the expense of the interests of the masses. But, ultimately, his thinking in this direction remained without concrete follow-up, more in the nature of a conviction about what the Congress should be doing. Perhaps his efforts were not implacably resolute; perhaps the preoccupations of the freedom movement left him with little time for the structural reordering he desired; perhaps it was the influence of Gandhi, for whom he had unbounded love but with whom he also disagreed on several points of both strategy and policy, that made him temper his more radical inclinations with compromise and consensus. Whatever the causes, he remained a figure seeking to empower the masses but unable to fully act on his intentions. He spoke and wrote about the concerns of the masses, but less from constant association and more as a theorist dilating on the oughts, or as an 'internationalist' who, from his readings of Marx and other socialist writers, was aware of the historical imperative for his organization to be more attuned to the needs of the peasants and workers.

We see, therefore, that in spite of the politics of Gandhi and the intentions of Nehru, the middle class, and some elements of the upper classes, remained at the helm of the freedom movement. One factor, perhaps not as obvious as those discussed earlier, which helped preserve this social immobility was the growth of the communal problem. The British policy of fanning suspicions between Hindus and Muslims to divide and rule needs no reiteration. But the reason why this stratagem succeeded so spectacularly is that at the very outset there were elements in the middle classes of both communities who saw the possibility of personal gain in such a policy. It was once again Nehru, the uncannily astute observer, who put his finger on the genesis of the problem. 'It is . . . extraordinary,' he wrote in the 1930s, 'how the bourgeois classes, both among the Hindus and the Muslims, succeeded, in the sacred name of religion, in getting a measure of mass sympathy and support for programmes and demands which had absolutely nothing to do with the masses, or even the lower middle class. Every one of the communal demands put forward by any communal group is, in the final analysis, a demand for jobs, and these jobs could only go to a handful of the upper middle class . . . These narrow political demands, benefitting at the most a small number of the upper middle classes, and often creating barriers in the way of national unity and progress, were cleverly made to appear the demands of the masses of that particular religious group.'[18]

It was more than evident that both the Hindu and Muslim communities were inegalitarian, and each preserved an elite segment that was less than inclined towards a genuine empowerment of the masses and the inevitable socio-economic destabilization that this would involve. The conjuring up of an external threat to the community enabled these vested interests to divert attention away from pressures for the internal restructuring of their communities. The very process of a freedom struggle was unpredictable; it could, at any stage, trigger off unintended consequences, such as a questioning of the raison d'etre of the ordained order of things or the erosion of long-standing vested interests. The dangerously leftist critique of Nehru and Gandhi's movement to give pride and dignity to the harijans were pointers in this direction. But if the entire community could be perceived to be threatened by another, then any unrestrained tendencies towards internal reform could always be foiled by the need to close ranks in order to face the external threat. After 1909, when the Morley-Minto Reforms introduced the system of separate Hindu-Muslim electorates, the communal question had become a significant issue. This, naturally, consolidated the conservative, middle-class leadership in both communities and checked the forces of radicalization within the movement. Even before 1916, for instance, Motilal Nehru postponed the possibility of a break with the excessively moderate tactics of some of his colleagues in the Congress until 'some solution for the Hindu-Muslim question was found'.[19]

More than the sincere liberalism of Nehru, it was Gandhi's decisive contribution that postponed a flare-up in communal relations much before 1947. His basic approach was that the Hindus, as the majority community, must show a disproportionate tolerance and indulgence towards the demands of the Muslims. His unshakeable faith in the possibility of communal amity, and the force of his personality, kept the Congress in line with his approach. But there were some of his Hindu colleagues who always felt that this degree of magnanimity was misplaced. And the unstated quid pro quo that they extracted for going along with him was that he would use his authority to keep in check hotheads like Nehru from achieving their radical intentions with regard to the socio-economic agenda of the Congress. As Ravinder Kumar notes, 'the fact that the liberation movement was basically middle class in character and tied to the vision of a market economy probably fed into the widening gulf between Islam and Hinduism within the sub-continent.'[20] For, 'Only a radical national movement held the possibility of forging unity between different religious communities; and since the liberation movement in India was middle class in character, it failed to tame the monster of communalism.'[21]

And so the Indian freedom movement unfolded, increasingly supported by the masses, but controlled from the top by a group of people, undoubtedly patriotic, committed and sincere, who had similar origins, similar constraints and similar interests, and who genuinely believed in their historical destiny to steer India towards liberation from colonial servitude. It is important to remember that this class of people retained their pre-eminence in the freedom movement not as a result of a cynical or premeditated pursuit of power; their position was the consequence of a historical inheritance. They preserved and perpetuated this inheritance, but without the slightest dilution of their commitment to the goal of independence. These were by and large good people. Some of them, like Dadabhai Nauroji, had distinguished themselves in their rigorous analysis of the impact of colonialism and imperialism. Others, like C. Rajagopalachari, even when pursuing less idealistic or radical policies, such as opting to participate in the Legislative Council elections (against the inclinations of Gandhi, who wished to persist with constructive work in the villages, and the advocacy of Nehru and others for a boycott), remained convinced that their actions would help in the ultimate cause of freedom. Many were capable of great personal sacrifice, and some of the examples that they set became part of the folklore of the freedom struggle. But it was precisely for all these reasons, perhaps, that these people entertained no self-doubt about their right to lead. The societal structure thus remained frozen to their benefit in the very midst of the flames of idealism.

The Constituent Assembly met on 9 December 1946. It was elected on a severely restricted franchise of barely eleven per cent of the population of British India and the princely states. Not surprisingly, it largely brought together people from the upper and middle classes to debate and finalize a Constitution for independent India. Since the Muslim League boycotted the Assembly, the vacant seats were filled by nominating a group of eminent people. These were people in a familiar mould: English-speaking, inured in Western political concepts, and well versed in British Constitutional Law. Under the initial Chairmanship of Dr Sacchidanand Sinha, the Assembly began its proceedings by discussing rules of procedure in a manner that would have done the British parliament proud. In his inaugural address Dr Sinha first dwelt on aspects of Constitution-making in Europe and America and then thought it profitable 'to turn to some aspects of the question in our own country'.[22] When Dr Rajendra Prasad was elected the Chairman of the Assembly, the first seven speakers who rose to felicitate him spoke—in unintended tribute to that prophetic strategist Macaulay—in English. Khan Abdul Ghaffar Khan, who was probably less comfortable about shedding his ethnicity, or, given the remoteness of the region from which he hailed, less exposed to the impact of mainstream British colonialism, was the first delegate to express his felicitations in Hindustani.

The important point is that none of the members of the Assembly believed for a moment that their vision of India could in any way be at variance with what the rest of the Indians wanted. The Assembly was the end product of a historical process which had created a certain class of people, largely homogenous in their conditioning, exposure and thinking, who had never been seriously challenged in acting on behalf of the Indian people. The fact that they were elected on a limited franchise, or came largely from a privileged background, never corroded their confidence in the pureness of their intentions or their ability to draw up the political edifice of independent India. Their conclusion was, of course, a foregone one. As K.M. Munshi, one of the nominated luminaries to the Assembly, confessed: 'Most of us have looked up to the British model as the best . . . why should we go back upon the tradition that has been built for over a hundred years and buy a novel experience?'[23]

Today, with the hindsight of sixty years, there are many voices which have questioned the decision of the Assembly to opt for the Westminster model for India. It is not the intention here to go into the merits of this debate except to highlight how smoothly—without any substantive opposition—this decision was taken by the Assembly. And the reasons for this are not difficult to understand. The upper- and middle-class elite which the British had helped create in India in their own image could not so easily wrench itself away from the ideological umbilical cord with the 'mother' country. This was not peculiar to India's colonial experience: former American colonies, for instance, opted for the presidential system. But in India the outcome was more predictable. For, 'in no other colony did there develop such a large stratum of urban professionals steeped for the most part in the values of bourgeois liberalism. This educated middle-class elite, which provided all the leaders of the National Movement, came to oppose British rule in the name of the most advanced bourgeois democracy, represented by Britain itself.'[24]

Nehru had said quite bluntly that the Constituent Assembly was not a revolutionary body. He had also expressed the hope that perhaps at a later stage a more representative body would be convened to write a Constitution more in consonance with the needs of the people of India. But this sentiment, along with many of his other radical intentions, remained in the nature of a critique, not a basis for action. In his autobiography he argues for the creation of an altogether new state, a root and branch change. And he is ruthlessly critical of some of the elements in the middle-class condominium at the helm of affairs. 'There is a great deal of talk of safeguards in these days of constitution-making,' he wrote. 'If these safeguards are to be in the interests of India, they should lay down, among other things, that *the ICS and similar services should cease to exist* [emphasis mine], in their present form and with the power and privileges they possess, and should have nothing to do with the new constitution.'[25] He is equally forthright on the question of the English language. 'Some people imagine that English is likely to become the lingua franca of India. That seems to me a fantastic conception, except in respect of a handful of upper-class intelligentsia. It has no relation to the problem of mass education and culture. It may be . . . that English will become increasingly a language used for technical, scientific and business communications, and especially for international contacts . . . but if we are to have a balanced view of the world we must not confine ourselves to English spectacles.'[26]

Nehru wrote these lines in the 1930s. Perhaps if Independence had come then, when his views had a nascent intensity, he would have done more to implement his ideas. But by 1947 he was older, more pragmatic and more constrained by the moderating responsibilities of leadership. The imminence of Independence and, most importantly, the events leading to the unprecedented trauma of Partition left him or the freedom movement with little time to consider or pursue ideas for the empowerment of the masses—ideas that existed, at least in theory, as part of the Congress agenda.

Some of the peasant agitations of the 40s, and the greater
incidence of workers' protests just before 1947, were
significant pointers to areas of policy-making which would
require attention. But these could be taken up after
Independence. The immediate goal was to ensure the end of
British rule and preserve the unity of India.

The increasing communal strife preceding 1947 also almost
overwhelmed the voice of Gandhi, the one man who had
given to the national movement an idiom comprehensible to
the masses. As we have seen, Gandhi did not seek a radical
realtering of the existing social structure, but his was an
extremely powerful voice of exhortation in favour of the
needs of the deprived. He did not seek to dispossess the
privileged; but he never failed to urge this segment to look
beyond its interests and devote itself to the needs of the vast
numbers of the poor and destitute. His own example proved
quite transparently that he judged the worth of the privileged
by their ability to be sensitive to the conditions of the
impoverished and exploited masses. But the gathering clouds
of communal violence deluged his appeals for social
concern—a few days before Independence he was in a Muslim
house in Beliaghata, one of Calcutta's poorest quarters,
seeking to douse the flames of Hindu-Muslim violence. In
spite of the immediate task at hand, however, his commitment
to the long-term goal never left him.

When the ministers of the West Bengal government called
on him on Independence Day, his advice was: 'Beware of
power; power corrupts . . . Do not let yourselves be entrapped
by its pomp and pageantry. *Remember, you are in office to
serve the poor in India's villages* [emphasis mine].'[27] And just a
few days later, he wrote the following lines for an unknown
visitor: 'I will give you a talisman. Whenever you are in doubt,
or when the self becomes too much with you, apply the

following test. Recall the face of the poorest and the weakest man whom you may have seen, and ask yourself if the step you contemplate is going to be of any use to him. Will he gain anything by it? Will it restore him to a control over his own life and destiny? In other words, will it lead to swaraj for the hungry and spiritually starving millions? Then you will find your doubts and your self melting away.'[28]

It was a powerful test, given with the utmost sincerity. It would remain a valid reference point to judge the behaviour of the Indian middle class during the freedom movement and, far more significantly, in the decades to follow 1947.

But on that hot and muggy night of 14 August 1947, there was a genuine sense of jubilation among all Indians—rich or privileged, poor or weak. The achievement of freedom and the end of British rule was a victory important in itself. It was a transcendent moment uniting all of India in triumph. And yet, when at the stroke of the midnight hour Nehru spoke his famous lines about India's tryst with destiny, his words had a special meaning for the educated few, who had not only been witness to or participated in the drama of the national movement, but had given it its ideology and direction as well. The rest of India did indeed awake to hope and freedom, but it were the middle and upper classes that fully understood the real meaning of the end of colonial rule in the context of the prospects that had opened up for the direct assumption of power. For it was the middle class, above all, which enjoyed 'the crucial advantage of affiliation with a "world consciousness", thus having access to vastly superior ideological resources for running the machineries of a "modern" state'.[29] On 15 August 1947 the bells of freedom tolled for all Indians, but they tolled specially for those who inherited the paraphernalia of giving shape to independent India.

The Age of Hope

Freedom came in 1947, but the nature of the entrenchment of the middle and upper classes under British rule, and their leadership of the freedom movement, ensured that the institutions built up during the colonial era remained largely intact. There was an Indianization of the apparatus of governance, but the apparatus itself was adopted with few, if any, changes. The newly anointed Indian head of state, Governor-General C. Rajagopalachari, moved into the newly vacated Vice-Regal Lodge. Prime Minister Nehru took residence in the palatial premises of the former Commander-in-Chief of the British Army. A parliamentary form of government, patterned overwhelmingly on the British system, was in the making in Parliament House. The Indian Civil Service, that pinnacle of middle-class aspiration, was retained in spite of the trenchant criticism by Nehru just a decade ago. The mode of selection to the ICS and the other administrative services remained the same as during the Raj. The judicial structure as evolved under British rule continued. The armed forces preserved their British traditions and hierarchies without modification. The education system and its syllabi saw no substantial change until many years later. And English retained its primacy as the language of usage in government and in the echelons of society which mattered.

This continuity, both in form and substance, in spite of such a significant rupture with the past in terms of the end of colonial rule, is not difficult to understand if seen from the point of view of what the Indian middle classes expected from Independence. Their aim was the end of British rule. In this respect their outlook was unhesitatingly anti-colonial. But political independence meant the absence of the British. It did not mean a jolting discontinuity which would end a system of governance, or jeopardize a socio-economic matrix in which the middle classes had acquired a stake. This commitment to the existing order of things sans the British, or to put the same thing differently, this aversion to drastic or uncontrolled change, was not without some redeeming aspects. In the years leading to independence, 'it helped galvanize social energies of the people to fight against foreign rule without maximizing internal schisms.'[1] In the years after independence, 'it insulated the fragile institutional structure of democracy from being overwhelmed by the populist pressures released during the independence movement.'[2]

There are no accurate figures for the numerical strength of the middle class in 1947. It would, however, be accurate to say that in relation to the absolute numbers of the poor, it was a minority not exceeding ten per cent of the population. Like middle classes in other societies it was not an undifferentiated monolith. It had its unifying features, both in ideology and aspirations, but within this broadly defining framework it had its segmentations in terms of income, occupation and education. Apart from the vast majority of the agricultural poor, it did not include unskilled and semi-skilled manual workers, skilled manual workers, petty clerks and employees such as postmen, constables, soldiers, peons, etc. At the other end of the scale it excluded the rich industrialists and capitalists, the very big zamindars and taluqdars, and members of the princely families. In between these areas of exclusion, its main adherents came from those in government service, qualified professionals such as doctors, engineers and lawyers, business entrepreneurs and the more well-to-do traders, teachers in schools in the bigger cities and in the institutes of higher education, journalists, the partially or fully educated among the middle-level peasantry, the white-collar salariat in the private sector, legislators, and a substantial section of university students.

The upper castes dominated the Indian middle class. Prominent among its members were Punjabi Khatris, Kashmiri Pandits and South-Indian Brahmins. Then there were the 'traditional urban-oriented professional castes such as the Nagars of Gujarat, the Chitpawans and the CKPs (Chandrasenya Kayastha Prabhus) of Maharashtra and the Kayasthas of North India.'[3] Also included were the 'old elite groups which emerged during the colonial rule: the Probasi and Bhadralog Bengalis, the Parsis, and the upper crusts of the Muslim and Christian communities.'[4] Education was a common thread that bound together this pan-Indian elite. The kind of education varied. Some, belonging to the upper spectrum of the class, had their higher education in England. But almost all its members spoke and wrote English, and had had some higher education beyond school. Income was another distinguishing factor. Here again there were variations. Given the price levels and the perception of needs in those days, anything in a broad income band from Rs 1200 to Rs 12000 per annum was sufficient to entitle one to membership of the class. But, objective criteria apart, what gave the Indian middle class a unifying and distinctive feature then was a certain commonality of approach and thinking, an attitude towards the nation and society, a sense of idealism and high-minded purpose transcending purely individual concerns. In short, an ideological framework to which it owed allegiance.

Conventional theory attributes to the middle class qualities of balance, prudence and stability. This point of view was probably first articulated by Aristotle who said that 'the best political community is formed by citizens of the middle class.' Aristotle argued that the middle class does not, unlike the poor, covet its neighbours' goods, and others do not covet its assets. That state is good, Aristotle asserted, where the citizens have a moderate and sufficient property. But the good Greek thinker, whose views have been somewhat uncritically subscribed to through the ages—for obvious reasons—by members of the middle class itself, also said that the positive features of the class are in evidence where it is the largest and the strongest class, or at least where it is large enough numerically to provide a moderating ballast to society. Where the middle class is sizable the state is likely to be well administered and free from factions and dissensions. But in India, in 1947, the middle class was a small percentage of the population. Above it were a handful of the very rich capitalists, or members of the hereditary aristocracy, and below it the vast majority of the unempowered peasantry and workers. From where then did this class, which had for decades enjoyed a power and influence disproportionate to its size, get for itself, in the years just after Independence, an ideological framework that combined elements of a respect for ethics, social sensitivity, self restraint and idealism?

The answer to this question is important in distinguishing the different behavioral patterns of the middle class in the sixty years since Independence. It is important also in highlighting a very important insight into the psyche of this class in societies which have recently emerged from colonialism with very wide economic and social disparities, a disrupted indigenous tradition of social sensitivity, and an inability to act collectively action except against the external enemy, viz, the colonial power. In such societies, once the external enemy is vanquished the nascent middle class, in spite of the qualities generally ascribed to it in conventional theory, is incapable of evolving a paradigm of conduct from within itself. In order for it to have ideological mooring, there must exist, outside and above it, an ideological inheritance powerful enough to hold it in thrall. If such a legacy exists, the middle class, like litmus, will absorb it. If it does not, members of this class will run amok in the individual pursuit of the many new opportunities for self gratification, unrestrained by the tempering influence of a larger or ennobling cause.

Fortunately for the middle class in India, the freedom movement had generated a powerful ethical and intellectual legacy quite distinct from the anti-colonialism inherent in a liberation movement. This legacy was symbolized in the compellingly charismatic personalities of Gandhi and Nehru. For the educated Indian, Gandhi stood for the pursuit of morality as an absolute end in itself. His consistent stress on the means being as important as the end and his emphasis on uncompromising probity in public life were internalized by the middle class as an imperative, valid not only during the course of the freedom movement but also in the conduct of the affairs of the newly independent state. Nehru's vision of a modern Indian state, dismissive of the obscurantisms of the past and striving towards progress on the foundations of science, technology and industrialization, also had an irresistible appeal for this urban-centric class nurtured on Western concepts of rationalism and liberalism and impatient to get on with the task of 'nation building'. At the same time, the concern of both Gandhi and Nehru for the poor was perceived as being far more than merely an emotional awareness of the deprived; the middle class understood this concern to mean that both the State and society need to have a sensitivity towards redressing the problems of the poor. Gandhi's life-long work for the upliftment of the harijans and his identification with the destitute had lent credibility to his unceasing exhortations on the need to work for the lowliest and the humblest. Nehru, too, as the spokesman of the Congress Left, was identified with the ideological assertion that the needs of the impoverished peasantry and the proletariat must be addressed as an intrinsic part of the exercise of building a modern and progressive nation.

A natural corollary to such a concern was to categorize as vulgar the ostentatious display of wealth. Gandhi's spartan lifestyle and his ability to live what he preached had a special fascination for the middle class. For its members he became less an example of austerity in the tradition of the mahatmas in India and more a symbol of voluntary restraint of material wants in a poor country like India. His austere lifestyle was not viewed as something to be emulated in an absolute sense; it was internalized more as a guiding principle: high thinking and simple living. If Gandhi was revered for actually having the courage to live like those below, Nehru, the patrician hero, was admired for effortlessly being able to renounce the comforts and perquisites that were his by virtue of belonging to a class above. Few in the middle class took to spinning or the regular wearing of khadi; but the purity and simplicity associated with that cloth underlined the essential point that such lifestyles need to be voluntarily restrained that are jarring or incongruent in a country as poor as India.

Charkha, khadi, the swadeshi movement and the economic dependency and exploitation intrinsic to colonialism had made self-reliance a far more self-evident aim in newly independent India than it is generally regarded today. Gandhi's stress on cottage industries and his somewhat pastoral vision of self-sufficient village communities was taken cognisance of by the middle class. But it was Nehru's vision of an awakened India, invulnerable to outside manipulation and moving towards the creation of a modern and industrialized economy on the basis of its long suppressed indigenous strengths, that had a far greater appeal for this class. Memories of the struggle for freedom were still fresh. Patriotism had not as yet become a tired and clichéd slogan to be used for partisan political ends. And self-reliance, both in the economic sense and in the political sense of being resistant to external pressure, was accepted as a valid policy paradigm to ensure that independent India would be able to stand on its own.

Another message indelibly identified with both Gandhi and Nehru was that of communal tolerance. While Gandhi made no secret of his belief in religion—religious symbols occurred frequently in his writings and public pronouncements—there was not the slightest doubt about his catholic spirit and respect for all religions. He genuinely believed that Hindus and Muslims could live together in peace and amity. His efforts to douse communal passions in the years leading to Partition, and after, constituted a deeply moving and powerful influence in reinvesting hope and faith in the possibility of communal harmony. Nehru, quite unlike his mentor, was not religious in the conventional sense. In keeping with his espousal of the modern and rationalistic outlook, he shied away from religious imagery and ritual. He believed that religion at the level of ordinary practice led to orthodoxy and prejudice and a narrowness of vision which was at fundamental variance with the aim of inculcating a scientific temper and building a progressive India. But the common ground of both Nehru's supra-religious modernity and Gandhi's eclectic religious faith was a fundamental opposition to communalism. It was this sentiment which was internalized by the middle class with selective elements of the outlook of both. The members of this class were not unhappy with the sanctity given by Gandhi to the religious domain. Yet, they, like all Indians, were also deeply influenced by his advocacy of communal harmony. And while they were less than entirely comfortable with the stridency of Nehru's convictions against the role of organized religion in society, they were willing to accept the argument that a modern and progressive State was required to be above all religions.

There were essential and theoretically irreconcilable differences between the outlook of Gandhi and that of Nehru. These were recognized by both leaders, and Nehru, in particular, analysed them with considerable candour in his autobiography and other writings. The variance of viewpoints is reflected also in significant segments of the correspondence between the two leaders. But preoccupations with the negotiations for the transfer of power in the final phase of the freedom movement, the emotional burdens of Partition, and, finally, the euphoria of freedom itself helped in pushing these differences into the background. Moreover, Nehru was transparently sincere in his public pronouncements of a blind faith in and love for Gandhi, who was equally overt in his affection and admiration for Nehru. But the bulk of the middle class was not really aware of or overly interested in the intricacies of their theoretical differences. And from their words and deeds it culled out a composite ideological framework whose principal elements can briefly be recapitulated as follows:

(a) An acceptance of the role of ethics in society, probity in public life, and the link between politics and idealism;

(b) A belief in the vision of an industrialized India, rational and scientific in outlook and modern in the Western sense of the term;

(c) A social sensitivity towards the poor; a belief that the state and society must work towards their upliftment;

(d) A reticence towards ostentatious display of wealth, which was seen as something in bad taste and incongruent in a country as poor as India;

(e) An acceptance of the goal of self-reliance, reflecting an optimism in India's intrinsic economic strengths and the political need to be insulated from external manipulation;

(f) A belief in a secular state, above religious divides.

In addition to this distillation from the Gandhi-Nehru legacy, there were other supplementary supports that reinforced the ideological moorings of the middle class. The first was a belief that freedom in 1947 was the culmination of a genuine mass movement. Nehru, because of his honesty and intellectual objectivity, could admit the middle- and upper-class orientation of the freedom struggle even when its manifestation on more than one occasion was that of a mass movement; but the middle class as a whole had neither this objectivity nor this insight. This, of course, was rather convenient: if the freedom struggle could be projected as a mass movement involving all classes of people, it bestowed legitimacy to the beliefs and agenda of those who were at its helm, and who became with independence, its principal beneficiaries.

A second aspect of the scaffolding supporting middle-class attitudes and thinking was a belief in the uniqueness of the Indian liberation struggle. There is little doubt that in many ways the struggle was unique. A largely non-violent agitation succeeded in vanquishing one of the world's most powerful colonial empires, and it did so on the universal principles of freedom and equality without professing a hatred for the enemy. There was thus a heightened moral dimension to the pursuit of an even otherwise just cause. And the halo bequeathed by this moral heritage was specially claimed by the average middle-class Indian. It gave to his views and opinions a self-righteousness and a sense of moral superiority that was often quite irksome to a foreign observer. But it also helped to nurture his continued acceptance of the role of the moral in the public realm, which was a positive factor in the years just after independence.

A third strand contributing to the weave of the middle-class Indian's thinking was a romanticization of India's past. The basis for this was not any serious study or analysis but an emotional pride in a mythical past where India, prior to her humiliating subjugations, was a land of prosperity and plenty, culturally efflorescent, morally awakened, and politically powerful. It was this India which, it was believed, had nurtured a moral legacy of rectitude in public life, a voluntary renunciation of violence, religious tolerance, and democratic participation. Gandhi's invocation of Ram Rajya undoubtedly contributed to the conjuring up of such a historical vision. But even the consciously intellectual Nehru was not always immune to such sentimentalizations. 'And yet India with all her poverty and degradation had enough of nobility and greatness about her,' he wrote. 'Behind and within her battered body one could still glimpse a majesty of soul. Through long ages she had travelled and gathered much wisdom on the way, and trafficked with strangers and added them to her own big family and witnessed days of glory and decay . . . but throughout her long journey she had clung to her immemorial culture, drawn strength and vitality from it , and shared it with other lands.'[5] Somewhat bemusedly Nehru also succumbed to the temptation of giving his country an anthropomorphic form: 'India becomes Bharat Mata, Mother India, a beautiful lady, very old but ever youthful . . .'[6] The attempt to make ahimsa or non-violence a bequeath of the past was particularly laboured. In the case of Gandhi, faith easily triumphed over historical accuracy. Certain leaders, like Ashoka, were selectively highlighted for their principled pacifism, and others forgotten. The amazing thing is that even Nehru, for all his emphasis on the dispassionate analysis of historical forces, concluded: 'Right through history the old Indian ideal did not glorify political and military triumph, and looked down upon money and the professional money-making class.'[7]

Perhaps Nehru symbolized at its most refined the middle-class susceptibility to glorify India's past. And in analysing the influences that moulded middle-class thinking we are concerned with the strength of this belief, not just the historical evidence to support it. Our concern is also with the impact of such influences. A belief in a once great India enabled the educated middle-class Indian to overarch his immediate past and seek confidence and reassurance in an idealized remote. This quantum jump reinforced his desire to take India forward so that it could resurrect its past greatness. In this endeavour he perceived the primacy of his role as self-evident. For he was educated, culturally literate if not accomplished, and above all, conscious of the heritage which needed to be reinvoked. His claim, therefore, of being the chief spokesman of India's past was valid, and little more needed to be done to re-evaluate or question this interpretational monopoly.

The accommodation of an idealized past did not in any way mean a rejection or dilution of the project of modernity and progress, to which the middle class remained firmly loyal.

The two were not contradictory; both had their own place in a perspective which sought to invoke the past not to replicate it in exact detail in the future but to recreate, through the opportunities available in the present, the grandeur and prestige that was assumed to have existed before.

A fourth aspect of middle-class thinking was the conviction, accepted almost as axiomatic, that parliamentary democracy as it had evolved in Britain was the model on which to structure the Indian polity. This was not surprising since, as has been already shown, the middle-class Indian was the most porous repository of the western values of democracy and liberalism. He was against the British in their colonial avatara; but he was an admirer of Britain in terms of her internal achievements and her credentials as the mother of all democracies. At the same time, his intellectual distance from the masses in his own country gave him little opportunity, and even less inclination, to seriously consider alternatives to a system of governance which a certain kind of education and exposure had convinced him was the best for his country.

These then were the elements that coalesced to form the ideological framework of the Indian middle class at the time of independence. Not all of them were in perfect harmony, and some, such as a pride in India's past prior to her subjugations, contained in them the seeds of communalism. But whatever its shortcomings, this framework, and, in particular, its derivations from the Gandhi-Nehru legacy, helped motivate this class to play a role in nation building with both optimism and idealism. The important thing is that there was an ideology, a vision, a calling which the middle class could owe loyalty to. It was this loyalty to something other than merely its own gratifications that gave it a larger cause and purpose. This is not to state that the middle class had completely transcended its self-interests—in any society, to expect this to happen with respect to any class is utopian—but its natural proclivity, in the absence of a larger ideal, to a cynical, spiralling materialism was kept in check. The fact that during this phase, in the form of Nehru and other stalwarts of the freedom movement, ideology coincided with leadership that was both charismatic and respected was also a factor of considerable importance. The middle class, in order to have a vision beyond its immediate material interests, has always needed to have something to look up to: either an ideology which is more than the sum of its own interests, or a leader whom it can respect and repose confidence in. In the years after 1947 it had both; but as we shall see later, in but two decades from then it was groping to find both.

How did this ideological mooring mould and influence the lifestyle of the middle class? It is difficult to answer this question merely by a surface observation of the way its members lived, for in this respect nothing changed dramatically after 1947. Within the bureaucracy it was the handful of officers in the ICS who represented the pinnacle of aspiration and set the standards of behaviour. In the private sector it was a group of Indians working in senior management positions in the more well-known British firms in India, based mostly at corporate headquarters in Calcutta but also in the other big towns, who were considered the achievers fit for emulation. A young ICS officer in charge of a district or sub-division in 1947 still lived in good colonial style. More often than not he had half a dozen servants, at the very minimum, to help support his lifestyle: cook, bearer, chaprasi, chauffeur, mali, ayah, bhishti, sweeper, dhobi, etc.—all living in the servant quarters in one corner of the compound of his sprawling bungalow. He lived in the Civil Lines, the cleaner, more expansive, less populated area built by the British to accommodate the burra sahebs, away from the din and chaos of the congested old city. In the evening he went to the Officer's Club, accessible, as its name suggests, to but a few of his own ilk. His take home salary was in the vicinity of Rs 400 a month—negligible by today's standards but not insufficient given the price levels prevailing then.

Outside the portals of the heaven-born service, as the ICS was then called, those in senior government service had a similar if scaled down lifestyle. A new entrant to the Indian Administrative Service (the successor service to the ICS), even while on training, had a room bearer exclusively to himself who served him chhota haziri in his room and kept his breeches shining for the mandatory lessons in horse riding. Of course, there were variations of nuance and scale in the perquisites available to support the desired lifestyle, but the standards set by the upper echelons in government were a reference point for the aspirations of the middle class as a whole. Those not in government but with the required income base sought to approximate the establishments of the big babus and ended up with many of the same accoutrements of social standing. Perhaps the most stubbornly insular in the continuity of the British milieu were the private sector box-wallahs in Calcutta, who, at least in the early years after 1947, continued to work under English CEOs and measured their own progress in terms of the extent to which they could emulate their masters' mannerisms and lifestyle.

For a more complete understanding of middle-class behaviour, we need to look beyond this seeming continuity of colonial lifestyles, to try and see how the ideological legacy of the middle class influenced its attitudes and priorities in everyday life. As discussed earlier, one discernible trait was the acceptance of the role of the moral in society. The term moral is used here not in an absolute or very narrow sense but more in the nature of a generally accepted ethical yardstick to which people were expected to conform in public and personal life. Thus, for instance, an officer was expected to be beyond the temptations of personal gain and honest in his advice; a judge was supposed to keep a certain distance from lawyers in order to project and preserve the impartiality expected from him; a lawyer was expected to be honest with his clients and never collude with the opposite side; a businessman was expected to pursue his goal of profits but by ethical means; a teacher was expected to judge his students strictly on merit; and a student was expected to rely solely on his performance and not on the influence or money of his parents.

These are but some examples that illustrate the prevalent notions of right and wrong. Obviously there were the exceptions to the rule, but the important point is that these were regarded as such and attracted social opprobrium. Moreover, the middle class extended the ambit of its expectations of moral uprightness to those outside its purview and specially to those above it. The worth of a successful politician, for example, was to be judged by his personal probity and not only by the money he had acquired or the power he wielded. Similarly, a rich industrialist who had a reputation for unscrupulousness was held in bad odour. Of course, society still had its normal ebb and flow. Thus, a businessman still sought to cultivate a useful bureaucrat as and when possible. The difference was that when he brought a gift to further his cause, a senior bureaucrat—and he still set the standards—would more often than not return it, or keep something negligible as a symbolic gesture, as for instance two or three pieces from a basket of fruits or a box of sweetmeats. Moreover, gifts were the exception rather than the norm, given only on special occasions and kept within inexpensive limits.

Such parameters of social interaction were linked to another aspect: a conscious ceiling on material wants. Undoubtedly, there was less money in circulation then and fewer opportunities for its use. But if less was available, less was also sought. This had little to do with the facile generalizations, popular with some commentators in the West, and accepted uncritically and self-righteously by some sections of the Indian intelligentsia, that Indians were essentially other worldly and above the temptations of material wealth. On the contrary, the general approach was that the rich were entitled—within reasonable limits—to their goodies, but the middle class, while not against such goodies, had other priorities. Among these were a good education for the children, the availability of wholesome food, the inculcation of the correct family values, and a basic but unostentatious standard of living. Education, and in particular higher education, was given great importance. This emphasis was traditional, a part of historical memory, for the middle class owed its very emergence to the opportunities grasped in this field. With the coming of Independence and given Nehru's vision of progress and industrialization, there was a great sense of anticipation that the opportunities for those who had the right education would multiply manifold. Degrees in the fields of medicine and engineering were specially valued, as they are today; but then there was a sense of exhilaration, of entering new areas of learning and of making a pioneering contribution in the building of a modern India.

The joys were simpler then; even recreation needed a minimal materialistic base. To visit a cinema hall once in a while and see a film with the whole family was the high point of entertainment. There was no television and no video recorder; the radio was there but not yet the transistor. Films were popular but even more so their songs—the count down of the most popular Hindi film songs on *Binaca Geet Mala* every Wednesday was something never to be missed. There were few major newspapers and even fewer magazines. The pan-Indian sway of *The Illustrated Weekly of India*, an English journal, was unchallenged. Family ties were stronger; and while these were occasionally stifling, they also were a source of joy and support.

Material pursuits were thus subsumed in a larger framework that did not give them the aggressive primacy that they have acquired today. There was less of the feeling that one must have it all in the shortest time possible. Even the more well-to-do families felt that to flaunt their assets was in bad taste. Indeed, there was a sense of slight disdain for those who lived only at the level of their material acquisitions. There were other countervailing concepts such as status and respect which had a higher priority in the scale of social values. Status, and the respect it earned, was not so directly linked to what one owned; it still had more to do with what one did or what one had achieved. Keeping up with the Jones' was somehow a less compulsive pursuit than keeping up with the image of refinement associated with a restraint on materialistic exhibitionism in a poor country—an ideal directly imbibed from Gandhi, Nehru and the freedom movement.

In fact, social sensitivity towards the less fortunate was a natural extension of an attitude that saw purpose and meaning in life beyond mere individual gratification. This sensitivity did not necessarily translate itself into something as dramatic as a renunciation of what one possessed, or a headlong plunge into social work. Indeed, as we shall see later, the middle class would remain resolutely resistant to any attempts to dilute its basic economic interests. But, even with this as a premise, the middle-class world view—at the subjective level of its own thinking on what should be done and what should be of concern—included the belief that the needs of the poor must be addressed. This belief underwent a further transference: from a concern at an individual level to a faith in the State as the principal agency to achieve the desired goal. Of course, such a transference was rather convenient, because it demanded no immediate sacrifices at the personal level. No immediate sacrifices at a personal level.

Some objects of desire were not so readily available because of the restriction on imports and the emphasis on self-reliance. Also, it would have been nicer if salaries could have been a little higher and taxes a trifle lower; but, by and large, life as inherited, if not entirely as desired, continued without inconvenient upheavals. In the absence of pressures compelling any basic change in lifestyles, the concern for and awareness of the poor largely manifested itself in the form of a paternalistic sensitivity to their travails. At the same time, given the avowedly socialist goals of the state, there was this diffused conviction in a middle-class person that he was contributing, either through his work (specially if he was in government) or through his taxes or both, towards the fulfilment of the welfare policies of the State. The important point is that in the years immediately after Independence, the middle class believed that the professed bias of the State towards the poor was valid and necessary, and it was prepared, at least in theory, to accommodate interests outside its own narrow ken.

Perhaps the most seductive goal for the middle class was the pursuit of modernity. It was also the most complex and problematic. 'Modernity was interpreted in the Nehruvian sense of shedding the shackles of the past and adopting a rationalist and scientific outlook. Such an approach it was felt would equip an individual to tap the possibilities of the future in a modern and progressive India. The image that beckoned was that of 'the "new man" or the "modern man", the "citizen of the new state", the "man in the era of science", the "industrial man", and so on.'[8] 'India must break with much of her past and not allow it to dominate the present,' wrote Nehru in his book titled, ironically enough, The Discovery of India. 'Our lives are encumbered with the dead wood of this past; all that is dead and has served its purpose has to go.'[9] Other social thinkers were equally categorical in this prescription. In the fifties D.K. Rangnekar wrote: 'The young Indian must come round to a rational and objective view of material advancement. He must be able and willing to tear himself away from his family ties; flout customs and traditions; put economic welfare before cow worship; think in terms of farm and factory output rather than in terms of gold and silver ornaments; spend on tools and training rather than on temples and ceremonials; work with the low caste rather than starve with the high caste; think of the future rather than of the past; concentrate on material gains rather than dwell on kismet.'[10] The fledgling publicity apparatus of the state carried on similar exhortations against the social evils associated with the past, as did the popular media. Films like Awara helped popularize modern concepts of egalitarianism, of equal opportunities for all, notwithstanding the hierarchical stratifications of the old order. Others like Do Bigha Zamin and Sujata brought out the inequities of the decadent feudal order and the caste system.

The problem was that however appealing the image of the modern man and of a modern society might have been, the past could not be so easily wished away. For one thing, the very nature of the colonial experience was such as to nurture a nostalgia for an idealized past. Nehru himself conceded this: 'The rising middle classes wanted some cultural roots to cling on to, something that gave them assurance of their own worth, something that would reduce the sense of frustration and humiliation that foreign conquest and rule had produced.'[11] Moreover, as we have observed earlier, for all their social activism and modernity of outlook, both Nehru and Gandhi romanticized the past. Nehru, in particular, wrote and spoke of the dead weight of the past almost as much as he did of its glorious legacies. In terms of a purely rational analysis such an approach was not incompatible, for the past did have elements deserving of both praise and criticism. But for the middle-class person such an intellectually nuanced projection blurred the message and fostered an effortless schizophrenia: an endorsement of the project of modernity in the public realm and a retention in the private domain of many of the orthodoxies and rituals incompatible with such a stance.

This duality was also due to the fact that society, as a whole, was not fully prepared to absorb the project of modernity. In Europe, 'the strong independent State with a fairly effective government and a common pattern of law enforcement and observance preceded nationalism, and both preceded democracy. The states in South Asia were created anew, partly as an effect of rising nationalism. And they were immediately given a readymade democratic ideology . . .'[12] This telescoping of the historical process created a constituency professing allegiance to certain values associated with modernity, viz, democracy, rationalism and egalitarianism; but it did not allow these to seep in and effect a substantial or transformational change. The patchwork acceptance of the ideal of modernity led to its own distortions. It prevented a serious or objective evaluation of the modernistic critique of the practices and institutions of the past, while at the same time allowing these very institutions and practices to persist, in the shadow, as it were, of the overt pursuit of modernity.

Thus, in theory the caste system was rejected as a relic of the past, inimical to the creation of an egalitarian society because it was suppressive of such normative values as the dignity and equality of human beings. In practice, however, the middle class remained upper caste in character, and, except for an excessively westernized fringe, allowed considerations of caste to govern important decisions relating to ritual and marriage. Its approach to the newly christened scheduled castes continued to hover between sufferance and disdain. Open hostility would bring into question its credentials to be modern; but in private the harijans of Gandhi were still quite readily given the derisive label of chamars. There were, of course, honourable exceptions to the rule; but what has been stated accurately portrays the behaviour and attitudes of the class as a whole. The amazing thing is that this reluctance to jettison considerations of caste overlapped with a respect for Gandhi and his crusade against the ostracization of the harijans. It was almost as if the Mahatma had already done, on behalf of the middle class, enough for the atishudras; now that independence had come it was time to applaud the nobility of his work and get on with the actual task of governance. Of course, the morally persuasive force of his example could not but compel a toning down of the virulence underpinning the rigidities in society, and the official policies of affirmative action could also not be derided publicly. But neither Gandhi nor the much desired aspiration for modernity constituted a pressure strong enough to force a qualitative change of attitude. This was all the more so because the social structure that gave sustenance to such attitudes had remained largely unchanged. The atishudras were not a part of the middle-class elite that assumed the mantle of governance after 1947, and the latter was under no great pressure to accommodate them in its fold: Gandhi died in 1948; and a leader like Ambedkar who could have made a nuisance of himself in aggressively raising the issue of social restructuring was 'domesticated, for all practical purposes, by the Mahatma and (his) national presence . . . marginalized by his political heir.'[13]

There is a telling incident which convincingly illustrates this contradiction between ideology and practice. Jamnalal Bajaj, one of India's better-known capitalists, was an ardent follower of Gandhi. His wife, who became a widow in 1942, followed in her husband's footsteps. After Gandhi's death, she transferred her loyalties to Vinoba Bhave, widely recognized as Gandhi's successor. 'I walked with Vinobaji for years,' Mrs Bajaj told Ved Mehta, who was interviewing her for his book Mahatma Gandhi and His Apostles. 'Ten or fifteen miles a day, begging land for the poor. It was very hard, changing camp every day, because I never eat anything I haven't prepared with my own hands. Everyone knows that Moslems and Harijans have dirty habits.' And, having said this, the lady, who was chewing betel, spat.[14]

Nowhere is the dichotomy between the ideal of modernity and the hold of tradition brought out more vividly than in the field of religious beliefs. Nehru believed that the secular temperament and the secular state were an intrinsic part of the 'modern' man and of 'modern' society. Gandhi drew the inspiration for his message of religious tolerance from the best in all religions. He was thus quintessentially religious in preaching communal harmony. Nehru, on the other hand, was a professed agnostic. The spectacle of organized religion filled him, as he confessed in his autobiography, with horror. In his last will and testament he wrote: 'I wish to declare with all earnestness that I do not want any religious ceremonies performed for me after my death. I do not believe in any such ceremonies and to submit to them, even as a matter of form, would be hypocrisy and an attempt to delude ourselves.'[15] This was much too extreme a position for the average middle-class person. He was, by and large, against communal hostility and discord, but was unwilling or disinclined to transcend the role of religion in his life to the extent that Nehru claimed to have done. At the same time, given the bias of state policy under the influence of Nehru, he could not bring himself to publicly discount the Nehruvian definition of secularism. The result, again, was a curious hybrid of public posturing and private compromise.

The public acceptance of secularism, internalized as the shying away from an overt expression of interest in religion, prevented many of the secular concepts in religion from being more fully explored. There are many concepts in Hinduism, for instance, which have the potential of being harnessed in an entirely non-communal manner for the public good. These include the notion of sewa or socially useful voluntary service; the emphasis on dharma, or right conduct, and the causal cycle of karma, or the belief that good actions reap good rewards; and the conditional legitimacy given to the desire for material things by making artha one of the four purusharthas or goals of life and not something to be pursued in exclusion. Concepts of a similar social value are easily identified in the other major religions of India as well. But is was unfashionable in the Nehruvian paradigm of modernity to go deeper into any aspect of religion aside from stressing the equality of all religions in the eyes of the State. This was undoubtedly of inestimable value in a nascent polity recovering from the aftermath of Partition. And yet, it also served to make the actual practice of religion an almost surreptitious exercise, to be carried out discreetly, away from public scrutiny or debate. This, in turn, allowed many superstitions and prejudices to continue unchallenged; many rituals, inherited as part of long-established tradition, continued to be observed in the privacy of most middle-class homes. There was nothing particularly wrong in this, except that, given the modernist imperative to transcend the influence of religion, there was no serious effort to know or keep in touch with the philosophy behind these rituals. The hold of the past ensured the continuity of traditional religious practices; the aspiration to be modern resulted in these practices surviving only as mechanical ritual.

It is difficult to say whether there was a conscious hypocrisy or deceit involved in this process. For most educated Indians it appears to have been more in the nature of a tacit acceptance of the unavoidable gap between Nehruvian precept and traditional practice. For instance, the special Kumbh mela at the Sangam at Allahabad in 1953 attracted large numbers of educated Hindus. Their dip in the holy waters was an act of faith at a personal level. Their rejection of religious ritual as inimical to a rational and scientific outlook was an act of conformity to the dominant secular ethic. Both co-existed. Of course, Nehru, uncompromisingly consistent in his views, did not participate in the Kumbh mela celebrations. But it is also significant that, in spite of the expressly stated views in his last will and testament, his last rites were performed in accordance with Vedic ritual and to the loud incantations of priests.

The distinction between what the middle class sought to be, or what it thought itself to be, and what it actually was, is important for the shadow it casts on future events, such as the furore among its members over the implementation of the Mandal Commission Report, and the rise of religious fundamentalism. The important point for our analysis at this stage is to understand the shadow play between the persistence of tradition and the appeal of modernity. The contradiction between the two occurred because they were posited as essentially representing two different ways of life. The Nehruvian model was heavily influenced by Western concepts of modernity; for the middle class this was part of its appeal. But the very stature of Nehru was such that little effort was made to modify his vision to include indigenous elements in order to evolve an authentically Indian idiom of change in continuity. The dilemma was all the more acute for the educated Indian, because his education exposed him to the new, even when he could not quite give up the old. The contours of his search for identity could be seen in more than one area of social interaction. Modernity, as per Western liberal ideology, implied the ability for rational calculation, a separation of the personal and the professional, the dispassionate pursuit of efficiency, the absence of emotion and sentiment in work, and a liberation from favouritism and group allegiances. But in India, even for the educated, all of these could be nullified by traditional loyalties to family, kin, community and caste. The hold of the joint family was particularly strong. Job opportunities did lead male members away from the family home—often the immediate family, the wife and children, accompanied them—but geographical distance did little to dilute the strength of ties to the larger family. 'Even in nuclear families, nuclearity is only residential, and functionally the joint family obligations in performance of rituals, kinship and marriage obligations and in ownership of assets and properties and sharing of economic responsibilities are maintained.'[16] What is interesting is that recent studies have shown that institutions like the joint family and traditional caste occupations played a significant role in capital formation and the development of a marketing network. But in terms of conventional thinking the middle class had already made a black-and-white demarcation: the joint family, with its web of obligations, responsibilities and control, was an institution of the past; the nuclear family, with its greater sense of freedom and autonomy in decision making, was (in accordance with the social pattern in the West) an institution of the present. It is undeniable that economic developments were corroding the age-old foundations of the joint family system. But in respect of this institution and that of many others, the middle class, caught in the penumbra of the past and the present, the traditional and the modern, was unable to develop an authentic paradigm synthesizing both. And this would have important consequences for developments in the future.

~

Looking back, it is clear that almost immediately after Independence the direction of State policy was being dictated by middle-class interests. This was not the result of a conscious or pre-planned strategy, but a consequence of the predominant position of the middle class in the influencing and making of State policy. If questioned, a middle-class person would have emphatically denied such an accusation. Under Nehru the policies of the new State were clearly to be for the betterment of the downtrodden and the poor. This was quite clear even before Independence. Speaking in the Constituent Assembly on 20 January 1947, Dr Sarvepalli Radhakrishnan had proclaimed: 'We are not here asking anything for a particular community or a privileged class. We are here working for the establishment of Swaraj for all the Indian people . . . We are here to bring about real satisfaction of the fundamental needs of the common man of this country.'[17] Nehru, in his very first speech in the same Assembly, was even more emphatic: 'Well, I stand for socialism, and I hope India will stand for socialism and that India will go towards the constitution of a Socialist State, and I do believe that the whole world will have to go that way.'[18] The middle class was both reassured and inspired by such a vision, and its faith in the bonafides of the State in forging an interventionist policy for the benefit of the poor was unquestioned. The State elite that inherited power at the time of Independence enjoyed enormous prestige, and there was also a sufficiently unified sense of ideological purpose about the desirability of using State intervention to promote economic development. To this end, the State did seek to exert pressure on the proprietary classes. But even while it sought to formulate goals and policies as an autonomous actor, 'neither at the behest of nor on behalf of the proprietary classes, it could not ignore the serious constraints on the framework of policy actions, and certainly on their effective implementation, posed by the articulated interests of those classes.'[19]

In this dialectic between belief and practice, intent and reality, the middle class was a gainer in two ways. First, because it believed in the socialist rhetoric of the State, it was rid of any sense of guilt or cynicism in the perpetuation of its interests at the cost of those for whom the policies were ostensibly being implemented; and second, because of the facade given to State policy by socialist rhetoric, it could pursue its own interests with a minimum of friction or challenge. From the beginning, the State in India was an inordinately powerful player. It was not only the principal organ to make policy but also the chief implementing agency. Its powers were further enhanced by the policy of planned economic development adopted by Nehru; such an enhancement was also inherent in the 'top-down' model of development, both in the economy and in the social sectors. In 'an interventionist state in a poor economy, those who control state power tend to exercise enormous influence,'[20] and in newly independent India the upper and middle classes were the most strategically placed to control state power. Their representatives ran the all-powerful bureaucracy; they were fully represented in the legislatures; they were at the helm of business and industry; they had an outlet for their views in the media; and, in the countryside, they owned most of the land. The result was that the interests of the middle class hijacked the agenda of the nation, even as its members continued to believe that the State was rightly biased in favour of the less privileged.

It is not the intention here—nor would it be feasible in the space of one book—to enumerate in the fullest detail how the middle class influenced, overtly or insidiously, the making and implementation of State policy so as to further and—at the very least—preserve its own interests. But a few important examples will suffice. In an overwhelmingly agricultural country, where the vast majority of the poor were landless or marginal peasants, the professed policies of the State were for structural reform in the countryside, their main elements being land redistribution, investment in agriculture, and community development. But the interests of the rich and middle-level peasantry, dominant both in the Congress and the State apparatus, stood in opposition to the achievement of these goals. Thus the Zamindari Abolition Act was enacted in 1955, and although official statistics claimed in 1961 that the rights of zamindars had come down from 43% to 8.5% of the cultivated areas, 'a closer look at the situation gives rise to the strong suspicion that the connection between these statistics and social realities in the countryside (was) largely fortuitous.'[21] Nehru's thinking on agrarian cooperatives was largely scuttled by his own party. There was a general consensus among policy makers on the need for land ceilings so that the surplus land made available could be distributed among the poor and landless farmers. 'However, agriculture being a state subject, the central leadership could only set guidelines and attempt to persuade state leaders to institute land ceilings and implement redistribution. The state leadership of the Congress virtually everywhere had no interest in such proposals which could only antagonize the party's predominant rural supporters, the principal land-controlling castes in the countryside. Virtually everywhere, therefore, land ceilings legislation was a farce and land redistribution practically non-existent or cruel to those who "benefitted" from it by receiving barren, unproductive, or alkaline soil to farm without the resources to make use of it.'[22]

This gulf, between an intent motivated by a concern for the deprived and a reality conditioned by unyielding class interests, is seen also in the Community Development Programme launched in the mid-fifties. The aim of the Programme was to democratize village communities so as to make them a more effective agent in the task of economic development, and in theory the Programme as drawn up by middle-class bureaucrats sitting in the cities appeared attractive. But the developmental inputs it generated were largely appropriated by the dominant groups in the countryside. Moreover, the funds allocated to it were insufficient. By 1956 only a quarter of the rural population had been covered by the Programme. However, the same year saw the creation of a full-fledged Ministry of Community Development in Delhi. The same malaise afflicted the attempt at introducing democratic local government through the well-conceived system of Panchayati Raj. Under this new system, the numbers of block development officers increased three fold between 1959 and 1962. But while the bureaucracy proliferated in the villages at the lower-middle-class level, the official machinery proceeded very cautiously with regard to changes in the existing rural social structure. And, as a prescient observer said bluntly then: 'To democratize the villages without altering property relationships is simply absurd.'[23]

The city-based socialists saw the countryside in black-and-white terms—a few rich landlords and a vast, impoverished peasantry. But there was also a numerically small but significant segment of middle-class peasants. In fact, the impact of the tenancy legislations of the Nehru period, and that of several measures in the actual implementation of official policy in the rural sector, was to promote the interests of smaller landlords or richer peasants. This class of agriculturists had aspirations to middle-class status and lifestyles, but its day, as we shall see later, was yet to come. In the early years after the freedom movement the vision of the ensconced middle class was overwhelmingly urban. In keeping with the Nehruvian concept of progress, its goal was to achieve industrial and technological modernity. 'The economy based on the latest technological achievements of the day must necessarily be the dominating one,' Nehru had declared almost a decade before Independence. 'If technology demands the big machine, as it does today in large measure, then the big machine with all its implications and consequences must be accepted.'[24] And when after Independence Nehru described the large factories and plants as the new temples of modern India, he was voicing a sentiment readily shared by the urban-centric middle class. It must be emphasized again that this approach was not consciously anti-rural; there was this general feeling that industrial progress would have beneficial spin-off effects for the agricultural sector as well. What can, however, be said is that the more articulate and influential members of the middle class had a lesser interest in the rural sector, and their priorities played a crucial role in the moulding and direction of State economic policy. One aspect of this was that alternative strategies for economic development were ignored. For instance, one such strategy could have emphasized with great relevance 'heavy public investment in irrigation, flood control, and drainage; in biological research and agricultural extension; and in the provision of off-farm employment in the rural areas through the encouragement of small scale industries.'[25] But for the middle class such a strategy would have hardly conformed to the grandiose plans for capital intensive heavy industrialization which, in accordance with Nehru's thinking and the economic history of the West, would soon, it believed, place India in the ranks of the economic powers of the world. There was also the memory of the colonial experience: Britain had won and India had lost because of the former's technological superiority. The consequence of such a bias in favour of industry contributed to the neglect of agriculture: in a country where eighty per cent of the people, and the overwhelming bulk of the poor, were agriculturists, the allocation for both agriculture and community development in the first three five-year plans did not exceed fifteen per cent of the total outlay. In fact, the basic direction of the policies, at least at the level of implementation, was such that by the 1960s 'the main benefit of increased income and expenditure accrued to the upper, middle and richer sections of the population. The bottom forty per cent, that is, virtually all the poor, did not benefit at all from the economic changes that occurred . . .'[26]

While the needs of the bulk of the rural population were

neglected, the urban-oriented policies of a State-controlled economy were found particularly conducive by the battalions of professional bureaucrats. The levers of the 'permit-licence-quota' raj[27] were largely in their hands. By wielding the 'weapons of monopoly control, foreign exchange regulation, industrial licencing and credit and input rationing to keep the industrialists on the defensive and to increase their own political leverage and corrupt income'[28] they acquired a strong vested interest in the perpetuation of the system. Moreover, 'through their education and personal relationship with the bureaucratic personnel, the more successful and politically astute among the professional and urban intellectual classes generally could gain preferential access to the privileges of education, housing, foreign travel, scarce consumer goods, and good jobs for themselves and their children.'[29]

The richer farmers and the established industrialists and businessmen were, of course, not too happy with the socialist pattern of the economy; but they had the wherewithal to manipulate the system, often with the support of bureaucrats. Entrepreneurs in the private sector at the smaller level were still a nascent tribe; in time, and in spite of the policies of the State, their numbers would increase and they would be aggressive entrants to the middle-class bandwagon. But at this time they were not a major factor to disturb the cosy condominium between the political leadership, the policies of the state, and the aspirations of the articulate middle classes.

There were other areas—the sector of health, for instance[30]—in which the interests of the dominant coalition, of which the urban middle class constituted an important part, hijacked the policies of the State, to the enduring detriment of those for whom the policies were supposedly formulated. Education provides a particularly striking example. A decade and a half before Independence the

Congress Provisional Governments in the states had introduced a Scheme for Basic Education. In the Constitution adopted by free India in 1950, Article 45 provided for free and compulsory education for all children until the age of fourteen. The middle classes of India had always accorded great importance to education and this statement of intent could not but have had their support. However, their demand was not for basic education which they had already acquired, but for higher education. It was their pressure, notwithstanding the importance given at the policy level to primary education, which led to a most remarkable—and improper—growth in higher education. Given that resources were both scarce and finite, such a growth could only have taken place at the cost of other educational priorities. Not surprisingly, today India sends about six times more people to the universities and other higher educational establishments than China; however, roughly half of India's population is illiterate, while China's adult literacy rates are close to eighty per cent. In fact, there is little doubt that the lopsided development of education in India is directly linked to the structure of Indian society, and 'that the inequalities in education are, in fact, a reflection of inequalities of economic and social powers of different groups in India. The educational inequalities both reflect and help to sustain social disparities . . .'[31]

Today India has the largest number of out-of-school children in the world and one of the world's largest reservoirs of trained and skilled manpower. The illiterate children come from poor households, mostly in the rural areas. The trained manpower has a largely middle-class and urban background. The responsibility for this telling dichotomy has to be laid squarely at the threshold of those who, in the initial years after 1947, were powerful enough to influence the direction of education policy in their own interest. What is equally telling is that in spite of the socialist inclinations of the State, 'the education of children of poorer social groups and less privileged classes and castes (could) be fairly comprehensively neglected without this becoming a politically explosive social scandal, as it would have undoubtedly become had more powerful people been at the neglected end.'[32] Indeed it has been plausibly argued that the educated elite saw in the neglect of basic education an opportunity to enhance their 'scarcity value'. 'In a country where the overwhelming majority are illiterate or drop-outs at the primary education level, the educated elite enjoy a high scarcity value for their education and profession. By managing to direct educational investment away from the masses, they have been able to protect their scarcity rent . . .'[33] It is another matter that even the increase in the number of higher educational establishments could not, in time, keep pace with the numbers from the middle class who sought to avail of their benefits. In such a situation, the obtaining of a degree soon became a substitute for the quality of education. The distortion of educational priorities had thus consequences which fell flat between two stools: basic education was neglected, but higher education became in time equally devalued, and shoddy.

Apart from a few very elite institutions, the indifferent level of training imparted in institutions of higher education is an important input in studying the evolution of the middle class in the years ahead. Universities were quintessentially middle class bastions, both at the level of the faculty and students. The middle class represented a continuity in educational traditions between pre- and post-colonial India. It, therefore, largely ignored the need to critically re-evaluate the content of syllabi and courses of the pre-1947 period, so long as the end result was a degree, and with it the possibility of a job. The erosion of standards in teaching and learning had become visible even in the first two decades after Independence. It is tempting to quote here the findings of a sympathetic observer who, in the mid-sixties, wrote a monumental work on the unfolding drama of development in Asian countries. His comments cover South Asia as a whole but have a special resonance for India:

Every Western visitor to South Asian universities is struck by the uncritical attitude of the average student: he expects the professor and the textbooks (often only certain pages are prescribed reading) to impart to him the knowledge he needs, and accepts what is offered to him without much intellectual effort of his own other than in listening, reading and memorizing. His submissiveness in this respect stands in curious contrast to his readiness to protest if he feels that requirements in examinations are unduly taxing. He is also aggressively conscious that as a university student he belongs, or will belong, to an elite group . . . Teaching in South Asian schools at all levels tends to discourage independent thinking and the growth of that inquisitive and experimental bent of mind that is so essential for development. It is directed toward enabling students to pass examinations and obtain degrees and, possibly, admittance to the next level of schools. A degree is the object pursued, rather than the knowledge and skills to which the degree should testify.[34]

The role of such an educational system, structured in response to middle-class needs but woefully inadequate in making an average middle-class person into a creative, normative and intellectually well-equipped citizen, cannot be overestimated in understanding and analysing the behaviour and reactions of this class in the future.

This class, specially those of its members at the policy-making levels of government, must also, in substantial measure, bear the guilt of having deprived India of the self-respect of having a national language of its own, and of making the knowledge of a certain kind of English into one of the most invidious systems of social exclusion. The question of a national language for independent India was undoubtedly a complex issue which generated a great deal of heat in the Constituent Assembly. As early as 1925, the Congress had adopted a Resolution that its proceedings shall be conducted as far as possible in Hindustani. But, given the linguistic predilections of the pan-Indian middle-class leadership of the freedom movement, little progress was made in the implementation of the Resolution and English remained the official language of the Congress. The debates in the Constituent Assembly on the question of a national language clearly brought out the divide between the votaries of Hindi and Hindustani from the North and the members from the South who advised moderation. Dr Rajendra Prasad, the President of the Assembly, himself put his finger squarely on the problem when he said: 'Whatever our sentiments may dictate we have to recognize the fact that most of those who have been concerned with the drafting of the Constitution can express themselves better in English than in Hindi.'[35] After interminable drafts and discussions a compromise was arrived at. Hindi in the Devanagiri script was to be the official language of the Union. However, English would continue for a period of fifteen years to be used for all the official purposes of the Union for which it was being used immediately before the adoption of the Constitution, and if need be its lease of life could be further extended beyond the period of fifteen years through Parliamentary legislation. The intention of the Constitution-makers was crystal clear:

English was to be progressively phased out to make way for Hindi as the national language. Article 351 laid out the policy guidelines framework through which this was to be achieved: 'It shall be the duty of the Union to promote the spread of the Hindi language, to develop it so that it may serve as a medium of expression for all the elements of the composite culture of India and to secure its environment by assimilating, without interfering with its genius, the forms style and expression used in Hindustani and in the other languages of India specified in the Eighth Schedule, and by drawing, wherever necessary or desirable, for its vocabulary, primarily on Sanskrit and secondarily on other languages.'

The charge against the English-knowing members of the middle class in the higher echelons of the Union administration and in the states, and their supporters in the professions, the armed forces, and in the corporate world, was that they had no intention ever of seriously implementing the stipulations of the Constitution. They were used to English as the language of usage; for many of them English had replaced the position even of their mother tongue. In Nehru, whose first language was English (and he had the honesty to admit this), they had a powerful patron. The result was that many of the policy measures that could have been taken in the early years after 1947, when patriotism was high and memories of the freedom struggle still vivid, to strengthen the cause of the national language, were ignored or implemented indifferently. The linguistic chauvinism that later erupted could perhaps have been preempted by a more persistent and imaginative handling at the very outset. The cynical could even argue that the hardening of positions by the time of the linguistic reorganization of states was a rather convenient development for those who had always remained unconvinced of the need to replace English.

The public motivations of the members of this pan-Indian English-speaking elite, in keeping with their self-conscious image of themselves as the 'Architects of Modern India', was always high-minded: the preservation of the national perspective and the unity and integration of India. It is true that, in time, the excessive zeal of the propagandists of Hindi made the implementation of the language policy difficult. But it is also true that influential bureaucrats (in collusion with their mentors in politics), did little to counter the chauvinisms on both sides of the divide through resolute policy initiatives. There was little incentive for those who had been trained to dispose off their files in English, and whose knowledge of Hindi was minimal or inadequate, to devote time to the implementation of the guidelines of Article 351, or dwell overtime on the formulation of a workable three-language formula, or ensure the allocation and optimum utilization of grants for the teaching of Hindi in non-Hindi-speaking states.

The one point on which the proponents of English were united was that Hindi was being made into an unspeakably difficult language by the 'narrow-minded' experts entrusted with its development. The criticism was valid, but for the wrong reasons. The motivation behind the plea for Hindustani, made forcefully and pertinently by people like Maulana Abul Kalam Azad, was not to maim the development of Hindi, but to enrich both Hindi and Urdu through the retention of a language which had become the lingua franca of the common man, specially in large parts of Northern India. However, the essential sentiment of the English-speaking upper middle class was not for an enriched blend of these languages but for an anaemic by-product which could be easily understood by them. To make Hindi simple, and not to creatively extend its reach and enrich its texture, was their simplistic demand. The humiliation inherent in such an approach for a newly independent nation, proud of its culture and heritage, was largely unfelt by them. What would be the reaction in England (or among the brown sahebs of India) if an influential lobby seriously argued for the deliberate pauperization of the English vocabulary! Hindi was a language with centuries of evolution and a sophisticated and extensive vocabulary. It could not be crippled or retarded simply to make it more comprehensible to those who had developed a greater facility in English. The same was true for the regional languages, whose development was also held to ransom by the preference for English of the ruling elite. The development of Hindi and the regional languages, as part of an overall and cogent policy backed by the requisite political will, should have been the norm in post-colonial India. To say that the perpetuation of English was in the national interest was a transparent attempt to give the cloak of ideology to a dominant sectional interest. For, how could a language spoken by less than one per cent of the population become a vehicle for national unity? Unless, of course, those who constituted that one per cent were also those who were running the country and interpreted the national interest from the very limited perspective of their own interests.

The truth is that English had become an instrument for social exclusion: the upper crust of the Indian middle class presided over this linguistic apartheid; the rest of India consisted of victims and aspirants. The ability to speak English with the right accent and fluency and pronunciation was the touchstone for entry into the charmed circle of the ruling elite. It was the criteria for social acceptance. Those who could were People Like Us. Those who could not were the others, the 'natives', bereft of the qualifying social and educational background. Even before Independence, but as close to it as 1944, Gandhi had warned: 'Our love of the

English language in preference to our own mother tongue has caused a deep chasm between the educated and the politically minded classes and the masses. We flounder when we make the vain attempt to express abstruse thought in the mother tongue . . . The result has been disastrous . . . We are too near our own times correctly to measure the disservice caused to India by the neglect of its great languages.'[36] Nehru had said with equal perception: 'The British had created a new caste or class in India, the English-educated class, which lived in a world of its own, cut off from the mass of the population . . .'[37] In pre-colonial times, this linguistic divide, while evident, was somehow enveloped by the larger task at hand, the struggle for freedom. Moreover, in spite of their knowledge of English, many of the stalwarts of the national movement 'lived and by and largely operated in the milieu dominated by the regional language and culture. It was not accidental, for instance, that Gandhi's *My Experiments with Truth*, Tagore's *Gitanjali* and Tilak's *Gitarahasya* were written originally in Gujarati, Bengali and Marathi respectively.'[38] In post-Independence India the English-speaking upper classes had little or no such redeeming features. But since they were at the pinnacle of the social order, their unrepentant and insular choice of this language set the norm, the standard of emulation, for the lower middle classes seeking upward mobility.

It is not surprising, therefore, that the formative years after Independence saw the mushroom growth of 'English-medium' schools. The tragedy was that in this process of mindless emulation, a real opportunity to give to English its appropriate role as the most easily accessible 'foreign' language in the overall structuring of the educational curriculum was lost. And since those who had not 'inherited' the usage of English as part of their social background could never acquire the same facility in the language, the nation produced a generation of linguistic 'half-castes'—insecure in English and neglectful of their own mother tongue. It also fostered a deep sense of inferiority in many talented people who, while excelling in their studies in spite of the burden of education in a foreign language, were unable to acquire the fluency in English of their social 'superiors'. None of this, of course, was of much concern to the self-assured world of the English-speaking elite. Its members had little reason to displace a language which provided them effortless social standing, access to the best educational institutions and the best jobs. The policy of 'benign neglect' of the language issue, for which Nehru has been recently praised, suited them rather well. This smug linguistic security would be challenged in the years to come, but the damage done in the foundational years of the Republic would leave a permanent scar. The members of the upper middle class who were (and are) both the beneficiaries and the perpetuators of such a system would do well to ponder over a charge made recently that 'no source of inequality in our society operates in as subtle and intractable a manner as language. Competence in English usage has become the single most important yardstick of a person's eligibility for negotiating the opportunity structure that can be availed of in a modern economy.'[39]

∼

The Indian middle class was the midwife of a compromised state—radical at the level of policy, self-serving at the level of practice. The evolution of this class under British rule, the position of vantage it enjoyed in 1947, and the tenacity of class interests in any polity are all elements in understanding why this happened. In his autobiography Nehru quotes approvingly a perceptive remark by the British writer Professor R.H. Tawney: 'The plutocracy consists of agreeable, astute, forcible, self-confident, and, when hard pressed, unscrupulous people, who know pretty well on which side their bread is buttered, and intend that the supply of butter shall not run short . . .'[40] The qualitative difference in the years just after 1947 was that even in pursuing its supply of butter the middle class was bereft of that soulless pragmatism, that complete lack of idealism, that is the bane of its members today. The Gandhi-Nehru legacy and the memory of the freedom movement gave a wider framework to the narrowness of the middle class' interests. In this sense the role of the middle class was constructive, for it became, in terms of its expectations from itself and from society, the harbinger of a positive value system on an all India scale. The gulf between precept and practice existed; but it was much less blatant than it is today; and the presence of an ideological framework made the presence of this gulf less visible, and therefore less accepted. The State enjoyed legitimacy, not only for its professed intentions but because it had widely respected leaders at the helm. The State was expected to deliver on its promises (this faith was in itself excessive, and this would have its own backlash in the years to come). Given the constraints placed on its functioning by the interests that controlled it, the State could at best usher in a 'passive revolution', whereby the demands of the new polity would be 'satisfied by small doses, legally, in a reformist manner . . . in such a way that it was possible to preserve the political and economic position of the old . . . classes.'[41] The genesis of the Indian State was such that it could not but be 'soft'—soft on all the hard rhetoric that could undermine the socio-economic structure that underpinned it.

There was thus the illusion that things were moving more or less as they should—at least for the world inhabited by the middle class. There was general political stability. The political monopoly of the Congress, the party that fought for and won independence, was largely unquestioned. The leadership was respected. The economy seemed to be trundling along. Per capita income, ahead of population growth, increased steadily, if marginally, by two per cent a year from 1951 to 1961. Industrial production was on the rise. The signs of change were visible. Newspapers wrote about them. Films romanticized them. Abroad, India's prestige was high. Nehru was a much admired leader worldwide. India occupied the moral high-ground in international relations: the policy of non-alignment gave it both a platform and self-respect. At home, the pressures were nowhere as great as they are today. The cities were manageable; municipal facilities could cope; water and power were available; admissions to schools and colleges posed little problem; there were less mosquitoes, less pollution and less filth, and on the whole less people trespassing on protected territory. The sway of the traditional middle class was mostly unchallenged. The cake was growing—albeit slowly—but the claimants were largely the same. Demands, from normally quiescent quarters, could occasionally be heard, but there was no jostling and aggression. All in all, there was a diffused sense of buoyancy and promise. After centuries of subjugation, India was on the move, on the path to resurrection.

But, alas, for the Indian middle class, this illusion would not last long. The defeat of India by China in 1962 and the death of Nehru in 1964 signalled a new phase in the evolution of the Indian State. It was the beginning of the end of the age of innocence. And, with it, the profile of the middle class was bound to change irrevocably.

The End of Innocence

The war with China in 1962 was the first serious blow to the easy confidence and sense of well-being of the middle class. The war was fought in the remote Himalayan mountain ranges, away from the cities of the mainland. No bombs fell on Delhi or Bombay or Calcutta or any of the cities which were the habitats of the educated classes. But the impact was psychological, not physical. The principle of non-violent non-cooperation on which the freedom movement was fought and won under Gandhi had, as we have discussed earlier, bequeathed a moral legacy, and its worldwide recognition had in turn fostered a sense of both pride and security. In Nehru, the nation had a much respected and admired spokesman of this legacy. His message, and the example of India's non-violent overthrow of colonialism, had a special relevance to the newly independent countries of the Third World. China was an Asian country, and a neighbour, with whom friendship and solidarity was part of the Nehruvian world vision. Its invasion of India and India's humiliating inability to adequately repulse the attack seriously corroded some of the assumptions on which the middle class had structured its hopes and expectations. Gandhi's faith in the near universal efficacy of non-violence was dramatically revealed to be what the middle class had always partly suspected it was: utopian. Nehru's belief in the natural solidarity of the colonized and his faith in the bonds of affinity that should exist between two Asian neighbours, based on shared principles and historical memory, were exposed to be the romanticizations of a man out of sync with the realities of the real world.

As often happens in such situations, the erosion of the sheen of trust and faith could not be restricted to only one area of assessment. If Gandhi's principle of non-violence had little relevance in the real world of international relations, was it realistic to expect that his idea of morality in public life would be relevant, given the compulsions of politics within the country? If Nehru's theorizings in diplomacy could be so rudely undermined by the ground realities of force and power, how valid was his espousal of the need to usher in socialism? Nehru's high-minded idealism in terms of his expectations from China had taken a severe beating. And, as a consequence, idealism per se was devalued in the estimation of his erstwhile believers. The retreat of the Indian army symbolized the retreat of idealism in the face of the compulsions of the real world. Moreover, the unpreparedness of the armed forces brought into question, for the first time in a focussed manner, the faith in the legitimacy of the State. For the middle class, the government that assumed power in 1947 was not the result of the normal equations of politics. It was a government that had emerged from the crucible of the freedom movement. It had a special sanctity, and this sanctity was extended to the party from which it was drawn—the Congress—and the State which it had the mandate to run. The intentions of such a State could never be doubted, and the presence of leaders who had themselves played a crucial role during the freedom movement prevented any skepticism from creeping in. But the debacle of 1962 found the State to be wanting both in respect of its promises and its abilities.

In the aftermath of 1962 there was a sense of bewilderment. Educated Indians had caught a glimpse of reality behind the comfort of illusions, and suddenly the institutions and beliefs of the past seemed inadequate when confronted with the uncertainties of the future. Expectations appeared more vulnerable now, and assurances less predictable. It was the beginning of a process. Assumptions were still sustained by the habit of belief, but the buoyancy and optimism, the faith and sense of purpose rounding the edges of middle-class aspiration were eroded. Sometimes it takes an outside observer to presciently sense the prevailing mood. V.S.Naipaul visited India for the first time in 1962. He travelled extensively in the country and met a large number of Indians, many of them from the cities. The year 1962, he wrote, was 'the last year of post-Independence glory for the Indian middle class, when (until the Chinese war blew away the fantasy) India seemed to have made it and Independence was still seen mainly as a matter of personal dignity, an Indian voice abroad, "Indianization" at home, a new kind of job, a managership, an appointment in the new diplomatic service, a new glamour, a conscious display of national costume and "culture".'[1]

Nehru survived 1962 politically. There was anger against him, and his attempts after the war to protect Krishna Menon, the Defence Minister, who was the real target of middle-class indignation, did not help his case. To decry his 'wooly-headed' idealism became a popular pastime in middle-class homes; from a man of vision, he was increasingly being regarded as a visionary. But there was also sympathy for him. His bonafides were not questioned. He had lost credibility, but not his appeal. The more indulgent were prepared to see 1962 as an error of judgement, the less forgiving as a monumental blunder of a good man. Even his defence of Krishna Menon recalled, at least for some, a value system of the past—to stand by a colleague when the chips are down. The role of idealism in the affairs of the State may have become less self-evident, but the transparent lack of guile in a man who personified such idealism still invoked understanding and even respect. There was a softer edge to political discourse; differences, across the political divide, were not harsh and shrill; and criticism, even when trenchant, was awed into restraint at the thought of who was the target of such an attack. It was perhaps for all these reasons that the middle class, after the initial shock of what had happened, rallied round remarkably well to contribute to the war effort. Patriotism and nationalism were at a pitch, but untainted by any notion of manipulation or partisan gain. And when Nehru wiped a tear on hearing Lata Mangeshkar's rendering of the lines *'Ae mere watan ke logon, zara aankh mein bhar lo pani, jo shaheed huen hain unki, zara yaad karo qurbani'*, there was hardly an Indian who could remain untouched by the innocence and pathos of the moment.

Nehru died on 27 May 1964, at the age of seventy-five, after having served as Prime Minister of free India for an unbroken period of seventeen years. For an entire generation of middle-class Indians, his was a presence taken almost for granted. People were aware of the persistent health problems in his last years, but the very fact that he could ever cease to be was somehow incompatible with the sheer familiarity of his persona. He had been around for so long, and in such an intrusive and paternalistic way, that it was expected that he would always be around. Nehru himself had encouraged this familiarity. He spoke and wrote about almost every important issue, and in a manner that the hopes and dreams of post-1947 India got inextricably linked with his personality and his utterances. He was loved by every Indian, but he symbolized a special assurance for the educated classes who had inherited the fruits of Independence. For them he was the bulwark of a value structure, an order, with which they could identify and which preserved their interests. He was not only living proof of the validity of a certain past, but also the guarantor of a future in which their pre-eminent participation would be ensured. In terms of his vision and his convictions he was hardly a spokesman for middle-class interests, but once this class understood how to get along quite satisfactorily in the gap between what he said and what actually happened on the ground, he became, notwithstanding his radical views, the most refined patron of a certain social structure with which it could identify. If in 1962 he was the focus of the middle-class Indian's anger and dismay, he remained, even after the event, and in spite of his obviously failing health, the rallying point for the nation to seek to transcend the humiliation of defeat. The damage could not be undone, but, while he lived, Nehru was a reminder of the relevance of the past and the continuity of a shared experience. He was the only leader in independent India who could sustain for close to two decades a national consensus, and ensure that this consensus was acted out in conformity with certain civilizational values, both in action and discourse.

The Indian middle class of post-1947 India was a part of this Nehruvian consensus. The events of 1962 dealt a body blow to some of the assumptions underlying this consensus, and loosened the hold of the Gandhi-Nehru legacy on which it was built. And when Nehru died, this consensus lost its most influential and persuasive spokesperson.

In seeking to survey, at a macro level, the developments in the three decades following the death of Nehru, it would be useful to identify certain dominant trends and correlate their impact on the evolution of the middle class. The first trend of importance was the visible retreat of ideology from public life and the corresponding transparency of the quest for power as an end in itself. As we have noted earlier, the middle class in India, as in many developing countries, needed to have an ideological framework, which it could identify with and owe allegiance to, in order to give a sense of purpose and context to its role in national life. The erosion of ideology, and the manner in which this class internalized this development, is thus of critical importance for the purposes of our study.

The political shenanigans that followed the brief interlude of Lal Bahadur Shastri's Prime Ministership immediately after Nehru's death made it rather obvious, specially to the educated classes, who followed the bitter acrimony between the two factions of the Congress Party as headline news in the morning newspapers day in and day out through most of 1968 and 1969, that the real tussle had little to do with issues and more with just the naked pursuit of power. This was a distinct break from the past. There had been struggles in the higher echelons of the Congress or in the government even before. For instance, Nehru's differences with his Home Minister, Sardar Patel, or his points of divergence with the President of the Republic, Dr Rajendra Prasad, were not entirely unknown. But these were always subordinate to a joint commitment to a larger cause, a greater goal, that transcended individual predilections. There was also the memory of the freedom movement and the influence of Gandhi, reinforced by the stature of the leaders themselves. The struggles within the government that resulted from such differences were thus played out far more discreetly. In fact, the underlying assumption behind these differences was that on a point of principle the leaders were prepared to differ, and even renounce political power before 1947 and in the years immediately after Independence, before there was more than one occasion when Nehru and other leaders were prepared to resign on a matter of principle.

It is perhaps because power has always had such an irrepressible appeal in the Indian tradition, that it has prompted an equally strong espousal of self-imposed restraints on its untrammelled pursuit. And the ability to renounce power has held a special fascination for Indians. Gandhi's adoration as Mahatma had undeniably something to do with his disdain for personal political positions. He was the unquestioned leader of the freedom movement, but he sought neither the Prime Ministership nor the Presidency. Such an indifference to power per se kept a check on the tendencies, always there in others, to uninhibitedly seek it. In any case, Nehru's pre-eminent position as a leader, and the banyan-like sway of the Congress across the nation, made it unnecessary to make a visible departure from this tradition. Till Nehru's death, both the principle and the facade were largely preserved.

Lal Bahadur Shastri's term as Prime Minister was much too short—a little over a year and a half—to allow the dilution of the assumptions of the past to overtly manifest itself. On his untimely death in January 1966, Indira Gandhi became Prime Minister. Initially, at the time when her name first came up as Shastri's successor, she continued the earlier tradition of devaluing the lure of political office. 'While (Morarji) Desai staked his claim to Prime Ministership most stridently, Indira maintained a low profile and dignified silence . . . (and) . . . kept up the pretence of being a reluctant Prime Minister even after she had been duly elected.'[2] Historians will debate whether this was just a ploy or the result of the as yet unshakeable hold of the expectations of the past. But this pretence was perceived to have been discarded with dramatic transparency in the months that were to follow. It is not the intention here to go into the details or assess the merits of the bitter and public fight for supremacy between Indira Gandhi and the clutch of old Congressmen collectively known as the Syndicate. But the rumours and invectives, the allegations and counter allegations, the partisan use of ideological labels such as 'progressive' and 'reactionary', and the accusations of the inculcation of personal loyalties over any consideration of principles, were sufficient to bury the faith in the mandatory role of idealism in public life forever. The change in the style of dissent and debate in the most visible rostrums of the nation, and the questionable methods employed to sustain this change of style, left little room for a more charitable interpretation by even the most indifferent observer. The middle class was certainly neither stupid nor indifferent. It held the ringside seat to these developments, and was witness, on an almost daily basis, to the reduction of ideology and principle to the level of manoeuvre and tactic. Colleagues in the cabinet were dismissed without notice; letters between leaders in the same party were deliberately leaked to the press even before they reached the addressee; individuals, prominent on the public platform, changed sides without the slightest qualm of conscience; and statements were made when it was obvious that they meant something quite different even as they were uttered.

The impression of a general sense of political mayhem was compounded by the disintegration, after the general elections of 1967, of the near monopoly of political power held since 1947 by the Congress. In several states non Congress governments came to power. These represented, as we shall discuss later, new interests clamouring for political power on the national stage, and were even less restrained by the memories and legacies of the past. Moreover, they were quick to internalize and emulate the fall from principle of the standard bearer in these matters—the Congress. The result was the most sordid display of opportunism and venality at the state level in many parts of the country, where coalitions were made and broken and made again with all principles thrown to the winds. For the first time since Independence, it became common knowledge that legislators were willing to switch sides for a price. In Haryana, they were labelled, in typical rustic humour, as *Aya Rams* and *Gaya Rams*, birds of passage, bereft of all principles and commitment.

On 1 November 1969, the nation saw the rather unusual spectacle of two simultaneous meetings of two wings of the Indian National Congress, each claiming to be the real party. The formal split in the once invincible behemoth was completed by the end of the month. Prime Minister Indira Gandhi was triumphant. Earlier in the year, in August, she had ensured the victory of Vice-President V.V. Giri to the Presidency, even though her party's official candidate for the job was the hapless Sanjiva Reddy. At the time of the split, the bulk of the Congress remained with her. Her next move was to try and wrest control of those states still ruled by Congress legislators owing allegiance to the Syndicate. 'To achieve this result all scruples were once again thrown to the winds and Indira's men went on a spree to buy over Congress (O) legislators in the states.'[3] In the general elections called by her in 1971, Indira Gandhi's wing of the party achieved a two-thirds majority in the Lok Sabha, substantially more than the undivided Congress had in the last House. The Syndicate was routed and left to fester as an inconsequential rump.

These developments, and the manner of their unfolding, have been described in some detail because they are of crucial significance in the kind of impact they made on the psyche of the middle class at a time when it was specially susceptible to internalizing such an impact. The defeat in the war with China had caused shock, disbelief and questioning. The death of Nehru two years later had removed a beloved and reassuring presence that guaranteed a certain legacy and value structure. With the certainties of the past askew, the next few years were of critical importance in evolving the ideological framework for the future. As a factor of influence, the political arena has always had a disproportionate importance in moulding the normative structure in India. Perhaps this is the case in all newly independent countries, where intra-system autonomies have yet to fully develop and the pervasive role of the State and the activities and conduct and behavioral choices of its leaders spill over into areas far beyond politics. Indeed, the distinctive nature of the Gandhi-Nehru legacy was that it defined for the middle class a way of life, encapsulating aims and goals, needs and wants and rights and wrongs as part of a unified value system, a code of behaviour, that was projected and generally accepted as being more than just the soulless mechanics of politics. But politics was the best platform to project this way of life; it was also one rarely redeemed by privacy or shielded from public scrutiny. Thus, what political leaders did became a kind of powerful normative theatre influencing the way people thought they should conduct themselves in their own little worlds of endeavour. The strength of the Gandhi-Nehru legacy and the extended duration for which it was sustained by a towering leadership had created a dependency syndrome: the middle class expected the political leadership to provide the norms and standards to define the parameters of its own code of conduct. Its vulnerability in this regard made it all the more porous to the messages emanating from the new paradigm of politics in the second half of the sixties.

These new messages were neither diffused nor e
They were buttressed by clinching empirical evi
Together, they spelt out an alternative framework of cond
and ethics that, like acid on steel, quickly carved out a place
for itself on the neglected structure of the Gandhi-Nehru
legacy. The supporting premises of this new framework could
easily be codified.

First, they stood on its head the Gandhian maxim that, in
the pursuit of any cause, the means are as important as the
end. From the din and dust and the acrimony of the political
scene following Shastri's death, the one inference that came
through clearly was that almost any method was acceptable
so long as it achieved the desired goals. Secondly, and this
inference followed from the first, there was a conscious
devaluing of the role of ethics and idealism as an aspect of
public life. Indeed, oversensitivity to such considerations was
dismissed as a refinement unsuited to the world of realpolitik
where there was little place for the squeamish and the finicky.
Thirdly, and this was again related to the first and second,
there was the glorification of power as an absolute end in
itself: the net outcome of political activity must be the retention
and consolidation of power; if this is achieved, the activity,
however base its motivation and content, is sanctified.
Fourthly, the individual, for the first time perhaps in recent
history, was actually projected as more important than the
cause. In this sense, politics in modern Indian history had
come a full circle: first, in the years before Independence, there
was the cause, whose expression created leaders; then there
were the leaders who because of the cause they espoused
were in the reach of power, but had the capacity to deny it
should that be necessary for the cause; then there were, even
after Independence, both the cause and the leaders, inextricably
linked, neither diminishing the other; and finally there was

subordinated all causes.

most importantly, for it was a derivative
and had the potential for the most
uences in the long run, was the
of the need for a society to have a
kind of ideological binding, a binding
coercive sense but in the sense of a set
of beliefs, almost sacrosanct, that could inspire rectitude and
socially appropriate action. The blatancy of the play for power
had laid siege to the Gandhi-Nehru ideological inheritance.
But what was worse was the cynical and overt use of 'ideology'
in the pursuit of power. It is said that it was P.N. Haksar, Mrs
Gandhi's erudite and urbane Principal Secretary, who advised
her that 'the best way to vanquish the Syndicate would be to
convert the struggle for personal power into an ideological
one.'[4] Perhaps his advice was motivated by the best intentions.
It is also possible that Mrs Gandhi sought to follow this advice
without wanting to debunk the very tool she was being
recommended to use. But the struggle for personal power was
so transparent that it became obvious, at least to the middle
class, that ideology, however laudable the terms in which it
was couched, was only a means to achieve that end. And the
fact that this stratagem was efficacious, in that Mrs Gandhi
emerged victorious in the end, conveyed a double inference:
that ideology could be made to serve narrow, personal ends,
and that to do this was both justified and effective.

As we have seen, where its own tangible interests were
concerned the middle class was quite capable of pursuing
them, notwithstanding the presence of an ideology that
sought to emphasize a different set of imperatives. But the
Gandhi-Nehru legacy still acted as a moderating factor against
the unrestrained pursuit of such ends; it was severe with any
attempt to seriously undermine the role of ethics in society.

But now the middle class was left without such a moderating framework. It was placed in a moral vacuum, where those who were supposed to set the standards had themselves indicated that these were really not necessary. Deprived of the security of an ideological umbrella, the middle class sought comfort in the only other certainty looming on the horizon—the authority of an unquestioned leader.

The Indian middle class' propensity to abjectly capitulate before a paramount leader (of which the apogee would be reached during the Emergency declared by Mrs Gandhi) was thus directly related to the erosion of an ideological commitment as an effective countervailing factor to such capitulation. In the case of Mrs Gandhi, the starkness of this transition was cloaked by genetic continuity: she was, after all, Nehru's daughter. The assumptions of the past were adrift; but its memories, its associations with the struggle for freedom and the principles and leaders and assurances that it had bequeathed could not be so easily obliterated. There was a need to assume the continuity of the past, and this partially explains the middle class' other propensity to acquiesce so easily in the phenomenon of 'dynastic succession'. Significantly, the more the continuity of the past was threatened, the greater was the need to hold on to the fiction that it was preserved because the future was in the hands of a former icon's progeny. The pendulum of allegiance would then oscillate between faith in a leader and, when he or she was found inadequate, a renewed search for a lofty ideology. But the resonances of the past would weaken with time, and so would the search for ideology.

The rise of Mrs Gandhi as leader on the debris of the past was thus a watershed for the middle class. The support she received did have a lot to do with the middle class' fascination for aristocratic succession: her father and she symbolized the lineage of the wealthy and the elite, above the reach of the middle class and therefore something it could not help looking up to. But it is undeniable that in the aftermath of the 1971 Indo-Pak war, which ended with Pakistan's abject surrender and the creation of Bangladesh, there was also a respect for statecraft and the ruthlessness and pragmatism of a powerful leader. It was, in many ways, Mrs Gandhi's finest hour: an enemy nation had been dismembered and the pre-eminence of India established in the subcontinent. This was in strong contrast to the debacle of the 1962 Indo-China war which was widely seen as the consequence of Nehru's moralist assumptions. With the past in shadow and the future uncertain, Indira Gandhi now became for middle-class Indians not only a metaphor for a new code of ethics and the amorality of success, but 'a symbol, a leader, a Shekinah to lead them through the night, a pillar of fire.'[5]

∾

The devaluing of idealism, as an aspect of leadership and as a factor in society, was accompanied by an erosion of the legitimacy of the State as an effective economic actor. We have noted that in the model of economic development chosen by India, the State was mandated to play a pervasive and interventionist role. Its chosen bias was to channelize economic activity on a socialist path. This bias had a broad supporting consensus; it was considered appropriate that the State should play a role in the elimination of poverty and the promotion of equity and social justice. Some of the constraints imposed by such a policy orientation were irksome to certain sections of the middle class, who would have been happier with more freedom to obtain their objects of desire and less of the regulations and bureaucratic controls. But even if their support was occasionally less than enthusiastic, they did expect the State to construct an economic agenda that could effectively contribute to the amelioration of the conditions of the poor and underprivileged.

The manifest inability of the State to achieve its stated goals on the economic front thus affected middle-class thinking at two levels: first, it raised questions about the legitimacy of the role of the State in this sphere; and, secondly, it raised doubts about the principles that were behind the assumption of such a role. The questions and doubts had probably surfaced even during the time of Nehru, when the gap between rhetoric and performance had begun to become evident. The middle class was itself greatly responsible for the inadequate implementation of Nehru's vision of a socialist India. It was unwilling to sacrifice its class interests even if it believed that the policies of the State in favour of the poor were justified. Nehru was unable to prevent this subversion. His intentions were sincere, but he 'allowed old institutions to persist under a cloud of reformist rhetoric and bureaucratic make-work . . . The atmosphere of action became a substitute for action.'[6] He left a legacy where the professed intentions of the State were radical, but its delivery in spreading the fruits of economic progress was poor, and the performance of the economy as a whole barely adequate.

For all of this, the Nehruvian years were imbued with an optimism, not uncharacteristic of a newly independent country, where the promise of a new dawn cast a kinder light on targets and statistics. In any case, the moderate economic growth in these years was indulgent to the middle class. Its illusions were largely intact. Unfortunately, the death of Nehru was followed by the failure of the rains in two successive years, 1965 and 1966. In a country overwhelmingly dependent on the monsoons, the consequences were disastrous. Large parts of the country were caught in the grip of famine. The shortage of foreign exchange foreclosed the possibility of large imports of food grains on a commercial basis. Prices shot up, and for the first time large segments of the middle class—doctors, teachers, engineers, and the ever volatile student community—came out of their relatively sheltered burrows to voice their protest against the economic hardships. The launching of the Green Revolution—whose impact we shall discuss in greater detail later—and the coincidence of sufficient rainfall in the next couple of years salvaged the situation somewhat, but the weather gods again played truant in 1972, at a time when the granaries of the nation were severely depleted in feeding the millions of refugees from Bangladesh and by budgetary resources stretched due to the war which had given birth to that nation. Once again, the scarcity of food and the increase in prices fuelled widespread discontent. The drought persisted the next year, and lingered on in some parts of the country almost till 1975. The ill-conceived attempt by the government to nationalize the wholesale trade in food grains in 1973 only accentuated the grave situation. 'Food stocks began to disappear as soon as the decision was announced. Consumers unable to lay hands on grain panicked. The government was unable to help them. Food riots the country was spared even in 1966 now took place in Nagpur, Bombay and Mysore. In Kerala all schools and colleges were closed after students looted food trucks.'[7] The attempt at nationalization was abandoned, but the damage was done. In one year, from 1972 to 1973, prices rose by an unprecedented twenty-two per cent.

The legitimacy of the role of the State in the economic arena derived from its professed intentions. These intentions, which made the impoverished masses a focus of special concern, were articulated with conviction by the leaders of the freedom movement and sought to be implemented by Nehru, given his unambiguous socialist inclinations. At least at the level of theory and perception the middle class, as has been said before, acquiesced both in this arrangement and the approach. But when the State was revealed so obviously to have fallen short of what it said it would achieve, the whole consensus supporting its activities was ripped apart. For a country which had elevated the goal of self-reliance to almost an ideology, the compulsion of importing Public Law 480 wheat from the United States was extremely humiliating. The slogan of *Garibi Hatao*—Remove Poverty—adopted by Mrs Gandhi in the 1971 elections had had an undeniable populist appeal and had contributed to her victory at the hustings. The middle class, not unfamiliar with populist rhetoric, had accepted this as an inevitable, if unwelcome, aspect of a democratic polity: leaders and political parties needed to carry conviction with the bulk of the electorate, the poor and the deprived. But the economic woes of the early seventies revealed the almost unbridgeable divide between rhetoric and reality. The slogan of eliminating poverty sounded terribly hollow when even such a basic requirement as food was in short supply and prices were spiralling steadily. For the first time the illusions of the middle class and the money in its pocket were hit simultaneously, and sharply. The result was a breakdown of the pact wherein it was willing to repose faith in the economic intentions of the State. And from this it was but a short step for it to question the concerns that had in the first place motivated this reposition of faith. If the State could be such a failure in acting upon its professed concerns for the poor, and if the leadership could be so transparently cynical in projecting these concerns only for narrow political gain, what was there to sustain in the middle class a sense of social sensitivity, or keep in check its tendencies to pursue only its own interests? A concern for the poor and the underprivileged had been an important aspect of the Gandhi-Nehru legacy. It had animated middle-class thinking, although often the interests of this class had militated against the policies dictated by this concern. But from now on, even the concern would diminish. The poor would become an abstraction, an unavoidable hindrance best hidden, as far as possible, from view.

～

A third factor to critically influence middle-class attitude and behaviour was the legitimization of corruption as an accepted and even inevitable part of society. As always, the susceptibility of those in high places to this virus quickly broke down the immune system of those who looked up to them for setting the norms of behaviour. The unquestioned probity of Mahatma Gandhi had provided a powerful antidote to the uncontrolled spread of this disease. But the symptoms were beginning to become apparent soon after Independence when he was still alive. Gandhi made public a letter he received in 1948 from an irate citizen in Andhra: 'The taste of political power has turned their heads. Several of the MLAs and MLCs are making hay while the sun shines, making money by the use of influence even to the extent of obstructing the administration of justice in the criminal courts presided over by the magistrates . . . A strict and honest officer cannot hold his position . . .'[8] The scourge grew during the Nehru years, notwithstanding his own public image of rectitude. Over eighty thousand cases of corruption were referred by the Vigilance Division of the Government to the Home Ministry for further investigation between the years 1956 and

1964. In 1964 the Government of India Santhanam Committee Report on Prevention of Corruption candidly recorded: 'It was represented to us that corruption has increased to such an extent that people have started losing faith in the integrity of public administration. We heard from all sides that corruption has, in recent years, spread even to those levels of administration from which it was conspicuously absent in the past . . . The general belief about failure of integrity . . . is as damaging as actual failure.'[9]

What, however, gave a new dimension to the problem was the impression, as yet nascent, that corruption in high places could be condoned and escape retribution. The Prevention of Corruption Act of 1947 was undeniably, and perhaps deliberately, both weak and deficient. No conclusive legal action against an offender emanated from it to set a public example of the State's resolve in these matters. Even more damaging was the manner in which, in the 50s, certain well-publicized scandals involving people in the highest quarters were handled. T.T. Krishnamachari, Nehru's Finance Minister, was involved in the Mundhra case in which the Life Insurance Corporation was the loser by over one crore of rupees. Krishna Menon was in the shade in the Jeep scandal, in which hefty orders were placed with a dubious firm in Britain. Nothing happened to both of them. Krishnamachari resigned as Finance Minister but was brought back into the Cabinet later; Menon was made Minister without portfolio in disregard of the comments of the Public Accounts Committee, and later anointed as Defence Minister. And Nehru publicly gave a clean chit to both.

The perception that the malaise had become both chronic and endemic grew in the years after Nehru. Several incidents that attracted considerable media attention and comment contributed to this process. In 1969 it was revealed that

Jagjivan Ram, a Cabinet Minister in Indira Gandhi's government and one of her chief lieutenants in the party, had not filed his income tax returns for the last ten years. The revelation was made by no less a person than the Finance Minister, Morarji Desai. It is said that Desai was aware of this for some time but he chose to make it public at the time of the imminent Congress split to derive maximum political mileage. Whatever his motivations, the lapse—if it could be indulgently described as that—was serious enough to create a public outcry. But Mrs Gandhi did not ask Jagjivan Ram to resign or even pull him up. She nonchalantly dismissed the entire incident as the pardonable forgetfulness of a busy man.

Another incident which created a dramatic ripple was the somewhat mysterious and bizarre case of Rustom Sohrab Nagarwala. On 24 May 1971, Nagarwala, a retired army officer who had also worked for Indian Intelligence, was handed over sixty lakh rupees by the chief cashier of the State Bank of India, Ved Prakash Malhotra, who said that he did this on instructions received over the phone from the Prime Minister herself. Malhotra realized that he had been duped when he later reported to the Prime Minister's house the completion of his mission. Nagarwala was arrested and confessed to having impersonated the voice of Indira Gandhi on the phone. The incident hogged media headlines. There were tumultuous scenes in Parliament. And some very incendiary questions remained unanswered: 'Had the Prime Minister rung up Malhotra earlier? If not, how was he familiar with her voice? Could the cashier have drawn a large sum from the bank vaults unless there was a precedent for the transaction? And whose money was it anyway?'[10] The rampant speculation was hardly put to rest when Nagarwala was tried and sentenced to four years rigorous imprisonment in three days flat, quite a record for a country notorious for its dilatory judicial procedures. In jail Nagarwala retracted his confession and asked for a retrial. But before this could be considered he died of a heart attack in prison in March 1972, and there were loud whispers that the powers that be had had him silenced. The innuendoes became even more strident when six months later the police officer who had investigated the case at such tremendous speed also died, in a car crash.

In 1971, Sanjay Gandhi, the younger son of Indira Gandhi, was selected by her government as the only applicant to be awarded the licence to manufacture 50,000 Maruti cars a year. There were a dozen applicants for the licence to manufacture what was then euphemistically referred to as an inexpensive 'people's car'. But Indira Gandhi maintained that the fact that Sanjay's mother was the Prime Minister had nothing to do with his selection. These were matters decided quite independently by the appropriate government departments. In any case, a deserving young man should not, she said, be thwarted from achieving his life's ambition merely because he was the Prime Minister's son. An area of three hundred acres of prime farm land in Haryana, on the outskirts of Delhi, was quickly acquired for the young entrepreneur by that state's obliging chief minister, Bansi Lal. It was said that the land had been acquired at artificially low prices and in violation of a regulation that prohibited plant construction within a thousand metres of a defence installation. But such allegations were ignored, as were the loud charges of favouritism and nepotism.

Whether the allegations were true or not is not for us the critical issue. It is not our intention, nor is it relevant, to dwell on the merits of the controversies surrounding the incidents we have just discussed. Perhaps Jagjivan Ram was genuinely only guilty of forgetfulness; perhaps Indira Gandhi had no ulterior motive in making light of his lapse; perhaps the link between the Nagarwala case and the Prime Minister was the fantasy of a frustrated opposition and he died of perfectly natural causes in prison; and perhaps Sanjay Gandhi was the only qualified applicant to be awarded the licence for the Maruti car. Our concern is with the impact these incidents made on the collective psyche of the middle class, and how they were perceived by the overwhelming majority of its members. The revelation of Ram's unpaid taxes came at a time when allegations were rife that he, and several other ministers, had amassed wealth quite disproportionate to their known sources of income. The casual manner in which his culpability was condoned reinforced the growing impression that the standards to judge personal probity were flexible, and that if you were important enough and had the right contacts you could get away with anything. The fact that political parties needed money and that big businessmen were prepared to contribute to their coffers was not unknown. But speculation about the increasing and unsavoury nexus between politicians and big business reached a new crescendo in the months after the Congress split. The activities of L.N. Mishra, the Minister of Foreign Trade in Mrs Gandhi's cabinet and the party's chief fund collector, acquired a notoriety that made talk of corruption in 'high places' a commonplace in middle-class homes.

Given this scenario, the unanswered questions in the Nagarwala case not only added credence to the pervasive belief about corruption in the highest echelons of government, but also brought the allegations of corruption to the doorstep of the Prime Minister herself. And when the licence for the Maruti car was awarded to her son, the charges of nepotism found a believing audience in the average middle-class person. For him, issues such as these were now not confined only to hushed whispers circulating on the rumour mill.

Thanks to a largely free press, which had grown in quantum and reach over the years, they were discussed openly and critically in the morning newspaper that he read. He was aware, for instance, that the credentials of Sanjay Gandhi as the only suitable applicant for the Maruti licence were less than established. A drop-out from school, he had not even completed the course at Rolls Royce in England. There were also the rumours that he had access to vast sums of money, readily provided by shrewd businessmen who were only too happy to invest in his and his mother's goodwill.

. All these incidents, the rumours, and the investigative stories in the press now led to the birth of a new phenomenon: the 'folklore of corruption'. Corruption at the highest levels was now assumed to be the norm. Its existence was taken for granted. Allegations sprouted quick and fast from what was undoubtedly a fertile field of evidence. Suspicions matured overnight into beliefs, and beliefs, in turn, nurtured new suspicions. Nehru had labelled this the 'atmosphere of corruption': 'People feel they live in an atmosphere of corruption and they get corrupted themselves. The man in the street says to himself: "Well, if everybody seems corrupt, why shouldn't I be corrupt?"'[11] The atmosphere had become far murkier since him. In such a milieu, the emphasis on ethics in public life became the naïve remembrance of those incapable of seeing the new reality. This new reality dictated that honesty was the flip side of the coin of failure, and dishonesty was the unavoidable accompaniment of success. The successful were there for all to see. And as their number audaciously proliferated, the wall of reticence and inhibition against the means they had adopted began to crumble. The belief that corruption was rampant prepared the ground for it to grow further, casting a shadow on almost every aspect of the nation's life. And the perception that it was pervasive legitimized its existence.

In this process, the middle class was victim, critic and colluder, rolled into one. The correspondence between the perception of corruption at the highest levels and the escalation of corruption in the everyday world of the ordinary person's life, was mutually reinforcing. If those at the helm of the country could be corrupt and successful, what was there to hold back those who at a less spectacular level had there own little opportunities to make money? This logic was particularly appealing to the vast army of official functionaries—themselves mostly from the middle class with whom the rest of the middle class had inevitably to interface on an almost daily basis. The impression seemed to grow that almost no transaction requiring governmental clearance or sanction could go through without the mandatory payment of bribe. Corruption of this nature had existed even before, but the scale and blatancy with which it now seemed to be entrenched was something new.

As the victim of this escalation, the average middle-class person was a vehement critic of corruption. But in the general erosion of ethics, many of the newly corrupt were people from his own class. Ironically, even a person thus enriching himself would never miss a chance in private conversation to condemn the increasing corruption of those at the very helm of the nation. The denunciation of corruption of a greater magnitude and at a higher level fulfilled the psychological need to minimize his own divorce from ethics. Hypocrisy grew, but guilt was allayed. More importantly, a large number of those at the receiving end of the system seemed to realize, soon enough, that it is better to swim with the tide than to remain forever marooned on an island of principle. If the payment of a bribe could get a job done faster, it was better to pay than to fight. And once money could be paid to get what was legitimate, what was there to block the next descent on the slippery slope, when money could be paid to obtain what was not? The appeal of the 'short cut' to gain, pecuniary or otherwise, was powerful. But again, those who were willing to grease palms, for legitimate or illegitimate ends, were also vociferous critics in drawing-room conversations of the growing canker of corruption in society. The hypocrisy—and eloquence—of the middle class seemed to grow in direct proportion to the degree to which it was compromised. To accommodate its own interests it was prepared to lower its ethical threshold, while always retaining its 'moral' right to criticize the corruption at the very top. Indeed, the perception of corruption in high places provided it an alibi to justify its own departure from principles. This was visible even in matters less dramatic than the actual acceptance of graft. After all, if the Prime Minister herself was perceived to be unfairly pushing the case of her son, there could be little wrong in an 'ordinary' Indian espousing the case of a relative irrespective of his merits. If politicians could rake in the cash in bagfuls, how could it be wrong for a bureaucrat to accept from a businessman a Diwali gift far more expensive than the occasion warranted? The 'folklore of corruption' gave corruption acceptability; and the greater part of the middle class, bereft of its ideological moorings after the death of Nehru, had little resolve or inclination to resist this development. In fact, the truth is that the innocent profile of the middle-class victim could give way as easily to the indignant anger of the critic as it could to the satisfied smirk of the colluder.

~

The trends we have discussed—the retreat from idealism,

the reduced sensitivity to the poor, and the legitimization of corruption—coincided with a change in the character and structure of the middle class itself. The traditional middle class, whose elements we have described earlier, had ensconced itself under the avuncular idealism of Nehru. The new claimants to middle-class status came from a different background, and were weaned on the pragmatic realism of Indira. Indira herself once summed up this difference when she said, 'My father was a saint who strayed into politics. I am a tough politician.'[12] The times had changed, and those who scrambled onto the bandwagon now reflected this change, not only in their origins but also in their idiom.

There were several factors responsible for the expansion of the traditional ambit of the middle class. In the post-1947 years there was big business controlled by traditional business families, and below this identifiable strata a small but socially subordinate entrepreneur class and a large trading community. Both the latter segments had grown over the years but without an aggressive claim for upward mobility in the social hierarchy. By the mid-sixties, however, with two decades of capital accumulation and expansion behind them, the more successful in their ranks were on the brink of taking the great leap upwards. An important milestone in expediting this aspiration was Indira Gandhi's nationalization of banks in 1969. This made capital available for the first time and on a national scale to a large community of entrepreneurs and traders who had hitherto been outside the traditional borrowing and investing community. Along with the setting up of government controlled financial institutions, such as the IFC, IDB, and ICIC, it helped establish 'a crucial financial infrastructure for systematic capitalist development in the country'.[13] Statistics give an idea of the extent to which this one step contributed to the changes in the economic fortunes of the many. At the time of nationalization there were 10,000 bank branches and deposits valued at roughly 6000 crores. These more than doubled in the next few years and by 1990 there were over 55,000 branches with deposits totalling 129,000 crores. Of course, the availability of capital at concessional rates was only one among many economic factors in swelling the numbers of the enterprising. But there is little doubt that the 'nationalized financial system mobilized domestic resources and organized their disbursement for productive investments over a scale and with an efficiency which the private banking system could never have come close to matching.'[14]

The considerable growth in the small-scale sector also provided a fertile breeding ground for new entrants to the middle class. The share of this sector had steadily grown since the second five-year plan. It was government policy to provide financial and fiscal incentives to small-scale enterprises, albeit with chafing regulatory mechanisms. Overall industrial growth, low but consistent, had provided a generally enabling environment. The nationalization of banks facilitated much needed availability of capital, and the ancillarization and sub-contracting resorted to by larger firms diversified the opportunities available. But, over and above all these factors, tribute must be paid to the entrepreneurial skills and tenacity of these pioneers. Red tape and an extortionist bureaucracy were a major constraining factor. If, in spite of this, some of these nascent units flourished it was because the survival instinct was high and scruples limited: often family members pitched in to reduce the costs on labour, and paid labour was ruthlessly exploited to maximize output. Many professionals, recent beneficiaries of the expanded infrastructure of technical education, preferred the path of self-employment and set up units of their own. Between 1966 and 1978, almost half of all factories that started production were in the small-scale sector; the number of products exclusively reserved for the small-scale sector rose from 128 in 1971 to 844 by 1981; and 'the share of individual proprietors and private partnerships in the total stock of capital within privately owned enterprises in the factory sector steadily rose over the seventies.'[15] By the mid-seventies the small-scale sector had grown to within striking range of contributing almost half of the country's total industrial production. And the significant point is that its profitability was often higher than that of the corporate sector.

The income of the lower bureaucracy in charge of the myriad regulatory mechanisms overseeing this spurt in private entrepreneurship, grew in tandem. Every agency assigned to enforce rules had officials willing to use them as the easiest means of making money. With more money around, there were more people willing to pay. And with more people willing to pay, there were more officials willing to accept, at each stage of the economic process. A registered enterprise in the manufacturing sector was entitled to an import licence. This had a price. When the goods arrived, their clearance required the 'cooperation' of custom officials. At the time of production, inspecting officials had to be kept 'pleased', and minions running critical infrastructure departments such as electricity had to be kept 'happy'. The assessment of excise needed the 'support' of the officials of the excise department. When the product hit the market, the 'help' of the officials of the sales tax department was crucial. And at the time of the final reckoning of profits, income tax department officials had to be persuaded to be 'understanding'. This enumeration is but indicative. The maze of officialdom was labyrinthine, and its stranglehold complete. At the level of formulation many of the policies were enlightened, but at the stage of implementation there were always enough loopholes and discretionary powers to make the 'appropriate' ruling or stamp of a government functionary the single most important factor for profit. The lower official functionary, on the basis of his salary and what he could earn as extra, was, till the mid-sixties, generally resigned to his status on the fringes of the lower middle class. But now, with the increase in opportunities and money, his purchasing power and his pretensions looked decidedly upwards. The increasing acceptability of corruption reduced his need to cloak his gains. In terms of income and perquisites, which were there to see, he aggressively claimed a place in the middle-class pantheon.

The burgeoning black economy also created a source of disposable income for a new generation of carpet-baggers who now emerged from the woodwork to bask in the light of a less inquisitorial sun. The existence of a black economy was not unique to India. What was unique, however, was its size, conservatively estimated to be almost fifty per cent of the recorded economy, and thus 'significantly larger than in other industrializing countries such as Brazil, South Korea, Mexico (and China)'.[16] There can be more than one view on the impact of the black economy. At one level it provided resources for investments and, given its integration with the 'white economy', helped sustain the capital market. But its wide awning also provided shelter to a fast-breeding tribe of hoarders, speculators, middle-men, real estate operators, traders and rentiers. This tribe flourished in the interstices provided by an inadequate and colluding machinery of law enforcement. More often than not it had protection from the powers that be. It is difficult to put an accurate figure to its size. One estimate at the end of the eighties quantified it as close to fifty million, of which traders formed the single largest component.[17] The figure would be smaller for the mid-seventies, but even then its presence was visible, and growing. Its motivation was not profit alone but quick profits made as unproductively as possible. Money acquired so easily and in such amounts could not be entirely hidden. Much of it found expression in the status symbols of the upper-middle-class life.

But such changes were not confined only to the cities. There were pressures pushing for recognition in rural India as well. Even prior to 1947 the Congress party derived its strength in the countryside from the support of the dominant land-owning castes, and the instruments of agrarian reform it introduced after Independence, such as the Zamindari Abolition Act of 1955, changed the status quo only to the extent that they shifted power from a handful of very rich upper-caste farmers to a broad band of middle-level cultivationalists of the intermediate castes. Such relatively well-to-do farmers owned over sixty per cent of the total land area—each such farmer owned, on an average, ten acres or more—although their numerical strength was less than a quarter of the total agrarian population. And it was they who benefited the most from the Green Revolution, introduced from around the mid-sixties.

The Green Revolution itself was the consequence of the realization that attempts to boost agricultural production through 'ideological' measures such as land redistribution were not yielding the desired results. What was required was the application of new technologies such as high-yielding varieties of seeds and better fertilizers. The famines of 1965 and 1966 dramatically underlined the urgency to energetically pursue this alternative strategy of development. When the new technologies were made available, middle-level farmers were the first to adopt them. These were no absentee landlords but hands-on farmers who had for generations lived off the land. Moreover, their holdings were 'large enough to generate the capital or secure the credit to pay for the inputs of the new technology'.[18] Government policies, such as substantial price supports for agricultural produce, subsidized inputs on account of water, power, fertilizers, diesel, etc., institutional credit, and the near absence of taxation of agricultural wealth and income, also helped, particularly since the principal beneficiaries were not without the clout to manipulate the system to their advantage. As the surpluses from agriculture increased, many such farmers moved into lucrative off-farm activities such as brick kilns, flour mills, sugar cooperatives, transport companies, trading etc. There was also profitable diversification within agriculture, such as the setting up of dairy and poultry farms on a commercial basis and the renting out of tractors and other agricultural equipment. Capital outlay was still kept to the minimum; family labour rather than extensive use of wage labour or machines was still the norm. But it was clear that a new class of 'bullock capitalists' had emerged, and it soon began to take an interest in things not restricted only to the monsoons and soil quality.

With the formation of non-Congress governments in 1967 came the first inkling of the impact this new class would have on Indian politics. No longer was it willing to be taken for granted by the Congress. Charan Singh, who headed the ruling coalition, the Samyukta Vidhayak Dal, in Uttar Pradesh in 1967, became the most eloquent spokesman for this agrarian bourgeoisie opposed to what were perceived to be the pro-urban policies of the Congress. A consciousness of increased political and economic clout also prompted the more confident of its members to acquire some of the accessories enabling greater social recognition. Children began to be sent to better schools, preferably in the 'English medium'. Consumer patterns began to change. Material goods, hitherto considered unnecessary for the simple lifestyle of a farmer, began to be sought. And lifestyles as yet remote and shunned as '*shehri*', or of the cities, were emulated. The arrival of television in the countryside around the early and mid-seventies also played a crucial role in this process. The programmes telecast were elementary, the television sets black-and-white and usually not more than one for an entire village. The ostensible purpose was to provide a visual aid to spur agricultural productivity, and programmes such as '*Krishi Darshan*' were indeed very popular. But telecasting could not be restricted only to such programmes; and, inevitably, perhaps unconsciously, television also brought in images, in a more intimate idiom than cinema, of an alternative lifestyle, of the cities and the upwardly mobile, just at a time when there were people who were acquiring the wherewithal to adopt them. For a variety of reasons, therefore, a significant segment of the countryside began to emerge as an aspirant to middle-class status. It was the beginning of a process which would see its explosive culmination in the adoption of the Mandal Report about a decade and a half later.

~

The number of people clamouring for a piece of the middle-class cake had thus increased, but the size of this 'cake' had not. In fact, given the famine years of 1972 and 1973, and the financial burdens of the 1971 war, the cake appeared to have reduced in size. The asymmetry seemed all the more prominent when the physical possibilities of the economy were juxtaposed against the aspirations and expectations of the arrivistes. The highly unpopular rise in prices was not only due to shortages in agricultural production but also because there was, in general, more money chasing fewer goods of a certain preferred variety. The reaction against the shortfall was all the more aggressive among the new entrants because they were late arrivals; moreover, unlike the traditional middle class in the years after Independence, the edge of their wants was not dulled by the ideology of restraint and simplicity. They arrived economically and socially when the societal consensus on the Gandhi-Nehru legacy had broken down. They sought to emulate middle-class lifestyles when all that remained to be adopted was the exterior shell of material desires. In this ideological void, only two things seemed to matter: success, irrespective of the means, and money, regardless of its source.

The traditional middle class was disoriented, striving to come to terms with the new imperatives of the social order. Its task was made more difficult by the brashness of the new entrants who were impatient to move ahead, and had little qualms about flaunting the power and goods money could buy. This latter tendency created its own social tensions. There were some powerful but fringe movements which arose in protest against the breakdown of a value system and the erosion of social concerns. The extreme left Mao-inspired Naxalite movement of the late sixties, which had its leaders in the intellectual '*addas*' of Calcutta, and which spread like a rash among students in places as far away as Delhi, was one such. It faded away not only because its support base in the impoverished peasantry was limited but also because its essentially middle-class organizational hierarchy provided a relatively easy target for the coercive machinery of the state to overwhelm. 'But the movement's stated aims had stirred the best young men in India. The best left the universities and went far away, to fight for the landless and the oppressed and for justice. They went to a battle they knew little about. They knew the solutions better than they knew the problems, better than they knew the country . . . Naxalism was an intellectual tragedy, a tragedy of idealism, ignorance and mimicry: middle-class India . . . incapable of generating ideas and institutions of its own, needing constantly in the modern world to be inducted into the art, science, and ideas of other civilizations, not always understanding the consequences, and this time borrowing something deadly, somebody else's idea of revolution.'[19]

After the euphoria of victory in the 1971 war, middle-class India came back with a thud to reality: economic hardship, an ideological vacuum, disequilibrium in hierarchies, the swagger and insecurities of the newly arrived, and a perceived sense of severance from the past with no assurances of a faith-inducing value system in the future. The charisma of Indira Gandhi, till recently a rallying point for the whole country, began to quickly lose its sheen. The middle-class Indians' disillusionment with her appeared to be less on account of how she did what she did—for the methodology of her practice of power was no longer a cause of revelation—and more on account of her inability to do enough to stem their growing discontents. Jayaprakash Narayan's Nav Nirman or Reconstruction movement, launched in 1974, provided the ideological peg for them to hang their increasing dissatisfactions on. His call for a moral renewal found in them a receptive audience, for it seemed to be the only alternative left to find a more effective polity and leadership to protect their own interests.

Jayaprakash Narayan, a socialist and a Gandhian at the forefront of the freedom movement, had remained away from conventional politics in independent India. When he reappeared on the political stage in 1974, his ability to voluntarily renounce power gave him (for reasons we have touched upon earlier) an irresistible appeal to the middle class. His unquestioned personal integrity and his link to the stalwarts of the freedom movement only enhanced his moral authority. The JP movement, so named after him, against the perceived immorality and corruption of Indira Gandhi's regime, first gained support among the city-based youth wings of the opposition parties in Bihar. It acquired momentum in the student committees of Gujarat, where a series of spontaneous protests coalesced under the banner of the Nav Nirman movement. In both states the demand was for the dissolution of the local legislatures and fresh elections. The attempt by Mrs Gandhi to use the coercive apparatus of the State to quell these protests only served to give the movement further momentum and extend its reach to other parts of the country. JP now spoke of the need for a 'total revolution'—a somewhat anarchic vision of building everything anew—and of an even more incoherent notion of 'partyless democracy'. For middle-class Indians, however, the lack of ideological rigour was not of very great importance. Their support for JP was voluble so long as he could provide a successful platform to channelize their resentments against Indira Gandhi for her failure to deliver in accordance with their interests and expectations.

Nothing demonstrates this more convincingly than their support, even at the height of the JP movement, for certain actions of Mrs Gandhi which they found to be in conformity with such interests and expectations. In May 1974, the trade union leader George Fernandes, under the broad banner of the JP movement, called for a countrywide railway strike. The strike was brutally crushed by Indira Gandhi. Over 20,000 strikers were arrested; large numbers were mercilessly beaten up; and families of absentee workers were summarily thrown out of their railway quarters. The ruthlessness of the state machinery was widely known, but 'most of her middle-class countrymen, including those who accused her of authoritarianism, applauded Indira for her "firmness" in dealing with the railway strike. Their dichotomy was easily explainable. *They did not want their own rights and privileges to be touched* [emphasis mine]. Many, if not most, of them were also sticklers for all the Westminster norms being observed in Delhi, and were angry when Indira failed to do so. But they also wanted the trains to run regularly and did not want aggressive trade unionists to hold the country, or any business for that matter, to ransom.'[20]

The middle class was also enthusiastically supportive when in September 1974 Indira launched a nationwide crackdown against smugglers and other economic offenders. One hundred and thirty-four leading smugglers were arrested in a pre-dawn raid on 17 September. Applause for such 'firm' action involved both a hypocrisy and, later, an even more damaging indifference. The more well-known smugglers did not belong to the middle class. Stories of their opulent lifestyles, based on crime, political patronage, and official collusion, were the stuff of both reportage and rumour, and the cause of much indignation and resentment. The wings of such high fliers deserved to be clipped. But, and herein lies the hypocrisy, the middle class was itself the most avid buyer of smuggled goods even when the tainted origins of such goods were beyond doubt. Such double standards were consistent with its strident condemnation of corruption in high places and the acceptance of its unavoidability where its own interests were concerned. And when the draconian Maintenance of Internal Security Act (MISA) used for 'firm' action against economic offenders became, in but a short while, a rather convenient tool in the hands of Indira Gandhi against her political opponents, the middle class, in an ominous portent of things to come, remained largely indifferent to such abuse.

Indira Gandhi probably knew quite well which of her

actions would receive the immediate endorsement of her otherwise vocal critics from the middle class. On 18 May 1974, in the midst of the JP movement and the railway strike, India detonated an underground nuclear device at Pokharan in the sandy wastes of Rajasthan to become the sixth member of the exclusive Nuclear Club. The credit for this landmark event—labelled by the government as a peaceful nuclear experiment (PNE)—was certainly due to Indira and the dedicated group of scientists, also from the middle class, who worked to implement her vision. However, over and above the demonstration of India's technological abilities, the nuclear explosion fulfilled a deep-seated yearning in the educated Indian for greater military prowess as a defining aspect of India's search for 'self-respect' in the international community. It was a yearning often espoused in disregard of other priorities perhaps more relevant to the 'other' India where self-respect could still be defined by the availability of two meals a day. In this as in other things the middle class was insular in its vision and unwilling to concede a different perception of the national good. Mrs Gandhi was aware of this and through Pokharan, or the annexation of Sikkim the next year, she knew she could—irrespective of the self-evident merits of these actions—also stem the growing disenchantment with her as a leader.

The selective endorsement of some of Mrs Gandhi's actions even at a time when the JP movement had considerable support was not proof of how discriminating the middle class was. It was proof, rather of its ideological rudderlessness, where the only compass working was a perception of its own interests and expectations. JP's critique of Indira Gandhi was on avowedly 'moral' grounds. The middle class was willing to climb onto the 'moral' platform to the extent that this platform could accommodate its discontents. It was happy, for instance, if its anger against the rise in prices could be given a better projection through a 'moral' critique. But it was unwilling to allow its endorsement of the 'moral' to rein in its own proclivities to the contrary. Thus, its internalization of the 'moral' critique was both partial and selective and this was betrayed in the lack of consistency in its critique of Indira Gandhi's actions.

There were other elements as well, more perhaps in the realm of psychology, to explain its inconsistencies. The unambiguous assertion of authority has always compelled admiration in the Indian psyche. Conversely, and perhaps paradoxically, the prospect of disintegrating authority has only served to heighten the barely dormant tendencies towards the acceptance of anarchy in society. The obverse side of this 'authoritarian-anarchic' syndrome is the unqualified adulation of a strong leader at the time of his emergence, and the unconcealed glee at his discomfiture at the time of his downfall. Psychology apart, the essential reason for such wide swings of emotion and allegiance is the absence of an ideological mooring, an enduring belief in some sacrosanct norms and principles that could provide a consistent and unfailing criteria for the educated Indian to judge the actions of others and his own. The Gandhi-Nehru legacy had partially filled this lacuna; but its impact was, unfortunately, shortlived. Self-interest had, indeed, always remained an enduring beacon. But the expectations this generated could at best be only inadequately fulfilled by a system seeking to deliver on its promises without long-term or structural changes. The adulation of any leader, however strong, could thus not last for long. For, expectations would soon enough outstrip the inherent limitations of the system. And then the pent up frustrations would express themselves in a celebration of the leader's inevitable fall from grace. By being unable to see beyond its narrow self-interests, the middle class limited its intervention in the system to only the fulfilment of those interests. If it appeared that these were being catered to in the short run, it was willing to set aside even a pretence at normative convictions. The Emergency imposed by Indira Gandhi on 25 June 1975 provided dramatic proof of this myopia.

The 'remove Indira' campaign reached its crescendo on 12 June 1975, when Justice Sinha of the Allahabad High Court pronounced his judgement in an election petition against her. His historic judgement set aside her election to Parliament in 1971, and debarred her from elective office for six years. The electoral malpractices for which she was so convicted were, according to some, both minor and of a technical nature. But the judgement greatly weakened her moral right to continue in office, and was welcomed with great delight by her opponents. An appeal to the Supreme Court obtained only a conditional stay. She could stay in office, but not vote in Parliament. The 'moral' indignation of her critics at any further attempt by her to cling to office was now at its peak. This, indeed, was the dominant sentiment of middle-class India too. 'It had become fashionable to express one's commitment to JP and his movement, even more fashionable to say how much one hated Mrs Gandhi, how dictatorial she had become: the old comparison with Hitler and Stalin had returned . . .'[21]

On the night of 25 June Indira obtained Presidential assent for the imposition of Emergency rule. Almost immediately, JP was arrested, as were almost all her prominent political opponents. Democratic rights were suspended. Censorship was imposed all over the country. The scope for dissent was eliminated. Overnight, the world's largest democracy was converted into a dictatorship.

There was not even a semblance of protest by the great

Indian intelligentsia and its educated hangers on. Till twenty-four hours ago they had emphatically added their articulate voices to the cacophony of righteous condemnation of Indira's undemocratic ways. Now, they gave proof of the strength of their 'ideological' convictions by crawling when they had only been asked to bend. By the evening of the first day of the Emergency it became clear that there had not been even a semblance of credible protest anywhere in the country. JP's powerful movement had as it were disappeared overnight. The most spectacular capitulation was witnessed among the traditional 'guardians' within the middle class of the right to dissent and free expression—the journalists. 'The national editors had been forced to submit to censorship, but nobody had asked them to drop on all fours in front of the government. Nevertheless, the editors, urged on by proprietors with bad consciences who wished to placate Mrs Gandhi, had assumed this traditionally Indian posture of respectful subservience, and they remained in it, not looking particularly dignified, until the emergency was over . . .'[22] Even worse than the fulsome flattery of Mrs Gandhi were the media plaudits that heralded the arrival on the national stage of her second son, Sanjay Gandhi. Till only recently, his Maruti car project was the butt of relentless criticism. But now he was hailed almost as a messiah, a symbol of the dynamism of youth, and, more to the point, the best bet to be in the good books of his mother. Some 'intellectuals' remained critical in their personal assessment, but they chose silence as the better part of valour. Others decided that the best thing to do was to flamboyantly climb onto the Indira Gandhi bandwagon. The colourful artist M.F. Hussain, whose bare feet hardly detracted from his talents as a painter even if this made him an object of considerable curiosity for the middle class, drew a much publicized triptych in oils of Mrs Gandhi, representing her as the goddess Durga, triumphantly vanquishing all her foes. Only a year earlier he had been a prominent participant in JP's protest march to Parliament.

The bureaucracy, across the country, and at both senior and junior levels, also quietly accepted the new regimen. Indeed, even if some officials were persecuted for their 'deviant' behaviour or for not being sufficiently 'committed', the combination of strong political authority and the absence of dissent was generally welcomed by others in the clan as the 'appropriate' milieu for administering firmly, and if necessary, arbitrarily. It is true that the conditions of service made it difficult for officials to speak against their political masters, but it is also true that over the years bureaucrats had come a long way from being fearless implementers of correct policy. There was a time, in the years after 1947, when a politician would hesitate to ask an upright bureaucrat to do something which was not according to the spirit of the rule book. And if such an order was given, a bureaucrat would ask for it in writing, and then record his reasons for opposing it, unconcerned about the consequences. But, in tandem with the decline of ethical standards in society as a whole, the much vaunted 'steel framework' of the bureaucracy had long since ceased to be invincible. In fact, contrary to popular perception, it was not the unethical politician who first corrupted the bureaucrat; it was the ambitious bureaucrat who, quickly falling in tune with the changing times, first indicated to the politician that for the right rewards he was willing to be corrupted. From then onwards it became much easier to build the politician-bureaucrat condominium on the strong foundations of mutual gain, whether pecuniary or otherwise. This process had consolidated itself by 1975. Mrs Gandhi had therefore little to worry on account of the bureaucracy.

On the whole, and in striking illustration of the ideological barrenness to which it had been reduced, middle-class India accepted the suspension of democracy with a readiness that transparently betrayed the sole reference point that animated it: its own narrow self-interest. Most of its members had supported the JP banner as the only available avenue to effectively give vent to their economic discontents, specially with regard to the rise in the cost of living. But the unending political turmoil generated by the movement was proving to be tiresome; and its excessive emphasis on the moral, tedious. Mrs Gandhi could now impose some 'authority', and dispel the fear of chaos and disorder. Many of the steps taken by her regime seemed to provide proof of such an intention. Trains were running on time; some notorious hoarders and smugglers had been arrested; there was to be a crackdown against speculators; traders had been ordered to display prices; commodity prices were to be rigorously monitored; government servants had orders to be punctual and less often on tea-breaks; the law and order situation was better and petty criminals were at bay; and corruption had at least become more 'rule bound and predictable' and restricted to a 'monopoly' of those close to the regime. What more, after all, could one ask for in a democracy?

The plight of the common man was, however, not quite as comfortable as that of his middle-class countrymen. Sanjay Gandhi was determined to use the draconian powers under the Emergency to get rid of slums and enforce family planning. The poor were the primary targets of both endeavours. Slums in the city were certainly an unsightly reminder of the grim problems of poverty and unemployment. The remedy, of course, was to try and tackle the underlying systemic reasons for the poor and unemployed from the countryside migrating to the cities. To wish them away as part of some 'beautification' programme was hardly the remedy; and to brutally enforce such an elitist vision through the coercive machinery of the State was hardly the right policy. The move to restrict families to two children was in conformity with long-stated policy. It could even be conceded that this policy needed to be more energetically and imaginatively implemented. But the move to enforce it by such clumsy methods as giving mandatory vasectomy 'quotas' to every petty official dealing with the unempowered public was a terribly foolish way of achieving the desired goal. Nor was it intelligent to make—as allegedly happened in innumerable cases—vasectomy a punishment for any and every offence. Distortions in the implementation of such a policy were inevitable. Every case of an innocent victim, or—in the case, for instance, of an unmarried man, an ineligible victim— received the widest publicity through a rather efficient whisper campaign organized by the underground opposition. Thus, even as the bulk of the middle class in its urban citadels was singing paeans to Mrs Gandhi, the opposition to the Emergency in the country as a whole was growing.

It is interesting to examine why Sanjay Gandhi's slum clearance programme and his attempt to enforce the small family norm had (and continues to have) the enthusiastic support of large numbers of the middle class. Those who lived in slums were not from the middle class. They were the poor, who defiled the aesthetics of the neighbourhood, spread disease, fostered criminals, and laid claim—illegally— to already scarce municipal services. If they could be somehow removed from vision and tucked away in a less noticeable part of the city, it was all for the good. Of course, most middle-class homes needed domestic help to clean the toilets or wash clothes and utensils, and many of those who provided these services lived in these slums (which explains why every middle-class or affluent neighbourhood sustains its own satellite cluster of *jhuggi-jhonpris*). But no matter. What would have been really nice was the removal of the eyesores that were their habitats without the loss of the support services they provided. If they had now to travel long distances—expending time and money—from their new areas of rehabilitation to reach their traditional employers on time, it was their problem. Sanjay Gandhi, cutting through the red tape of rules and electoral sensitivities—for, unfortunately, these recalcitrant slum dwellers also had votes—was helping to achieve this desired state of affairs for the middle class. Of course, in this process there would be some unavoidable instances of hardship and the use of excessive force, but these could hardly be helped. The essential thrust of the young man's policy was correct and such labels as 'fascist' and 'undemocratic' were only an attempt to besmirch his no-nonsense panache.

The poor, the average middle-class person also believed, had this tendency to multiply like rats. Their increasing numbers were a burden on the economy, an impediment to growth and prosperity which was now within reach but for these unwashed masses. It was pointless to work for a reduction in their numbers through such long term—and ineffective—measures such as education and economic development. Such an approach was unrealistic, and even if it worked would take far too much time. What was needed was some 'firm' action to prevent them from multiplying, even if it meant the use of force and the curtailment of their democratic rights. Only such measures would work with 'these people' who would otherwise remain steeped in ignorance and superstition. Sanjay Gandhi's family planning drive was, thus, on the right track. As always, some instances of excess and abuse were unavoidable in the strong implementation of any good policy. But so long as they happened to these other people—who, in any case, had a tendency to exaggerate—it was all right. The important point was that as a result of such strong-arm tactics there would, hopefully, be less of the 'other India' to pull down those who had arrived, or were impatiently waiting to arrive. And this could only be for the good of all concerned, including, of course, the nation.

Unfortunately for the middle class, the poor far outnumbered it, and by the time Mrs Gandhi called for elections in January 1977, it was clear that the wind was blowing strongly against her. It was time, therefore, to dump her and shift sails to join the winning flotilla. And this is precisely what many prominent members of this class did. The adulation with which they had greeted her suspension of democracy was matched by the enthusiasm with which they celebrated her defeat on the restoration of democracy. Even the pretence of principles, of consistency in thought and action, of some beliefs over and above the perception of self-interest in the immediate context, was over. The years between 1964 and 1977 had taken their toll. The die was cast. From now on the pendulum would swing mechanically across the political spectrum. The moral opposition to Indira Gandhi led by Prime Minister Morarji Desai assumed power in 1977, only to quickly fall apart on the sharing of the spoils of power. Mrs Gandhi was back in office in 1980. And so the process continued, with the middle class increasingly proving itself to be convictionless, remarkable only for the extent of its material wants. But even with regard to the latter there were changes taking place, and, for the purposes of our study, we will examine at this point at least two subsequent events: the initial appeal of Rajiv Gandhi, and the impact of the Mandal Commission Report.

~

Throughout the seventies, and at a rate disproportionate to the growth and expansion of the economy as a whole, the middle class had continued to consolidate its economic position. Prices had risen, but so had incomes. The improvement in fortunes was particularly noticeable in the case of the self-made entrepreneurs and businessmen who had aggressively arrived on the middle-class stage only a decade or so ago. The 'new rich' may have lacked a certain kind of 'upbringing'—a point of comment for the more exclusive in the traditional middle class—but they also had much more of what really mattered: money. 'Upbringing' could not be bought for money; but money could certainly compensate for it by bringing in more of the things—a car, a TV, a music system, the entire range of 'foreign goods'—that now even the more 'well-bred' hankered for. Things were generally looking up even for the salaried class, even though in comparison to the new money in evidence they had reason to lament their perennially deprived status. 'We are only middle-class people' or 'We are "service" people' were by now worn out phrases, revealing not only a tinge of regret for what was beyond reach, but also an inability or a refusal to see the unbridgeable gulf that still separated them from the really deprived.

The improvement in economic status was both gradual and dramatic. Some of those who travelled by bus had bought a scooter; those with a scooter had graduated to a car. The old Philips radio had given away to a Sony transistor; and the transistor to a black-and-white television. Savings, garnered with difficulty, had yielded dividends; an expanding economy, and bureaucracy, had provided an opportunity for both husband and wife to work. Ancestral properties, long neglected, had grown in value. A fan in summer had been replaced with a 'cooler'; a cooler, in the more well-to-do homes, with an air-conditioner; houses had been renovated to include modern fittings and sanitaryware. More houses had telephones. More people were travelling abroad, on leisure or 'excursion fares', or on employment, sending much of their savings home. Families went out to eat once in a while; children got their way oftener about the need for new clothing; and the young, only recently employed, began to think of what their fathers could not contemplate till close to retirement: investment in property.

There were dramatic manifestations of this gradual economic consolidation. In 1978 Prime Minister Morarji Desai decided to auction the government's gold reserves to raise money and inhibit the smuggling of gold into the country. To the surprise of the government, the price of gold did not come down after the auction. It rose higher, thereby indicating that there was now a wider and stronger spectrum of monetary surplus in the upper echelons of the economy that could not only absorb the excess but also ask for more. The spectacular increase in the value of real estate made this trend even more obvious. Between 1980 and 1982 land prices more than doubled in the major metropolitan cities of the country. The sudden surge in demand took a lot of people by surprise. Retired couples living quietly in Delhi in unassuming houses financed by taking government loans repaid over years, suddenly found brokers offering sums for their property which left them dazed. The new demand for housing made the earlier pace of municipal growth look prehistoric. Cities grew both horizontally and vertically at a rate that consigned all earlier notions of size and suburbs to history. Building activity tried to meet the demand; but there were more people wanting to buy than there were properties available. And prices continued to rise. As did rents.

By the early eighties the indications were all there that

the 'dominant proprietary classes', with strong representation from the middle class, had considerably grown in strength. Pranab Bardhan has divided these proprietary classes into three broad categories: the industrial bourgeoisie, the rich farmers, and the professional classes. The problem was that the State itself had lost its 'autonomous' role in regulating the inter se conflicts of these dominant interests. One manifestation of this was the increasing and unproductive proliferation of subsidies to placate these competing interests. 'When diverse elements of the loose and uneasy coalition of the dominant proprietary classes pull in different directions and when none is individually strong enough to dominate the process of resource allocation, one predictable outcome is the proliferation of subsidies and grants to placate all of them, with the consequent reduction in available surplus for public capital formation. Huge subsidies from the Government budget are required every year to maintain high support prices for farm products, while the vocal urban consumers (as well as the industrialists whose wage costs will go up otherwise) have to be pacified with lower issue price of grains at the public distribution points; to maintain low prices of fertilizers, irrigation water, power, diesel and so forth for rich farmers; to supply all kinds of underpriced public-sector-produced materials and services for rich industrialists; and to promote substantial subsidies to export interests.'[23] To illustrate his contention Bardhan provides some revealing statistics. In 1950-51, the total amount spent on subsidies by the Central and state governments was 0.4 billion rupees. By 1970-71 it had risen to Rs 3.4 billion. In 1982-83 it was close to Rs 40 billion. Similarly, the expenditure on the public bureaucracy rose by seven times in the period between 1950-51 and 1980-81. And, significantly, the per capita increase in income of a Central government employee was two and a half times higher than that of the national average.

The economic cake had begun to taste quite sweet; but there were too many knives in it, and no impartial master of ceremonies. Benefits, and a yielding state, had fuelled aspirations. But while the aspirants sought quick fulfilment, the state could not deliver, immobilized as it was by the conflicting demands of the very interests it had brought to maturity. There was a diffused sense among the beneficiaries of the need for a more effective and transcendent arbiter who could take all their interests a step further. For large sections of the middle-class, many of the instrumentalities of the part were perceived as both discredited and ineffective. Little could be expected to be achieved from a replay of the political process as it had unfolded over the years. The existing political leadership had also a fatiguing sense of deja vu about it. Umbrella organizations—such as the Congress party, which had in the past absorbed the pulls and pressures of the dominant coalition within its pan-Indian patronage system— were seen to be running out of steam. This diffused but identifiable sense of inadequacy was rudely jolted by Mrs Gandhi's tragic assassination in October, 1984. Her elder son, Rajiv Gandhi, an airlines pilot, who had consciously opted to stay out of politics, and had only reluctantly agreed to assist his mother after the untimely demise of his younger brother, Sanjay, in an air crash in June 1980, succeeded her as the Prime Minister of India.

Rajiv was forty when he became Prime Minister. His sheer paucity of years was as audacious as the fact that he had almost none of the traditional exposure to politics. For the middle class he represented something new, something different to the predictability of the past. The fact that he was not a 'professional' politician was his biggest asset, for this implied a certain innocence of the compromise inherent in the existing state of affairs. His youthful years promised a dynamism and the possibility of a future that could mark a new beginning. He was perceived to be free of the baggage of old ideology, pragmatic, with an open mind, and capable of taking decisions without the mandatory reference to the past. In his tastes and sartorial preferences, in his familiarity with computers and the latest technology he was a 'modern' man. At the same time his personality projected a certain 'gentlemanliness', quite in contrast to the manipulative and ruthless image associated with his brother Sanjay. He was good-looking, urbane, and with the right lineage. The serenity on his face in a moment of deep personal tragedy, as he lit the pyre of his slain mother, would etch itself on the minds of millions of middle-class Indians as they watched the live telecast of Mrs Gandhi's final journey.

Expectations had also come full circle. Earlier, in the years after 1947, the middle class had given allegiance to a leadership that had an aura of personal sacrifice, a long association with politics in the struggle for freedom, an unambiguous set of ideological beliefs, a professed disdain for material pursuits, and unquestioned personal integrity. Nehru fitted this bill. Some three decades later, his grandson was the hero of this class for a different set of reasons: he had had little or no involvement in politics, he was perceived to be free of straightjackets, ideological encumbrances, and in his demeanour and his inclinations he held the promise of a decisive push towards greater material fulfilment. By now the middle class was not only bereft of an ideological framework, it was generally tired of the deceit of ideology. If Nehru stood for ideology as a conditioning prerequisite for economic development, Rajiv stood for technology as the pragmatic precondition for economic change. This qualitative change in outlook corresponded to the felt needs of the middle class, which, after a period of economic consolidation, saw itself marooned on a plateau far below the summit of its material expectations.

Middle-class Indians saw Rajiv Gandhi through the prism of their own needs: the opening up of the economy, access to hitherto out-of-reach consumer goods, and technological progress. They had reasons to believe that these hopes would be fulfilled. By the time he became Prime Minister, after the assassination of his mother in 1984, Rajiv Gandhi had already acquired the image of a 'modern' leader. He was elected to Parliament in June 1981. The same year saw the commencement of production of colour televisions in India as a part of government policy. Next year in November the Asian Games were held in New Delhi. Rajiv Gandhi was in charge and did a commendable job in ensuring the meticulous planning of the event. The middle class shared his perception that the Games were 'a window for the world to see what India is capable of doing when we really mean business'.[24] In as much as the event was a success internationally, it was also a technological landmark internally. For the first time its inauguration was telecast live in colour, nationwide. To facilitate the fullest impact of this feat, individuals had also been permitted to import colour televisions on a differential rate of duty. Indians living abroad—and the middle class had now quite a few, specially in the Gulf, UK and USA— were allowed to send colour televisions into India for their relatives, and these came in sizeable numbers. These were propitious signs.

It is important to remember that Rajiv's own vision—and popularity—may have been much wider than merely the things which made him a messiah for the middle class. Our focus, however, is limited to try and see what were the reasons for his appeal to this particular segment. And to understand that notwithstanding his looks and lineage and youth and sincerity, he was doomed to fall prey to the same syndrome as those before him: the limitations of the system making it impossible for a leader or government to deliver in conformity with expectations. At the helm, Rajiv had commitments beyond pandering exclusively to the middle class. This was not only a matter of inclination or choice but of political compulsion: the bulk of the populace was not from the middle class, and its needs could not be ignored, because even though it was still ill-equipped to effectively give voice to such needs, it had, over the years, adapted rather well to democratic politics, and the verdict of its numerical majority could no longer be taken for granted. But the system, as it was structured and as he had inherited it, had its own limitations in catering to all the demands placed on it. Rajiv Gandhi's ultimate tragedy was that in spite of his sincerest intentions he fell flat between two stools: he could neither fulfil the heightened expectations of the middle class, nor could he restructure the system to effectively cater to the more assertively articulated needs of the poor.

The honeymoon was bound to be shortlived. The furore over the allegations of corruption in the import of the Bofors gun, which led to Rajiv Gandhi's defeat in the 1989 elections, was but a symptom of a deeper malaise, wherein disillusionment with a political leader, whatever his strengths or foibles, was an inevitable consequence of the limitations of the system. The personal charisma and talents of a leader who chose to operate within the system as it existed ultimately served only to raise expectations at a pace disproportionate to the abilities of the system to deliver. And, as had happened with other leaders in the past, once Rajiv's political ascendancy began to show cracks, the middle class revelled in his discomfiture with the same intensity with which it had celebrated his coming to power. The hypocrisy and double standards in much of its criticism were, if anything, even more transparent. The righteous cacophony over the payoffs in the Bofors case coincided with the acceptance of corruption, away from the public glare, in the everyday life of most of its members. The indignation over such trivial matters as his 'extravagant' holiday in the Lakshadweep islands with his family and friends was coterminous with a visible increase in conspicuous consumption among these same middle-class critics. The moral outrage over his capitulation in the Shah Bano case was accompanied by little signs of the desired social courage in the average middle-class person when it came to confronting religious orthodoxy and prejudice in his personal life.

~

V.P. Singh became Prime Minister when Rajiv Gandhi lost the elections in 1989. His term in office lasted less than a year, but it would leave a lasting legacy because of his announcement of the implementation of the Mandal Commission report on twenty-seven per cent reservations for backward classes in Central Government jobs. B.P. Mandal, who himself belonged to a backward caste, was appointed in 1977 to head a commission to identify backward castes and make recommendations for their advancement. He submitted his report in 1980, but neither Indira Gandhi nor Rajiv took any steps to implement it. On 7 August 1990, V.P. Singh, somewhat besieged by the infighting in the fractious coalition he headed, finessed his opponents by making the politically explosive announcement of the implementation of the Report.

The reaction took the country by storm. There were violent

student demonstrations in urban centres throughout the country. Some students immolated themselves in protest and became instant martyrs. Given the urban-centric nature of the media, the protests captured news headlines for days on end. Pictures in the newspapers and on television of the flame-engulfed body of the first student who immolated himself in Delhi fuelled angry denunciations of the report and of the unethical political expediency that seemed to have inspired V.P. Singh's action.

It is not our intention to go into such allegations, or to analyse the accusations as regards the methodology adopted by the Mandal Commission to support its recommendations. The seminal point for our purposes is that the implementation of the report, whatever the reasons behind the timing of the announcement, had brought to fruition a certain socio-economic process, wherein a significant section of the intermediate castes, specially in the rural areas, were demanding a share of the middle-class cake and made little secret of their intention to eat it too. As a result of the tenancy legislation of the Nehru period and the impact of the Green Revolution, many of these 'backward' castes had grown in economic and political power. Throughout the seventies and the eighties, the Jats, Yadavs and Kurmis in the north, the Kammas, Reddis, Vanniyars and Nadars in the South, the Kumbis, Patels and Patidars in the West, and the Marathas in Central India, to name the more prominent ones, had consolidated their status as powerful socio-economic groups in the rural areas. However, aspirations to middle-class status and lifestyles, which had only grown in intensity over the years, could not be sustained by agricultural incomes alone. In a generation or two even a land holding of a size within the ceiling limit permitted by the state (about fifteen to eighteen acres of irrigated land) gets fragmented. And without avenues for mobility to non-agricultural employment the younger generation of peasants finds itself exposed to unavoidable downward social mobility or even pauperization.'[25] This was all the more so because 'the incidence of farmers accumulating capital and investing their surpluses into business or industry are rare in our country. It has not happened in Punjab where the country's first green revolution took place. It has very partially happened in Maharashtra and Gujarat. Some evidence of such a transition . . . could be found in parts of Andhra Pradesh where rich farmers, particularly the Kammas and Reddys of the Krishna-Godavari valleys, due mainly to cash crop cultivation have slowly moved out towards industrial production graduating through commercial and real estate enterprises. Such mobility is however rare.'[26]

The rural middle castes had thus grown economically and wielded even greater political power, but these had not, from their point of view, translated into the desired employment opportunities which could fulfil or sustain the aspiration towards greater upward social mobility. A job in government held a special appeal. It had the aura of power and authority and made one a part of the establishment. This was of considerable importance to those who had traditionally been unrepresented, or at least under represented in the government hierarchy, still largely monopolized by the upper castes. A job in government signified status, security of tenure, and, given the pervasive level of corruption, opportunities, for those so inclined, to make money. In implementing the Mandal report V.P. Singh was helping to realize the felt needs of an important political constituency to become a part of the middle-class establishment on a more secure and institutional basis.

Singh described his move as representing 'a change in the very grammar of Indian politics'. He claimed that he had through Mandal facilitated the silent transfer of power away from the upper social strata. 'Today,' he said, 'an alternative rural elite is in the making.' There was an undeniable basis to the linkage Singh established between Mandal and the cause of social justice. Elites tend to be self-perpetuating; and the traditional upper-caste middle-class elite had made full use of its access to better educational opportunities and acquisition of skills in the professional and technical services to perpetuate its dominant role in the administrative and managerial services. In all the years prior to 1990, this elite was not particularly concerned about the fact that merit as a criteria for entrance to educational institutions and for jobs could hardly be operational when the bulk of the population was not even in a position to compete. So long as its hold on the benefits of the system was unchallenged and those who, at least under the Constitution, were equal claimants to such benefits were resigned to be on the fringes, everything appeared to be fine. It was only when this happy monopoly was challenged that merit, as against the accident of birth on which the reservations policy was based, suddenly became a major ideological issue. The city-based traditional middle class, somewhat cut off from grassroot realities and more susceptible to confusing theories for facts, was probably under the impression that caste, that 'anachronistic relic of the past', had faded away. The fact that it still existed may have come as a surprise to them; and it was only natural for that surprise to turn into outrage when its existence transformed itself into a challenge to their hold on the system. In any case, the argument that Mandal was opposed to merit rang a little hollow since, in the many decades before Mandal, the bureaucracy, or for that matter most institutions in the government arena, had really not distinguished themselves as symbols of great merit or efficiency.

The irony, however, was that the slogan of social justice rang equally hollow on the lips of the beneficiaries of Mandal. The neo-affluent and politically aggressive 'backward' castes identified by Mandal had little concern for social justice where their interests came in conflict with the needs of those for whom they should have been the spokesmen: the vast numbers of the poor and socially oppressed peasantry comprising the Dalits, or the scheduled castes, and the most backward castes who continued to live in absolute deprivation. According to a survey done by the Scheduled Caste Commission, till as late as the mid-eighties, over ninety per cent of the bonded labour in the state of Uttar Pradesh was from the scheduled castes. Most of the Dalits were either landless or precariously marginal farmers, whereas the bulk of the land was concentrated in the hands of the upper and backward castes, who, by virtue of their dominant position, had also siphoned off most of the benefits of schemes intended exclusively for the welfare of the scheduled castes. With increasing political awareness the Dalits were often more assertive on questions of land redistribution or minimum wages. This assertiveness brought them in direct conflict with the ascendant backward castes, and whenever this happened there was little ambiguity in the latter's choice between self-interest and the larger cause of social justice. Indeed, whenever the need arose, this self-interest was pursued with unrepentant ruthlessness. In Bhojpur, Bihar, the Bhumihars put together a private army—the Ranvir Sena—to suitably chastize the lower castes. It was this army which was behind the brutal massacre of the Dalits in Bathani Tola village. Another backward caste, the Kurmis, which owned large areas of land in central Bihar, had its own armed hoodlums, the Bhumi Sena, for the same purpose. And the Yadavs, also in Bihar, had christened their 'protective' force the Lorik Sena.

Clearly, those of the upper strata of these backward castes had enough economic and political clout to be virtually a law unto themselves.

It is also useful to remember that the other two principal recommendations of the Mandal report were the implementation of land reforms and the expansion of educational opportunities. Somehow, both these recommendations were rather conveniently glossed over by the very vocal supporters of the report. In Bihar, where Mandal was most loudly hailed as a messiah for the deprived, and which has had a backward-caste leader at the helm for some time, little has been done to implement the legislation on land reform. Nor is there any evidence that the Minimum Wages Act as applicable to rural labour is anywhere close to effective implementation. It is no surprise, therefore, that in a critique of the so called social justice platform, the Dalit Shiksha Andolan has come unhesitatingly to the following conclusion: 'On the basis of experiences in Uttar Pradesh, Bihar, Orissa, Karnataka and Andhra Pradesh, this organization opines that social justice is the ideology of the other and upwardly mobile backward castes. It does very little to the savarna dominated status quo and actually constitutes a programme of caste domination and hegemony which works against the Dalits.'[27]

The history of affirmative action in India also brings out clearly that an elite within the beneficiary segments tends to disproportionately benefit from such a policy, and then is able to generationally perpetuate this advantage. In time, there is nothing to distinguish this elite from the other privileged sections of society, but it continues to avail of the benefits originally intended to help the deprived. In the case of the Mandal report, the Supreme Court in a judgement in November 1992 declared that the socially advanced members of the backward classes, the 'creamy layer', would have to be excluded from the scheme of reservations. Subsequently, the Government of India, in September 1993, defined the broad criteria to identify the 'creamy layers': 'They are the children whose parents are holding constitutional positions, Class I and Class II officers, Colonel and above in the defence services, families owning irrigated land equal to or more than eighty-five per cent of the state land ceiling laws, or have a gross annual income of (rupees) one lakh or more.'[28] But the judgement, and the Central government directive, did little to stir the conscience of those who belonged to such privileged groups. On the contrary, the Kerala Legislative Assembly passed a bill to derecognize the entire concept of 'creamy layers', thereby inviting the threat of contempt of court proceedings from the Supreme Court. The governments of Uttar Pradesh and Bihar sought to subvert the Court's directive by redefining the categorization of the 'creamy layers' in a manner that would make it almost impossible to exclude even a very wealthy and well-established backward-caste person. The Supreme Court struck down the moves. The legal proceedings did little to disguise the transparent and brazen attempt by powerful vested interests to profit from a measure whose professed aim was to remove inequalities in society. The phenomenon was not new. Such interests, representing most assertively the upper strata from within the backward castes, had been steadily growing in power and influence—specially in the south but also elsewhere—much before Singh so dramatically made the 'politics of backwardness' a primary issue on the national agenda.

The truth is that under the garb of social justice the entire Mandal issue was an intra-middle-class struggle for the perks and perquisites that could be seized from the state. Those who opposed it used the argument of merit over birth as a stick to beat off encroachers from what they had come to accept as their exclusive turf. And those who supported it were themselves motivated by the most narrow self-interest, with little real concern for the requirements of justice for the vast majority of the poorest of the poor. If ideology was dead for those already on the middle-class wagon, it was even more glaringly non-existent for the new climbers. The aspirations of the latter for middle-class status and lifestyles had grown over time. And once they were provided the institutional scaffolding to achieve these, they had little to guide them except the dominant dictum in middle-class society: the means are unimportant so long as the end result of greater personal advancement can be achieved. Indeed, they were even more aggressive practitioners of this dictum, for as Paulo Freire has insightfully remarked, the 'oppressed', after replacing the perceived 'tormentor', tend initially to flamboyantly copy the ways of their tormentors. It was a strange and defeating process of Sanskritization, wherein those who ascended the social scale on the high platform of ideology were quickly and readily co-opted into the 'de-ideologized' milieu of those who had already arrived. Together, the old and the new members of the expanded middle class inhabited a landscape singularly denuded of any features of principle or morality. The real defeat was that of ideology, for two reasons: one, the very valid goal of social justice was overwhelmed by the cynicism of those who were its most eloquent votaries; and, two, the wave of caste consciousness that Mandal unleashed put on the backburner the real issues that needed to be confronted: poverty, illiteracy, disease and exploitation.

The Inner Landscape

We have seen, thus far, the evolution of the middle class as it has responded to external influences, in pace with the secular developments within the country. But our concern is also with the inner landscape of its thinking. It is important to go backstage, as it were, because it is there, hidden from public view, that we are likely to find, beyond the 'tidiness' of the middle class' own image of itself as a modern and rational entity, the scattered but powerful inheritances of the past, and the evidence of their patchy interface with the present.

We have noted earlier the persistence among middle-class Indians of tradition, even orthodoxy, despite their enthusiastic endorsement of the project of 'modernity'. This aspect is of critical importance to our analysis. Knee-jerk secularists, usually fairly ignorant both about ground realities and their own religion, will decry any discussion of the role and impact of religion in the life of the modern, educated middle-class person. But we must for the moment ignore the eloquence of such superficial critics. For, religion in all societies, be they modern or primitive, communist or capitalist, has always had considerable influence. And there can be no real assessment of some of the identifiable traits of the Indian middle class without taking into account the legacy that Hinduism—the religion of the overwhelming majority of the middle class— has bequeathed and the influence it continues to have.

It is a cliché to recall that Hinduism—the religion as it is lived by its countless followers—has no organized church, no one God, no paramount religious text, no codified moral laws and no single manual of prescribed ritual. The predominant emphasis is on personal salvation, a journey in which the individual is essentially alone with his karmas and his God. There is nothing wrong with such an approach in purely spiritual terms; it liberates the individual from the often stifling dogmas of organized religion and its prescriptive demands. However, in terms of the individual's relation to society, this very emphasis on the self as the centrepiece of the spiritual endeavour tends to stunt the growth of a sense of involvement in and concern for the community as a whole. This insensitivity to the external milieu, coterminous, often, with the most overt preoccupation with spiritual pursuits, has become so much a part of life that it is mostly not even noticeable to the educated Hindu. But it can come across as a startling revelation to the insightful foreign observer. Myrdal was struck by the callousness in personal relations in Indian society. 'Many of those who honestly advocate radical egalitarian reforms,' he wrote, 'reveal themselves as harsh, and sometimes thoughtlessly cruel, when they deal with members of the lower strata as individuals and not as a group to be cajoled.'[1] A.M. Rosenthal, writing in 1957, during the heyday of Nehruvian India, of which he was an admirer, was constrained to comment on what struck him about 'human relations' within Indian society: 'The heaviest handicaps under which India laboured through the centuries (was) . . . the individual's place in society and human relations within the society. An individual-to-individual callousness, despite

India's belief in her own spiritualism, was always part of India. No miracle has taken place. This callousness is still so strong in the country that it is the greatest danger for a foreigner living in India, for it is a frighteningly easy thing to find it creeping into one's soul.'[2]

It is easy to dismiss these comments as the biased and superficial inferences of foreigners. But a little honest introspection will endorse the truth of their comments. A pious Hindu will take a dip in the holy waters of the Ganga totally oblivious to the filth and garbage on and around the bathing ghat. The condition of things around him has little priority for him, for his concern is with doing that which ensures his own spiritual advancement. Temples in India will have their coffers overflowing with personal donations from the religiously active, but few of the donors would see much spiritual merit in using this same money for alleviating the misery of the thousands of the visibly poor around them. The donation to the temple deity cements the pact that each one of them has at an individual level with his saviour. The question of using one's wherewithal for the benefit of the deprived may fall in the diffused category of meritorious work, but is just not as efficacious, in terms of spiritual or material benefit, as the private world of personal religious endeavour.

The notion of personal salvation is not absent in the other great religions of the world such as Islam or Christianity. But there is a greater balance in them between the individual and his interaction with the entire community of followers. In Islam there is the Friday congregational gathering, where people from all sections of Muslim society meet as equals. In Christianity the community institution is the visit to the Church on Sundays. The very nature of such meetings emphasizes the importance of the collectivity over the individual. By contrast, in Hinduism there is no such institutionalization of the contribution of the individual to his community within the arena of spiritual search and fulfilment. It is not surprising, therefore, that 'welfare work in the slums and care of the poor in general was, and still is, a monopoly of the Christian missions.'[3] In many Western societies, whose achievements and material well-being are a matter of admiration for middle-class Indians, a traditional system of obligations at the micro level was gradually transformed 'from a network of individual relationships into obligations to the community . . . This was one aspect of the socio-cultural evolution by way of Mercantilism and Liberalism, industrialization and urbanization, which macro-sociologists have variously referred to as the shift from "status" to "contract", from "mechanical" to "organized" solidarity, from "Gemeinschaft" to "Gesselschaft" . . .'[4] In India, the emphasis in Hinduism on the self over the community has been an important factor in retarding the acceptance of such a sense of common obligations. Obviously, religion is not the only reason for this; the inequitable socio-economic structure was, and still remains, a powerful barrier to such an awakening. But certainly religion, as practised, has provided no countervailing moral imperative to enable an individual to identify his own spiritual growth with the welfare of the community. It is in this context that Swami Vivekanand had said that there is a need in India to integrate Sankara, the philosopher, with Gautama Buddha, the socially concerned humanist. More recent commentators, not professing to have the elevating evangelecism of Vivekananda, have said the same thing more bluntly: 'In the high Hindu ideal of self-realization there was no idea of a contract between man and man. It was Hinduism's greatest flaw . . .'[5]

A second aspect of Hinduism, of great relevance to our analysis, is the absence in it of a strong and unambiguous single ethical centre. There is nothing in Hinduism which categorically equates any action with sin. Indeed, there is no concept of sin in its operational lexicon. Any action considered wrong in a certain context is condoned and even lauded in a different context. The inference to be made is not that it espouses amoralism, but that it accepts a moral relativism which refuses to be straightjacketed by simplistic notions of right and wrong. Such a relativism reflected a metaphysical vision which, at one level, considered the world itself to be devoid of real meaning and therefore philosophically non-existent. If the foundation itself was considered to be both there and not there, part of the mysterious illusion of maya, how could it sustain a moral edifice which could lay claim to immutability? The Gita's strong espousal of right conduct as an end in itself—nishkama karma—coexisted with Krishna's own actions during the Mahabharata which justified the adoption of the wrong means if the ends they achieved were desirable. When Duryodhana, the arch villain in the epic, died, the heavens themselves rained down flowers on his body in recognition of his courage as a warrior. Yudhishtira, when questioned by Draupadi's father on the morality of her marrying all the five brothers merely said that morality is relative and has no final definition. In the Ramayana, the defeat of Ravana at the hands of Rama symbolized the victory of good over evil; but Ravana himself was one of the foremost disciples of Shiva and had won a boon from the latter in appreciation of his unwavering devotion. The Bhagvat Purana clearly acknowledges that the gopis of Vrindavan were married. When they left their husbands to frolic with Krishna their acts of adultery were said to be condoned because in the embrace of the divine flute player they achieved a personal salvation that rendered conventional notions of right and wrong meaningless. Such examples can be multiplied. The essential point is that Hinduism does not have a unified and unequivocal moral framework which could irrevocably restrain an individual's actions within the bounds of an identifiable code of conduct. An individual whose actions could be considered to be morally deficient at the level of perception and convention could still lay claim to spiritual redemption on the basis of his personal endeavours to please or appease his chosen divinity. For, the final goal was a personal moksha which, if the gods were benevolently disposed, rendered unimportant external approval or disapproval.

The absence of a moral code, binding on all, reinforced the doctrinal bias in Hinduism for the individual over the community. There were, of course, the loyalties of kin, clan and caste. At first glance it would appear that these could provide a transcending framework for the individual to acquire a wider and collective vision. But, paradoxically, these were in reality only extensions of the self. They restricted loyalties to narrow categories, while blurring a sense of obligation to the community as a whole. The fact of the matter is that whether as a result of his religious inheritance, or the rigidities of the social structure to which he belonged, or the absence of a moral imperative which stressed collective values, the average Hindu middle-class person had a very undeveloped sense of social sensitivity to the overall good of his community. He attached little priority to the need for an altruistic interface with society. His motivation to contribute to its betterment, without the notion of personal gain, was weak. He saw no great reason why he should identify his personal welfare with the well-being of even his immediate environment. His concerns were restricted to himself, his family, and, at a lower scale, his clan or caste. His cosmic view held an individual to be a microcosm unto himself. There was no need for his path to meander into the needs of others, who, even if they were obviously in need of succour, were only suffering the consequences of their own karmas.

Purists will protest at such uncharitable generalizations, and can certainly cite more than one reference in the very wide corpus of Hindu texts to the contrary. But their ability to do so is only evidence of the many contradictions between theory and practice in every Hindu's life: an extravagant humanization of divinity, and a metaphysical definition of the absolute as attributeless; the worship of Lakshmi as the embodiment of material fulfilment, and a strong philosophical tradition denying materialism; the concept of *Vasudhaiva Kutumbakam*, loftily demolishing barriers between all individuals in the world, and the inflexible structural rigidities of caste and hierarchy; the legitimacy given to realpolitik in the Mahabharata, and the absolute idealism associated with renunciation, forgiveness and piety; the glorification of women as goddesses, and their unrepentant subjugation in real life; the acceptance of the inexorable hold of destiny, and the legitimate space conceded for individual action; a concern for environmental purity, and the existence of even temples amidst the greatest filth and squalor. For every assertion, Hinduism can provide substance for a counter postulate. However, as has been stated earlier, our concern is not with endless theoretical intricacies, but with the influence of religion in terms of identifiable social behaviour. And here there can be little doubt that Hinduism, through its emphasis on personal salvation as an end above all others, and its often debilitating moral relativism, has tended to stunt the social virtues which could help cement an individual's commitment to the larger welfare of his community.

The Gandhi-Nehru legacy, by positing an unambiguous ethical imperative and strong social sensitivities, was a powerful attempt to counter the fragmented and individualistic vision of the educated Indian. It gave him a sense of national purpose, the fulfilment of participating in a joint endeavour with a larger set of norms and beliefs than he was accustomed to accept within the ambit of tradition. The struggle for freedom had already created a platform for strongly emotional collective aspirations on which this legacy could build. But, for reasons discussed earlier, the duration of this legacy was shortlived, too short for the process of transformation to be enduring. When its hold weakened, the old anomies resurrected themselves. And this time with stronger force because there was no ideological framework left to counter them.

Indeed, the rapidity with which the societal consensus forged by Gandhi and Nehru disintegrated is evidence of the weak foundations for such a consensus to hold in the first place. As the single largest beneficiary of an inequitable socio-economic structure, the middle class was always inclined to be motivated only by its own interests. But this proclivity was buttressed by a religious tradition which gave little value to enlarging this restricted ambit of interest. The intention in saying this is not to provide the bulk of the middle class an extraneous alibi to justify its behaviour, but to try and understand the combination of factors which could allow so many of its members to ignore, and sometimes not even notice, the appalling degree of suffering and deprivation at their very doorstep.

In the aftermath of sixty years of a socialist State, if we seek to catalogue the dominant social traits of the middle class, the first thing that comes to mind is a truly amazing imperviousness to the external milieu except in matters that impinge on its own immediate interests. In the beginning, in the years just after 1947, there was at least the awareness that India is a poor country and the poor exist and something needs to be done for them. No longer. The poor have been around for so long that they have become a part of the accepted landscape. Since they refused to go away, and could not be got rid of, the only other alternative was to take as little notice of them as possible. This myopia had its advantages: the less one noticed, the less reason one had to be concerned about social obligations; and the less one saw, the less one needed to be distracted from the heady pursuit of one's own material salvation. To get on in the world one had to restrict one's canvas, where all the discordance of other people's needs and conditions was best shut out. Thus it does not matter any more if in Delhi, the capital of the country, where so many middle-class ambitions and fantasies are played out every day, one-third of the population lives in slums, and one fourth has no access even to latrines.

The story is the same over much of urban India. From a bastion of the feudal aristocracy, the city emerged as a self-consciously middle-class citadel, but during this process of transformation the number of slums grew at the same pace, civic amenities plummeted, and pollution more than trebled. Surat, the diamond capital of the country, was until recently so filthy that it resurrected the plague virus from the rubbish heap of history. Till 1996, in Aligarh, a city associated for most of the middle class with education and learning, only six per cent of the city water was potable, the sewage system had completely collapsed, and thirty-four per cent of the population defecated in the open.[6] The startling starkness of poverty in the state of Bihar hardly needs elaboration. But in the capital city, Patna, multi-storeyed buildings have mushroomed and new boutiques open every other day in flourishing shopping complexes. What is even more revealing is that in a state where the concentration of the absolutely poor is one of the highest in the country, the money market is booming. 'Thousands of crores are put into the banking sector and even larger amounts are being garnered by institutions which claim that they are engaged in "para-banking" . . . These "non-banking financial institutions" mobilize huge deposits in small amounts from an enormous number of (largely middle-class) people and promise handsome returns on investment.'[7] In contrast to this preoccupation with speculation and quick returns, there has been no sign at all of any movement towards voluntary contributions to assist the neediest of the needy, whose numbers have so visibly increased in Patna itself. In the South, Tirupur, near Coimbatore, has emerged as a boom town of cotton knitwear exports from the country. Its success is a tribute to middle-class entrepreneurial skills and social insensitivities. Miles of farmlands have been acquired—often illegally—for upcoming mills and warehouses. New Esteems and Opel Astras jostle with scooters and mopeds on non-existent roads. Markets do brisk business when the city has almost no supply of potable water. And new houses and offices come up right next to sprawling slums and open sewers.[8]

These are but random examples, but they accurately illustrate the state of the rest of the cities. The issue here is not of poverty alone. Obviously, India is a poor country, and poverty cannot be pushed under the carpet. The issue here is the approach of the more well-to-do citizens of Indian society to this all pervasive poverty. For the burgeoning and upwardly mobile middle class of India, such poverty has ceased to exist. It has ceased to exist because it does not create in most of its members the slightest motivation to do something about it. Its existence is taken for granted. Its symptoms, which would revolt even the most sympathetic foreign observer, do not even register any more. The general approach is to get on with one's life, to carve out a tiny island of well-being in a sea of deprivation. The utter obsession with individual survival and betterment and the complete absence of a sense of social obligation is not unlike a system of apartheid, rendered more insidious because the perpetuators no longer even notice the conditions of those they have banished. The concern with personal salvation at the spiritual plane had assumed, at the temporal level, a Frankenstein form: the almost complete inability to see or identify with anything beyond the narrowest definition of self-interest. The absence of a strong moral imperative for social altruism had resulted, under the tutelage of unethical leaders and opportunistic politics, in a horribly bloated unconcern for society itself. The end product was the acceptance of a certain kind of lifestyle: insular, aggressive, selfish, obsessed with material gain, and socially callous.

Pankaj Mishra, in his brilliant book *Butter Chicken in Ludhiana*, insightfully captures vignettes of this lifestyle in small-town India. Of a visit to Muzaffarnagar he writes:

'The house I stayed at: it was in a large middle-class colony, typical of the thousands of such hodgepodge agglomerations of buildings that exist in cities all over India. The roads within the colony were all unpaved, and were most certainly unusable during the monsoons. Wild grass and weeds grew unchecked everywhere. At the back of every house lay gigantic mounds of garbage. Water spurted noisily from a leaking pipe and into a small drain someone had very cleverly directed to his garden.

It wasn't for lack of money that things were as they were: the houses belonged to extremely prosperous people. There were cars parked in front of every house; on the roofs were a surprising number of satellite dishes. The houses themselves were in a peculiar medley of expensive styles . . .

No, it wasn't for lack of money that such appalling civic conditions were allowed to prevail. If anything, the blame lay with the sudden plenitude of money: far from fostering any notions of civic responsibility, it had encouraged in its beneficiaries only a kind of aggressive individualism. The colony didn't matter so long as one could obtain, through bribing, through one's predatory prowess, illegal water, power, and telephone connections for one's house. Certainly houses were castles here and "Each to his own castle" seemed to be the operative motto, even as the garbage mounds grew higher, the wild grass lapped the high boundary walls, and one's customized Maruti 1000 frequently got stuck in the wet mud when the rains came.'[9]

The attempt to escape the external milieu, to build fences as a substitute for civic responsibility, nurtured its own sense of a siege mentality: if the unwashed masses seem to be climbing up the garden wall, raise the height of the wall; if there is not enough supply of water, dig a tube well, or add a water tank, or, best of all, siphon off the supply with a pump on the municipal line itself, irrespective of the consequences to the others; if the electricity is deficient, install a generator, or illegally increase the sanctioned load by bribing to the local electrical sub-station. The emphasis was on finding a short-cut, a quick-fix solution, which had to be efficacious even if unethical. In fact the siege mentality had little of the innocence or valour of those wrongfully besieged. Its origins lay in a cynical and deliberate withdrawal from a constructive interface with society; its motivations were based on an unyielding conviction that there could be no interest higher than one's own. Such a conviction was not restricted to a theoretical narcissism; it was easily identifiable in action. Contrary to the popular notion, most popular with the middle class itself, that it is the urban poor who are the least concerned about municipal rectitudes, the biggest offenders in the massive theft of electricity all over urban India belong to the 'affluent yuppie middle-class'.[10] Vehicles owned by the middle class are the largest cause of pollution in metropolitan India. If Delhi has 1500 tons of uncollected garbage every day, much of it is not generated in the squatters' colonies: a low-income-group colony produces only 0.3 kg waste per head, whereas a middle-class or rich colony produces upward of 1.5 kgs per head. Moreover, the lower income dumps have ninety-six per cent bio-degradable matter, whereas the garbage from the more affluent neighbourhoods have only forty per cent bio-degradable refuse. A typical middle-class colony of one thousand homes can generate an average of 5,200 plastic bags a day,[11] and these do not include the hundreds left scattered in public parks after a weekend of picnicking. A study conducted in the late 1990s showed that an important reason for Ahmedabad's critical water shortage was the consumption by middle-class localities of more than ten times their normal entitlement.[12]

One reason for the 'predatory prowess' was the perceived inefficiency of the system: it could not deliver in accordance with expectations, not even such basics as electricity and water, or such essential services as garbage removal. But this resentment at the State's limitations led to no desire to address the root causes of the problem. There was no introspection; it did not occur to the average middle-class Indian that in a country where scores of millions did not have even enough to eat, the State could, perhaps, have priorities other than only catering efficiently to the increasing demands of a vocal minority.

Middle-class criticism of the State for its inefficiencies and rampant corruption was certainly valid. But this criticism, in its intensity, was flawed, emphatically limited only to 'why can't the State do more for us?'; and it provoked no desire for organized action to rectify this state of affairs. The demands and the indignation displayed an acute sense of dependency: the State should deliver; it should deliver more of what we want; and if it cannot do so, we have the freedom to criticize, but no obligation to think or act beyond the articulation of our requirements.

The striking thing was that this constriction of outlook, unredeemed by any larger appraisal of what is wrong and what needs to be done, was sustained in circumstances which, by objective standards, were far from congenial. The Indian middle class has had to struggle to acquire or enjoy even the basic attributes of the conventional middle-class life. Till recently there was a queue for a telephone connection; a simple thing like a gas connection required the payment of a bribe or the use of influence; the purchase of a small apartment can mop up the savings of a lifetime; cars are, on average, more expensive than almost anywhere else in the world; the most incredible jostling precedes the admission of children to schools or colleges; and nothing can be taken for granted, not even assured and adequate supply of water or electricity. In the West, or in the emergent economies of South East Asia, these things would be considered the normal accoutrements of a middle-class home. Their inaccessibility for most middle-class Indians has not led to a sobering reappraisal of the dynamics between what is desired and what is possible, specially in a country so overwhelmingly poor as their own. On the contrary it has only served to give a frenetic edge to the aspiration to obtain the desired things by any means, good or bad. Simultaneously, it has fostered a constant sense of deprivation and a perennial susceptibility to wallow in self-pity, an almost reflex feeling that the middle class consists of the 'nowhere people' at the receiving end of an inefficient and inequitable system. And finally, it has given play to a tremendous obsession with 'status'. In a situation where things are difficult to get, and there are so many people around you defining their very existence by the ability to obtain them, the act of acquisition tends to disproportionately dominate the perception of social esteem. 'In order to gain and to hold the esteem of men it is not sufficient merely to possess wealth or power. The wealth or power must be put in evidence, for esteem is awarded only on evidence.'[13] Some degree of status consciousness is, of course, the trait of all middle classes. By definition, members of this class have to jockey to be above those they consider inferior, and strain to approximate those they know are above their reach. But it is the degree of this preoccupation, increasingly determined—specially for its parvenu elements—by the quantum of material possessions, that places the Indian middle class in a qualitatively different category. For, it must be one of the few classes in the world where the extreme sensitivity to intra-material hierarchies coexists so effortlessly with the most blatant insensitivity to the conditions of the world 'external' to such interests.

~

Did the frenzied absorption in worldly pursuits and the overwhelming preoccupation with material acquisitions reduce the role of religion in the middle-class person's life? The historical experience of Western societies was that the hold of the church declined dramatically in this century under the secular onslaught of a 'modern' and consumerist culture. 'The cement that held the communities of Roman Catholics

together crumbled with astonishing speed. In the course of
the 1960s attendance at Mass in Quebec (Canada) fell from
eighty to twenty per cent . . . Vocations for the priesthood
and other forms of the religious life fell steeply . . . Western
churches with a less compelling hold over their members,
including even some of the older Protestant sects, declined
even more rapidly.'[14] Was such a trend discernible in the
world of middle-class India, exposed to Western ideas of
rationality and progress, and fairly taken with the notion of
'modernity' and the Nehruvian critique of the obscurantisms
of the past? If such a trend was at all visible during the Nehru
years, was it sustained in the years after him? If so, in what
form? And if not, why not?

Nehru's aversion to the role of organized religion in society
was not, as we have discussed earlier, shared fully by his
middle-class followers. His vision of modernity held an
appeal for them; but it was hardly implemented in a
transformational manner. To endorse the Nehruvian vision
of emancipation from the dead hand of the past was to
subscribe to the dominant social imperative which was seen
as a means of inclusion in the liberal and progressive world
of the 'forward'-looking. Its espousal was part of the image
that the middle-class Indian wanted to project. In reality the
image slept quite easily with religious tradition, including,
for the majority, ritual, superstition, and prejudice. After
Nehru's death, and the demise of the Gandhi-Nehru legacy,
even the attempt to make public postures conform to private
actions was abandoned. Simultaneously, in tandem with
increased economic opportunities and mobility, traditional
support structures such as the joint family began to
disintegrate. This could, possibly, have liberated the
individual from the hold of tradition, and the compulsions
of conventional religious practice. To some extent this did

happen: the frequency of and familiarity with religious ritual was reduced, but, paradoxically, the need for the assertion of a religious identity increased.

There were identifiable reasons for this phenomenon. First, the breakdown of the extended family and the associated sense of belonging and security which it nurtured induced a hankering for a sense of belonging to some transcendent institution which could, through the medium of common belief, resurrect a sense of community. Secondly, for many middle-class families the degree and pace of change in the scope of one generation was both tremendous and traumatic. It was not unusual to find a person who had done his schooling in the village, college in the nearby town, and then found a job in one of the metropolises. Telescoped in the experience of a decade were the changes of a century: a new environment, new technologies, new values, new skills, new expectations and new lifestyles. Religion, by invoking the certitudes and simplicities of an idealized past, provided the most accessible crutch to stand up to the unpredictability of this rapid and demanding transformation.

Thirdly, the frenzy of a million individual endeavours that characterized the thrust and grasp of the urban middle classes created a pervasive feeling of being alone in a naturally hostile world, a world that was Darwinian in the survival of the fittest, and unkind to the unaggressive or the vulnerable. This feeling of being abandoned in a sea of constant strife and competition rendered the individual susceptible to any institution which posited counter values of peace and renunciation. Fourthly, the landscape of urban India where the largest concentration of the middle class lived was singularly deficient in institutions of community interaction. The elite had the memberships of clubs, but the clubs themselves were based on a stringent principle of social exclusion. For the great majority, the security of the mohallas or organically integrated habitats of the past were replaced by the anonymity and indifference of vast urban sprawls. The basic similarity in their material aspirations and the related concerns and anxieties rarely led to a common meeting point of solace and support. People lived in unfamiliar neighbourhoods without knowing who their neighbour was; joy and grief were largely nuclear phenomena. There was some evidence of community involvement in compact living spaces such as apartment blocks, but these were fledgling, more an indication of form than of substance, and hardly an effective antidote to the general feeling of rootlessness and alienation. Once again, religion was the refuge against this impersonal social structure. 'Much of the popularity of communal organizations . . . comes from their effective and organized insertion into the everyday life of urban neighbourhoods. Their ability to mobilize popular communal support is . . . also partly based on their ability to provide recreational, cultural and genuine welfare services . . .'[15]

Fifthly, in a situation where cynicism and corruption seemed to have compromised almost every secular institution, the appeal of religion, as the repository of absolute values, could not but grow. 'There is thus bound to be a palpable grief for the values of a lost—and retrospectively idealized—world when in the brave new one progress often turns out to be glaring inequality, rationality becomes selfishness, and the pursuit of self-interest and individualism comes to mean unbridled greed.'[16] And, finally, there was the tendency among the newly mobilized groups joining the middle class to assert their identity by appropriating the idiom they could best identify with. In this process, 'religious . . . ideologies often have proved more accessible, meaningful and effective in the defence of interests than more abstract and less familiar secular ideologies of class, nationalism, or citizenship.'[17] The notion of secular progress was accepted as almost axiomatic by the traditional middle-class elite steeped in the liberal political doctrines of nineteenth-century Europe and more at ease explaining India to a Western audience than having a conversation with an ordinary Indian. But their convictions were hardly as self-evident to the progressively less anglicized newer entrants to the middle class. Indeed, for them the assertion of a religious identity was often the most effective way to counter the smug assumption of ideological superiority of the already entrenched.

The existence of such powerful objective reasons did not mean that the middle class was in the throes of a religious revivalism. But what it did mean was that under the very awning of progress and modernization projected by secular India, there existed, contrary to the illusions of an overly westernized elite, a strong basis for the continued appeal of religion. And that, furthermore, the existence of this appeal created a psychological predisposition to support or condone the growth of organizations which sought to reap political dividends on the basis of this appeal. There was nothing wrong in a predilection for religion, but in a country of so many faiths there was the real danger of falling prey to an attempt to convert this predilection into a militancy directed against another religion.

For the reasons discussed above, the middle class was required to be specially vigilant to such attempts. That it was less than vigilant became evident in the build-up to the explosive Ram Janmabhoomi issue, and the demolition of the Babri Masjid in December 1992. To be fair, the bulk of the middle class was not in favour of such an extreme act of provocation. The actual act of demolition was the work of lumpen elements, led by committed cadres of the Bharatiya

Janata Party and its militant subordinate wings, who managed to give the fullest expression to their religious frenzy due to the indulgence of a prevaricating administrative machinery at the Centre.

It is a tribute to the momentum generated by the Gandhi-Nehru legacy in creating a general bias towards communal harmony that the first reaction of even the supporters in the middle class of the movement to construct the Ram temple, was one of shock at the destruction of the Masjid. But even if the middle class disapproved of the final act of violence, large numbers in it were guilty of having supported the growth of communal sentiments that led to the demolition.

This support was not necessarily overt or public. The specially anointed bricks for the Ram temple were not carried to Ayodhya only by middle-class hands. But the issue unleashed a wave of communal feeling that was readily internalized by most of the middle class. Mishra in his travels through small-town India found that 'The movement leading up to the event—the biggest of its kind since Independence—had received its most active support from middle-class populations in small towns and cities.'[18] Such a finding is not implausible because as a researcher has noted, 'the Hindu excluvism of the BJP party in India had substantial support among the new business and middle classes.'[19] It would be a safe generalization to say that the greater part of the middle class subscribed, in varying degrees of vehemence, to the BJP assertion that 'minority appeasement' had gone too far. It would also be fairly accurate to say that the call for Hindus to be proud of their religion—*Garv se kaho hum Hindu hain*—found a responsive resonance in most middle-class people, tired of hiding their feelings because of the Nehruvian definition of secularism as an aversion to the very practice of religion. There was also resentment at the use of the politics of secularism by the very political parties which spoke most stridently about the dangers of communalism. The general atmosphere of cynicism eroded the credibility of those who professed to oppose on principle the 'communal' politics of the BJP. The assertion of a Hindu identity, and its natural corollary, a heightened sensitivity to any perceived threat to this identity, created an enabling milieu for the kar sevaks to press on so militantly towards Ayodhya. When the Masjid fell, an entire generation of the middle class, weaned on the Nehruvian commitment to socialism, woke up to the debris of its own assumptions. Shock was followed by a sense of guilt; but guilt was not necessarily followed by a feeling of remorse. Instead— and this is important—there was in many cases an attempt to overcome guilt by a two-step manouvre: condemnation of the act of demolition, and an even more militant assertion of the reasons justifying the rise of Hindu assertiveness.

The fact of the matter is that the preoccupation with religion and religious concerns—the result of the absence, in recent times, of a strong ideological anchor in the secular realm— actually increased in the urban middle class after the Babri Masjid vandalism. One indication of this was the spectacular increase in the number of religious serials on television. The immensely popular Mahabharat and Ramayana, which ran to a mesmerized national audience for weeks on end, were followed by a spate of religious programmes which had the highest tele-viewer ratings and were a source of considerable profit for the producers and for Doordarshan. In many cities cable operators, responding to the demands of residential colonies or similar urban segments, began to telecast daily programmes with religious themes. The significant thing is that this demand for religious programmes increased after the Babri Masjid demolition. It was almost as if once the unbelievable had happened, the majority of middle-class people were suddenly released from the 'secular' inhibition of overtly seeking the role of religion in their lives.

The danger is that this increased religious consciousness that is the result not of any serious debate or discussion but of exaggerated grievances and popular mythological tele-serials, can often find communal political expression. Election results confirm that the most enthusiastic response to 'communal' politics has come from the urban middle-class voter. This is strikingly evident in the support base of the Shiv Sena in Maharashtra and of the BJP in states like Himachal Pradesh, Madhya Pradesh and Gujarat. Women in particular appear to be more easily influenced by religious chauvinism, more so women from the lower middle class, who, submersed in the grey vicissitudes of an impersonal urban existence, are quick to find in religious politics the black-and-white certainties of faith and familiarity. A survey conducted in Bombay in January 1996 among a thousand randomly selected women showed the widest support for the BJP and Shiv Sena among women from households earning between Rs 4000 and 6000 per month, the lowest of the income categories sampled.[20] It is this appeal of fundamentalism to women, and to the middle class as a whole, that led one commentator to make a historical comparison with the rise of Nazism in Germany. 'This is somewhat similar perhaps to what happened in Nazi Germany where the women and the middle classes in general became the foot soldiers of the Third Reich. Disenchanted with the effete politics of the Weimar Republic, they turned to the National Socialists to secure for them *kinder, kirke, kuche* (children, church and kitchen).' And while such a comparison may appear too alarmist or extreme for many, 'it is past time to note that Indian politics and society display many of the symptoms of a murderous pre-fascist stage which has already produced a multiplicity of localized *Kristallnachts* in numerous urban sites.'[21]

Admittedly, there is a section of the middle class, most noticeably from a Westernized upper segment in the bigger cities, which is forever ready to take up cudgels in defence of secularism. Unfortunately, the effectiveness of this cosmopolitan fringe is seriously in doubt. Its high-minded purpose has by now been overtaken by such a transparent cultural rootlessness that it can hardly convey its message with any semblance of credibility or impact. The criticism of what happened at Ayodhya rings true if the critic has, at the very least, some knowledge of what the Ramayana is about, apart from what can be gleaned from the abbreviated rendering of the storyline of the epic in an English anthology on Indian literature. Such critics must be informed, not only about the self-righteousness of their own stance but also about the culture and heritage whose aberrations they set out to criticize. A random survey will reveal, however, that many of the most vociferous proponents of secularism in the opinion-making salons of the metropolitan cities are ignorant of the line-by-line meaning of the national anthem! Gandhi was a convincing spokesman for communal harmony because he was so thoroughly familiar with his own religion, the essential tenets of other religions, and the idiom and substance of his own cultural milieu. It is neither possible nor necessary for every upholder of secular values to be a Gandhi. But an upbringing in liberal values is of little use if it becomes a barrier to a knowledge and understanding of one's own religion and culture—and the two are often inextricable. For the anglicized elite within the middle class, secularism has often become a stance, to be invoked, almost as a reflex, every time there is the slightest whiff of religion. For some of its members, faith is tantamount to medievalism, and all religious practice the equivalent of ritual and superstition. Such an attitude of disdainful dismissal would still be valid if it was not essentially rooted in a cultural nondescriptness, mistaken for too long as modernity, which leaves them as ineffectual clones of the 'British Fabian archetype' and aliens to their own cultural ethos.

Religious faith is a dynamic conditioning factor for the vast majority of Indians. To understand this, and to cull from this faith the imperatives for communal harmony, is one thing. To repeat the mantra of secularism without even a knowledge of such basics as the meaning and background of important religious festivals—which is very often the case with such critics—is quite another. A secularism based on such ignorance, on such a half-baked knowledge of one's own religion, becomes 'merely a fashionable opposition to theism and its inevitable morality'.[22] Indeed, this is the pity of it: the bulk of the present Indian middle class, coming to maturity after the demise of the Gandhi-Nehru legacy and relatively unexposed to the liberal Western doctrines of rationality and secularism, is increasingly susceptible to becoming cannon fodder in the hands of communal forces; and the liberal, Westernized fringe of the upper middle class, for whom secularism has always been an article of faith, is increasingly tending to maroon itself in a 'progressive' island of its own, cut off from the religio-cultural impulses that continue to animate the vast majority of Indians.

～

'But the real drive towards fascism will naturally come from the younger members of the middle class . . . This nationalist middle class is a favourable field for the spread of fascist ideas . . . If British control were wholly removed fascism would probably grow rapidly, supported as it would certainly be by the upper middle class and the vested interests.'[23] This was Nehru writing in the mid-1930s, but his comments have a relevance even today. There is little doubt that democracy as an institution has taken deep roots in India. The very fact that it has not only survived but grown in strength over the years, in stark contrast to the experience of many other countries which became independent around the same time, is perhaps one of the most outstanding achievements of the Indian polity, and an enduring tribute to the vision and perseverance of the founding fathers of the nation. Our investigation, however, is not about the institutional entrenchment of democracy as a system. That, happily, is a subject beyond the need of discussion. Our enquiry is about how deeply the middle class has internalized democratic values, as distinguished from its acceptance of democracy as a form of political activity. The enquiry is relevant, because although the educated Indian will be the last to doubt his own democratic credentials, there are good reasons to probe further the basis for such an assumption.

We have discussed earlier the tame acceptance by the bulk of the middle class of the suspension of democratic government when Indira Gandhi imposed Emergency rule in 1975. That mercifully brief period of undemocratic rule demonstrated one thing with chilling clarity: the middle class, notwithstanding its theoretical reiteration of the self-evident merits of democracy, could quite happily accept an alternative, authoritarian regimen, provided it perceived the latter to be more conducive to its interests. In other words, the commitment to democracy was as yet not strong enough to have a position in the scale of priorities above the pursuit of self-interest. An oft-quoted argument of the apologists for the Emergency is that a dose of authoritarian rule is often essential for the preservation of democracy itself. The cause for concern is that a large percentage of the middle class is as willing to subscribe to this argument today as it was during the Emergency.

An element of 'democracy fatigue' is certainly an important contributing factor in such an outlook. The endless shenanigans of politicians, the spectre of endemic political instability, the almost complete absence of norms and principles in the political sphere, and the absence of leaders of a pan-Indian stature has led to a disenchantment with the political process itself. Sentiments such as 'What India needs is a dictator' or 'What we need is someone who can wield the stick' are often reflective of the disillusionment of the average middle-class person with what the democratic system has come to mean in practice. Significantly, this feeling of disgust has prompted very few people from the traditional bastions of the middle class—the bureaucracy or the professional groupings—to seek to change the existing situation by venturing into politics themselves. The excuse for this coyness is that the world of politics is far too 'dirty' to allow 'good' people to enter or survive. There are undoubtedly valid reasons for such an appraisal. But the condemnation of politics and politicians has also become the most convenient excuse to remain in the niche of secure jobs, insulated from the uncertainties inherent in a political career. The comment of Bernard Shaw that politics is the last refuge of the scoundrel is perhaps the most widely shared perception of the middle class. And yet, the logic is strikingly circular: politics is dirty because good people do not enter it, and because good people do not enter, politics is dirty. The effect of such a Catch-22 argument is that it gives the middle class a moral perch to criticize the political scene, while justifying its reluctance to descend from this perch and do something to change things.

It is not the intention here to fault the middle class for its aversion to politics. Nor can it, in all fairness, be held culpable for wanting to do other things than fight elections. But it is worth pondering why that segment of society which professes the greatest affinity to democracy has opted to remain, by and large, merely a critical bystander to the progressive corruption of the democratic system. One reason, of course, is a sense of helplessness at the degree of venality in politics: what can an individual do when the very paramaters of political participation can so effortlessly overwhelm his reformist intentions? But this sense of helplessness is reinforced by the basic proclivity of the middle class—referred to earlier— to be so self-obsessed in its own material pursuits so as to withdraw from anything that does not directly concern its immediate interests. The emphasis is not on seeking change through involvement, but on restricting involvement even while harping on the need for change. This trend towards a withdrawal from the democratic process comes out clearly in a recent all-India survey which revealed that the turnout in elections is much higher among the disadvantaged, and that, more significantly, the opposition to the democratic system is strongest among the privileged sections.[24]

An important, and troubling, reason for middle-class disenchantment with democratic politics is the perception that the electoral system no longer serves its interests, either exclusively as it would like, or even preponderantly as was the case in the past. Elections are about numbers, and the rural and urban poor are many more in number than the middle class. Earlier, this vast numerical majority was mostly quiescent, and in the estimation of the privileged strata, well behaved. But the exposure to democratic politics can create its own momentum of empowerment; for the deprived, elections have become a means of obtaining what the establishment will not give otherwise. The finding that the disadvantaged are far more enthusiastic participants in elections only reveals that they have understood the value of their numerical weightage and the leverage this provides in electoral politics. Naturally, this numerical weightage is not a monolith; caste and other subjective loyalties are factors of increasing importance, both for the dispossessed and the upwardly mobile segments in the rural peasantry. And yet, the trend is unmistakable: democracy in India has ceased to be a genteel club where the poor are resigned to subordinating their interests in favour of the entrenched. The failure of the BJP's 'India Shining' campaign in the 2004 National Elections and the triumph of Mayawati's Bahujan Samaj Party (BSP) in the Uttar Pradesh Elections of 2007 prove this conclusively.

For the middle class, elections are today a far less predictable instrument to perpetuate its interests. Its commitment to democracy is thus less now than it was before, when it still felt that it could confidently perpetuate its interests through the democratic process. In such a situation it would be a fair inference to make that if another system, less democratic and more authoritarian, becomes available to better serve its interests, the middle class would have little hesitation in opting for it. This is neither an alarmist nor an extreme assessment; for, in any society where values become subordinate to interests, it is the fulfilment of these interests that will have priority rather than the preservation of the value structure. Democracy is about the empowerment of the largest number of people; self-interest is about restricting empowerment to a level where it does not threaten such a pursuit. The contradiction becomes all the more acute when the resources of the State are limited and there is no ideological framework of restraint and accommodation to constructively harmonize the two. 'It is necessary, therefore, to revise the traditional view of the urban middle classes as the main supporters of systems of political democracy. In developing countries, their expanding consumption demands can be met only by ignoring or repressing the needs of the majority.'[25]

A familiarity with the theory of democracy and the freedoms it promises does not necessarily translate into an acceptance of its restraints. There is good reason to believe that the educated Indian has always seen democracy more as a means of voicing his demands, or asserting his rights, or registering his protests, and less as a system of accepting community obligations, or restricting unreasonable interests, or tempering freedom with responsibilities. Prescient observers had occasion to comment on this tendency even in the early years after Independence. 'First of all,' Nehru said in 1958, 'a country which for a whole generation practised a certain technique of opposition to the government, when it has its own government, it is not easy to shift over or to make people think differently. It may be their own government, but people still have the habit of thinking of opposing the government . . . Secondly, they are apt to adopt that technique—just to press on some complaint or something, which is sometimes apt to be a nuisance.'[26] This culture of protest and demand, most handily used, ironically enough, by the better-off sections, had often very little to do with principle or democratic practice. In fact, the rejection of lawful authority for the most narrow and sectarian reasons was progressively made into quite a fine art. It is this that prompted another commentator, also a contemporary of Nehru, to say quite bluntly: 'While on the one hand, there is the cult of personality and submission to leaders without proper discussion and without proper criticism, on the other hand, we find an amount of indiscipline in our public life that is absolutely appalling.'[27] The reach and appeal of democratic politics grew in the years after Nehru, but so did this monochromatic vision of democracy as a means of 'obtaining' rather than 'giving', of asserting the primacy of the individual rather than of society, of having the freedom to demand rather than of sometimes conceding. Democracy became an unimpeded explosion of wants. The result was that while there was, over the years, greater democratic awakening, 'everyone awakened first to his own group or community; every group thought itself unique in its awakening; and every group sought to separate its rage from the rage of other groups.'[28]

An important aspect of the democratic temper is the spirit of enquiry, the ability to question the voice of authority. Such an ability falls somewhere between the reflex resort to protest and the obsequious renunciation of all scrutiny. To what extent do educated Indians possess this ability? There are several social thinkers and analysts who feel that the average Indian is far more susceptible to the idea of authoritarianism than he would like to acknowledge. It has been argued that the Indian ego is 'underdeveloped' because it is disproportionately dependent on outside 'props', such as the mother (who 'functions as the external ego of the child for a much longer period than is customary in the West'[29]), or clan, caste and religion. When in place, these props reduce the faculty of independent observation and judgement; when removed or weakened, as can often happen in an impersonal urban world, they create a sense of inadequacy, and a craving for the certainties of 'authority'. It has also been said that the 'controlled expression of one's aggressive drives is not emphasized in our traditional systems of child rearing. So when aggression breaks out, it breaks out in a primitive, chaotic fashion. This too is compatible with the authoritarian syndrome.'[30] Whatever the merits of such psychological analyses, there is little doubt that there is a strong premium on acceptance of authority in traditionally hierarchical societies. When the assertion of authority is weak, the seams of the social order no longer hold, resulting in a cacophony of individual wants, and a near anarchic release of suppressed aggressions. When authority is unambiguously asserted, the pendulum swings to the other extreme: abject capitulation. The Emergency was a striking illustration of such a syndrome. It is true that the assertion of authority is possible within the democratic framework. But the unsettling point is that the middle class has in the past easily fallen in line with an authoritarianism that was in violation of democratic governance. It is relevant in this context to consider the fact that the 'dispassionate ruthlessness of the Mahabharata and Arthashastra' have fostered 'a traditional concept of politics as an immoral ruthless statecraft.'[31] Has this legacy of the past been entirely replaced by the democratic experience of the past few decades? Or does it still linger as a residual inheritance that condones authoritarian tendencies, specially in the hands of a charismatic leader?

It is not easy to give emphatic answers to such questions. But it would be myopic not to take into account certain factors that do not render entirely improbable the susceptibility of the middle class to fascist tendencies. First, the present quality of political life, and the prospect of perennial political instability that looms large over the horizon, has brought middle-class faith in the political system to its lowest ebb. In fact, its disillusionment with democratic practice is, if anything, greater today than it was in the days preceding the Emergency. Secondly, its pursuit of self-interest as the sole motivating factor, to the exclusion of almost any consideration of the means, has grown over the years, not lessened. Thirdly, the enlargement of the democratic canvas has brought on the front burner issues and interests which have begun to pose a direct challenge to the traditional hegemony of the privileged. The enhanced appeal of communal forces, and the fact that the growth of democratic politics has not been accompanied by the requisite internalization of democratic values, are added reasons for concern. Ultimately, the democratic system will survive in India, not the least because it has increasing relevance and utility for the vast numbers of Indians less privileged than the middle class. But even in this process, it would be evading realities to believe that the support and cooperation of the middle class can be taken for granted.

∼

A factor of crucial significance in moulding the attitudes and choices of the middle class is the manner of its interaction with the West. That the influence of the West exists in strong measure is not in doubt. It had its origins in the nature of the freedom struggle and the impact of the values and institutions of the colonial power, Britain. As a colonial power, Britain was opposed; as a vibrant democracy, and a strong economic and military power, she was respected. But this respect did not have the distance of objectivity. For the bulk of the leadership of the freedom movement, and for the nascent Indian middle class, British rule was spectacularly successful in achieving a colonization of the mind. For those thus colonized, the colonial power represented in substantial measure a superior civilization, with its value structures and cultural ethos often preferred to indigenous tradition and heritage. Such a situation, where the emphasis on 'Indianness'—not an unusual aspiration for a newly independent country—was in real fact subordinated to a conditioned respect for the civilizational values of a foreign culture, could not but create its own existential dilemma. Nor was the dilemma new. Many decades before Independence, Raja Ram Mohan Roy, an eloquent voice for the rediscovery of India, maintained two houses, 'one in which everything was Western except Roy and another in which everything was Indian except Roy.'[32]

There are many examples of a colonial power leaving a lasting impact on the attitudes and lifestyles of the elite in the colonized country. But what must make the Indian example fairly unique is the enduring ideological hegemony of the colonial power even after its defeat, and the consequent failure of the elite to evolve a paradigm of modernization that fully took into account India's own culture, traditions, history and social specificities.

Admittedly, the task was not easy. Nehru, the icon of the middle class, himself confessed: 'I have become a queer mixture of the East and West, out of place everywhere, at home nowhere. Perhaps my thoughts and approach to life are more akin to what is called Western than Eastern, but India clings to me . . . I am a stranger and alien in the West. I cannot be of it. But in my own country also, sometimes, I have an exile's feeling.'[33] The realization of his dilemma was Nehru's greatness. To be unable to fully overcome it was his weakness. He was willing to split his name into Jawahar and Lal because the British, specially the BBC, found its length 'terrifying'.[34] In arguing the case of the present national anthem over its rival, he spoke of the sensational impact it created on an international gathering at the Waldorf Astoria Hotel in New York, and the enthusiastic endorsement it received from the biggest orchestra conductors in foreign countries.[35] As Prime Minister, 'he paid undue attention to and was guided by the advice and opinions of foreign commentators. Anxious that foreigners, especially the British, should think well of

India, he went out of his way to give interviews, some inordinately long, to foreign visitors even when they had little influence or power in their countries.'³⁶

The seeking of approbation from the West may have become a noticeable trait in Nehru, but it did not diminish him as an Indian. His formidable intellect and his genuine pride in being an Indian combined to make him more than an equal to those whose approbation he sought. But as a role model for lesser mortals, such as the average middle-class Indian, this 'looking up to' the West only strengthened the deep sense of racial inferiority bequeathed by the colonial experience. This inferiority manifested itself in more ways than one. First, it reinforced the tendency to seek solace in an idealized past whose achievements, imagined or otherwise, could reduce the erosion of self-worth. Secondly, it fostered an excessive sensitivity to any criticism or praise emanating from the West: the one was countered with disproportionate aggression, the other projected with unbecoming effusiveness. And thirdly, and this was by far its most debilitating consequence, it spawned a vast imitativeness which dulled the pursuit of excellence and creativity, and made most educated Indians—in their lifestyles and aspirations and cultural idiom—persistent and unthinking apes of anything Western.

There is hardly any area of achievement, aesthetics or lifestyle where this imitativeness, and the accommodation with mediocrity which it legitimizes, is not evident. The world of academia is littered with doctoral theses which have nothing more to contribute than extensive quotations from 'foreign' experts. The best works on India are still the monopoly of Western experts, or of Indians who have suddenly discovered their brilliance in institutions abroad. Scientists are judged by their 'foreign' degrees. The general impression of the middle class is that 'science and technology in India is second rate'.[37] Institutions of excellence have been patterned on those of the West, with little thought to curriculum and content as relevant to India. Some of the best and brightest students study here but their dominant interest is to go West, to somehow enhance their marketability by acquiring a Western degree. Most faculty members in such premier institutions have the 'mandatory' doctorate from the US, but that is probably the last time they did any worthwhile research. 'While a professor in a good management school in the US publishes annually three to six papers on an average, the eighty faculty members of (the prestigious Indian Institute of Management at Ahmedabad) together manage less than six in domestic and international journals combined, excluding the in-house journal of the Institute.'[38]

Lutyen's Delhi, even as a statement of imperial power, imaginatively incorporated Indian motifs and construction materials. But since then architecture in India has become a showcase of some of the most rootless—and ugly—imitations of Western design and concepts, a pathetic and tasteless hybrid that has prompted such clever appellations as 'Chandni Chowk Chippendale, Tamil Tiffany, Bania Gothic, Punjabi Baroque', etc.[39] Incredibly enough, even today new housing colonies in the capital of the country proudly give themselves names such as Beverly Park, Regency Park, May Fair Gardens and Malibu Towne! The melody and lilt of Indian film music, with its roots in the classical and folk traditions, has gradually given place to the simplistic obsession with the fast-paced beat of Western popular music. The beat can be catchy, but there is often a soullessness to it that bespeaks a mechanical grafting and an unthinking neglect of the possibilities and appeal of the indigenous tradition. If an earlier generation of upper-middle-class children came of age on the entertaining stories of Enid Blyton set in small-town England, ignorant of the extensive repertoire of folk tales and mythological stories in their own country, a new generation is being weaned on Barbie and Cindy dolls, completely clueless about the rich Indian doll-making tradition. 'Barbie and Cindy present addictive metaphors to the child's imagination, leaving a desert of sensibility behind when the child grows up beyond the doll-playing age.'[40]

Artistic talent has scandalously languished in India until recognition and acclaim has come from abroad. Once recognized in the West, all discrimination is thrown to the winds in lauding the new find. There is no balance, no equilibrium, that comes from a confidence in one's own worth irrespective of the certificates from others. The fashion conscious adopt the fads or the labels of the West with lightning speed. Women who still pronounce lingerie as 'lingeree' flaunt designer wear from the West as their most treasured possessions. If Victoria's Secret is still spelt correctly in the marquees of the bigger cities, the middle class in small-town India is not half that fussy: Western designer labels that look like the original and roughly spell the same way will also do quite well. Matrimonial advertisements in the newspapers have patented an expression which probably does not exist anywhere else in the world: 'convented'. Girls who are 'convented' are at a premium, not because they have graduated from a nunnery, but because they have studied in English-medium convents run by Christian missionaries and are therefore guaranteed to have shed enough of their ethnicity in favour of Western mannerisms that would be an asset to their 'educated' spouses. The examples are endless. Even dogs as pets have to be of a 'foreign' breed and are given the most pedantic English names, while the pups of the sturdy Indian 'mongrel' (the derisive appellation given by the British), the national breed in India, wander about homeless and emaciated on the streets.

There are, undoubtedly, certain areas of accomplishment which have remained impervious to this pervasive inclination to judge oneself by the approval of the West. It is also necessary to clarify that this is not intended as a critique of the West. Indeed, several aspects of Western influence have been positive, and have been synthesized with the Indian tradition with innovation and creativity. Our purpose is to identify the dominant trend, the most common inclination, the patterns of thought of the largest number of the middle class in their approach to the West and its influence on them. And in this respect the inferences are fairly clear. For a variety of historical reasons, which we have discussed earlier, independent India was not able to evolve an authentic cultural idiom of its own which could obliterate the sense of racial inferiority that the white-skinned created among their subjects. As a result, the tendency towards deferential imitation of anything Western has increased and not decreased in the years since Independence. Middle-class Indians are particularly susceptible to this tendency since economic change and mobility has diluted their traditional moorings, while the media revolution has exponentially increased their exposure to Western lifestyles and material achievements. The reservoirs of excellence that have confidently assimilated the influence of the West are the exceptions, not the rule. The young in the middle class are even more susceptible to blindly imitating the West than their parents were. Such a tendency, where a middle-class minority increasingly and unthinkingly accepts Western lifestyles and mores, while the overwhelming majority of Indians, half of whom are illiterate, are confined to an entirely different cultural space, can only dangerously widen the gulf between the two.

The consequences of this in the long term are unpredictable, but it will certainly increase the existing schisms and tensions in society.

~

One very fascinating and revealing aspect of the middle class in India is its attitude to sex. This attitude has been moulded by three conditioning factors: first, the legacy of the past, symbolized at its most clichéd by Khajuraho and the Kamasutra, with its refreshing openness to the issue of sex; second, the legacy of sex as taboo bequeathed by Mahatma Gandhi; and third, the impact of the media revolution, specially that of the electronic medium, and films, both Indian and Western.

The modern Indian has been separated for much too long from the legacy of the past for it to play a meaningful role in his life. Sex, in Hindu mythology and in the Hindu outlook on life, prior to the coming of the Muslims and prior to British Victorianism, was considered an essential part of refinement and aesthetics. *Kama*, or the pursuit of sensuous desire, was given a place among the four *Purusharthas*, or aims of life, along with *Dharma*, *Artha* and *Moksha*. Sexual desire was accepted as a valid aspect of life, and to acquire refinement and expertise in its expression was considered an attribute of the accomplished person. Vatsyayana's famous treatise on the art of love, the Kamasutra, written sometime between the first and the fifth century AD, becomes understandable in this context. Hindu mythological texts, predating the Kamasutra, are emphatic in the cosmological acceptance of Kaamadeva (the Hindu counterpart of the Greek Eros) as a primal force of attraction. Most Hindu gods and goddesses are fairly uninhibited in giving expression to the sexual urge.

Krishna, the celestial flute player, made the articulation of the erotic sentiment, *sringararasa*, a window to the divine. Much of Sanskrit poetry and literature is unabashedly erotic. And the temples at Khajuraho and Konarak, constructed as recently as the eleventh century AD, have boldly immortalized in stone the strength of an entire tradition which gave sex and desire a place in the sun, to be practised without a sense of guilt and with both elegance and restraint by the cultured person.

The coming of the Muslims about a thousand years ago imposed a new value system which frowned upon the importance given to physical desire in the Hindu world-view. Later, the British, as colonizers, sought to project the supremacy of their own race, religion and culture, by juxtaposing these to the 'moral degeneracy' of the Hindu religion and civilization. The Hindus were 'tied to hateful, horrible beliefs and customs . . . unmentionable thoughts'. Their culture had no 'moral codes . . . countenancing the greatest sensuousness'. Their form of worship was 'to a very large extent disgusting and even immoral'. For them Krishna the lover was, quite simply, an adulterer and a fornicator.[41] This deliberately unidimensional and mechanical assessment of the richness of the *sringara* tradition in Hinduism and the enlightened acceptance of *Kama* as an aspect of the divine in Hindu thought, was to a large extent internalized by the otherwise well-meaning revivalist and reforming movements of Hinduism in the nineteenth century. 'In one of the more ironic instances of transcultural transplantation, Victorian morality was made to become the touchstone' for reinterpreting Hinduism. The tendency to consider sex as something dirty was strengthened. It was to be banished to dark and dingy corners.[42] The new nationalism had little time or inclination to re-evaluate this derogatory assessment given by an alien culture and civilization. And the views of Mahatma

Gandhi on sex put the final capstone on this process.

The Mahatma had opted for celibacy at the age of thirty-three. He considered sexuality poisonous (*vishya*) and the sex instinct an enemy to be resolutely exorcised from the human system. He equated passion with impurity and distortion (*vikara*) and any thoughts of a sensuous nature as something to be ashamed of. For Gandhiji, sex was something to be abjured even in marriage:

> 'The very purpose of marriage is restraint and sublimation of the sexual appetite. Marriage for the satisfaction of sexual appetite is *vyabhichara*, concupiscence . . . if they (husband and wife) come together merely to have a fond embrace they are nearest the devil.
>
> The only rule that can be laid down in such instances (if a child is not conceived) is that coitus may be permitted once at the end of the monthly period till conception is established. If the object is achieved it must be abjured forthwith.'[43]

It is not the intention here to discuss the causes and origins of Gandhi's peculiarly inflexible views on sex. Definitive and persuasive work has been done on this subject. Perhaps certain early incidents in his life which he has talked about with candour in his autobiography played an important role in his lifelong association of sex with guilt. We know that he spent a major part of his life trying to overcome the urge for sex. The important point is that his views did not remain personal to him. He spoke and wrote about them extensively. Indeed, his personality was so towering and his contribution to India's freedom so pivotal, that his views on any subject could not be ignored. Gandhi's personality was not subject to compartmentalization. It had to be taken as a whole. He did not believe in artificial distinctions between political activity, economic upliftment and social reform. He lived life as he preached it. The net result was that along with his major legacies relating to swaraj, *ahinsa* and satyagraha, the emancipation of the downtrodden, etc., all his personal ideas on life and living, including on sex, were also internalized by the nation.[44]

There was thus the clash of two powerfully conflicting legacies: one, as historical memory, bereft of its societal context and its philosophical and cultural underpinning, but still recalled through a furtive reading of the Kamasutra or a quick glance at the photographs of Khajuraho as simply the legitimization of prurience; and a second, more recent bequest of Gandhiji, which categorically pronounced sex as evil and established an enduring association of sex with guilt. To this mixed approach was added the impact of films and the media. In the 1930s, Himanshu Rai and Devika Rani could exchange a kiss in films like *Light of Asia* and *Karma* without much ado. Most of the films of the silent era and the early talkies were quite uninhibited about showing a couple kiss. But middle-class prudery grew over the years. The result is that while the kiss has been substituted by the absurd depiction of two flowers bent towards each other or two cockatoos cooing, bawdy lyrics, suggestive pelvic gyrations, body-hugging clothes more provocative than nudity, and vulgar dialogues, replete with crude double entendres, have become the stock in trade of most commercial films in India. To this has been added the explosion on cable TV of Western television serials such as *Sex and the City*, *Baywatch* and *The Bold and the Beautiful*, whose sexual imagery, even if less vulgar, would leave all but the most daring Hindi film-maker asleep at the post.

The complexes the average middle-class person has about sex and its role in society are the result of all these factors: a past, which is remembered or invoked to justify sexual licence; a more recent heritage which considers the sexual urge wrong and associates it with guilt; and a present which is invaded, as it were, by the expression of sex as vulgarity or, as depicted in Western soap operas, fantasy.

One thing is certain: sex is very much on the middle-class Indian's mind, whether as desire or as guilt. But how does this interest express itself in society? An open expression of interest is taboo, because middle-class society, with the exception of a Westernized fringe in the bigger cities, is still conservative about interaction between the sexes. The sublimation of interest is becoming more and more difficult as the traditional restraints of the extended family, caste or clan weaken in the anonymity of the urban setting and the quantum, if not the quality, of sexually explicit imagery increases explosively. One outlet for expression is, of course, within the family itself. There is a view that Hindu society has always 'provided a wide scope for licentiousness within family relationships as a safety valve. The only restriction imposed on licentiousness was that it should be secret, always assumed but never paraded.'[45]

Outside the secrecy of the home, the principal attributes of the middle class' approach to sex are hypocrisy, guilt and aggression. Hypocrisy because the appeal of sex cannot be openly admitted; guilt because even when pursued it is considered as something wrong; and aggression because the conservative milieu for the interaction between sexes allows limited scope for more normal relationships to develop, and the dominant media message is that women are 'available' for the assertive male to have.

What is new is that under the facade of middle-class

prudery much more is happening in matters relating to sex than ever before. Old inhibitions remain but there are new curiosities and more opportunities for answers. There is still considerable ignorance and misinformation, but the 'Advice' columns of newspapers and magazines are flooded with letters from anxious middle-class readers on subjects which could never have been discussed so openly before. A survey of VCD vendors in cities, small and big, reveals a burgeoning middle-class clientele for pornography. A picnic with the family to a public park in the metropolitan cities can often be a rather embarrassing venture because of the number of couples in an advanced stage of foreplay behind every tree and bush. Beauty parlours, guaranteed to enhance sex appeal, have mushroomed all over urban India. A small town can often boast of several dozen such parlours. The 'look good' craze is not always a part of a 'know more' syndrome. Ignorance is often the most unfortunate adjunct of sex, because sex is still largely confined to the subterranean world, at odds with the middle-class' concept of propriety. Random examples can be amazingly revealing. For instance, in Gujarat, after the navaratras, among the main sources of revenue for Gujarati papers are advertisements offering safe abortions; a pointer to the increase in sexual activity, but also an indication of the degree of ignorance about contraception and safe sex.[46]

Nor is all such activity innocent. The revelation of a spate of sex scandals in small-town India—Jalgaon, Nasik, Chitradurga, Ajmer, Alwar, Jammu and Jalandhar—have shown the 'ugly eruptions of acne on the carefully made-up face of middle-class morality. Each story is distressingly similar—glamour-struck girls, unscrupulous men with powerful connections, sex, blackmail.'[47] Investigations revealed that the impact of the media can be a particularly culpable factor in small-town India. The attempt to copy MTV lifestyles in a conservative social milieu made innocent girls acquire a blatant but superficial image of modernity that made them easy prey to the machinations of the petty politician and the nouveau riche trader. It was, as someone remarked, 'a fatal cross-breeding of cultures', made more tragic and sordid by the attitude of the average Indian male to women.

In the absence of social norms which allow a more open interaction between the sexes, the middle-class male has had relatively few opportunities to meet women on the level ground of respect and equality. His traditional conditioning is to consider women as subordinate; his modern stance is to accept that they have equal status—but only in theory. The stereotypes of his upbringing tend to make him view the 'modern' woman, who can be seen to have stepped out of the traditional image in attire and demeanour, as 'available'. This is also the overwhelming message of popular Indian films: women can be 'had'—if the initiative is made with aggression. The effortless transformation of the 'modern' woman, dressed in the trendiest and skimpiest of Western clothes, into the sari-clad, demure and obedient wife, another frequent message of Indian films, reinforces the assumption that 'modernity' is skin deep, and that essentially nothing has changed in the traditional asymmetry between the sexes. It is for this reason that a rarely reported but pervasive problem of the working middle-class woman is sexual harassment in the work place, even if, with more middle-class women working, the work place has also become, across urban India, the most accessible 'social club' for middle-class men and women to meet with a relative lack of inhibition that would hardly be tolerated within the conservative confines of the traditional family structure. The gulf between a public posture of respect for the opposite sex and private accommodation of the male-dominant mores of the past is visible in other areas as well. Many educated Indian men will denounce the evil of dowry but will refrain from taking a strong stand where their own marriage is concerned on the pretext that they cannot go against the wishes of their parents. Dowry deaths are to a great extent middle-class India's preserve, and, ironically, here the women of the boy's family are often at the forefront in harassing and persecuting the wife.

The situation is not unremittingly bleak. More women are educated, and more among them are gradually asserting their identity and their opposition to the male-dominated assumptions of the past. Several women's organizations are doing pioneering work in hastening this process and providing useful support services to women who have stood up against the system. But the optimism must be tempered, for the distortions in the legacies of the past and the perversions of the present must still be strong to generate the kind of debate about—and opposition to—the fleeting nude scene in Shekhar Kapur's film *Bandit Queen*. Here was a film 'portraying a rebellious woman who refuses to succumb to the male-dominated system even after she is subjected to brutal violence and rape.'[48] The scene in question was perfectly in context. But many middle-class Indians, who live quite happily with the vulgarity and obscenity routinely present in Indian commercial cinema, objected to this 'assault on Indian culture'; and the judiciary pondered for weeks on the merits of this allegation.

∼

A certain placidity of temperament has conventionally been associated with the middle class: predictable goals, limited ambitions, the contentment of the humdrum and the routine, the simple certainties of a job, wife and family. It is an image which the middle class is happy to cultivate about itself: 'We are only middle-class people' is not an uncommon refrain, conveying a modesty of reach and a resigned acceptance of the parameters of effort and result. For many years after Independence such an image had a congruence with reality. People were happy with the manageability of their limited wants. There was much less competition; options and choices were fewer; there was an element of continuity even in change; the reference points were fixed; and ambition had a ceiling.

Today this image is not only misleading, it is so wide off the mark to be a matter of concern. Driven by the twin engines of material desire and the ceaseless competition to fulfil these wants, the Indian middle class appears to be close to a collective neurosis. The symptoms of this neurosis have been increasingly discernible over the past couple of decades. According to a WHO report of 2006, suicide rates (per 100,000) went up from 6.3 in 1980 to 10.5 in 2002—an increase of almost 67 percent. This statistic does not take into account those who failed in their attempt, estimated to be ten times the number of those who succeeded. Divorces have increased dramatically. Stress-related diseases have become commonplace. And worst of all, children are showing signs of stress-related symptoms that were till recently the exclusive preserve of adults.

What has gone wrong? There are visible signs of greater material success. The average middle-class family today has, for instance, many more consumer durables than that of a generation ago. But the possession of more seems to have fuelled the desire for more, in an endless rat race of want multiplying want. The problem is compounded because this race must be pursued amidst an avalanche of municipal concerns—about housing, transport, education, and even such basic amenities as adequate water and electricity supply.

Moreover, the new ethos of acquisition and competition does not seem to have obliterated a hankering for the easy-paced securities and assurances of the past. In order to enhance the family income, more and more men now seek out working brides; 'and yet, after marriage, (they) miss their non-working mothers' single-minded dedication to the family. The contradiction afflicts women too: much as they desire economic independence, they long for the securities their mothers enjoyed within the confines of the home.'[49] The institution which is under ceaseless pressure is the home. The demise of the joint family has given place to the nuclear family, where traditional family values of support and a sense of belonging and togetherness have often given way to individual pursuits and ambitions. Economic independence and education have made women more assertive, mostly for the right reasons. But this has also meant the destabilization of the traditional equilibrium of middle-class homes. If the mores of a male-dominated society are—ever so slowly—being eclipsed, so are the virtues of compromise and adjustment long considered an intrinsic part of marriage. Divorce has become a real middle-class alternative. One of the reasons for the spectacular success of films like, *Hum Aapke Hain Kaun* and *Dilwale Dulhaniya Le Jayenge*, was that they recreate an idealized world of the happy joint family and the slightly aimless but settled pleasures of a bourgeois existence, but without the strife and tension that have become their adjuncts in real life. Indeed, one of the few remaining constants of middle-class life is the addiction to Indian commercial films. Often entertaining and mostly escapist, these films, with their rags-to-riches fairy tales set to music and romance, sustain the middle-class dream, and provide an escape from the pressures and frustrations of the world outside.

But the compulsions of a frenetically competitive world are

never too far away. And by far the most unsettling aspect, with the most worrisome consequences in the long run, is the impact they are having on children. 'Childhood is now under siege in its own citadel: the middle and upper middle classes in the cities. It's the middle-class child, explain student counsellors and psychologists, who has to bear the brunt of a rapidly changing society in which restraining traditions have been offloaded in a single-minded pursuit of plenty.'⁵⁰ The pressures begin to mount on a child even as a toddler: admission to a good primary school is a fierce battle for seats are limited and applicants many. Ambitious parents begin to plan careers before the child has learnt to count upto ten. The pressures to do well in school are immense, for parents know that entry to a preferred college for a professional course will require the child to get marks in the nineties. The anxieties of the parents cannot but be absorbed by the child. Schools become competitive arenas and somewhere along the way the fun and abandon of being young is lost. With both parents working in many middle-class families, an entire generation of middle-class children are growing up as latch-and-key kids, coming to closed homes and the ubiquitous TV. When working parents try to make up by spending 'quality time' with the children, the 'guilt factor' often leads to an excessive indulgence which is harmful to the child. Another identifiable trend is that children are reading much less, specially for pleasure. If they read at all, it is books which can help them score better marks in entrance examinations, such as general knowledge manuals or encyclopaedias. The consumerist messages from society, and specially from television, are relentless. Children are growing up with a single-minded focus on acquiring these objects of desire, and are willing to orient their lives almost exclusively towards this end. The entire process is fostering a unidimensional outlook in life, where the determination to win the rat race is hardly counterbalanced by other values and virtues which are an essential aspect of the collective good of any civil society.

It has been said that GDH—Gross Domestic Happiness—is as important in judging the well-being of a country as GDP or Gross Domestic Product. The rise in GDP has disproportionately benefitted the middle class, inspite of all its protestations to the contrary. But on the GDH front, the report card is probably worse than it was thirty years ago. There is a great deal of entrepreneurial energy which is for the good; grit and determination, and the desire to succeed, are often dramatically in evidence. But there is a brittle self-centredness in all of this; there is no space in the average middle-class Indian's life for a nurturing and wholesome interface with society as a whole. The fierce pursuit of self-interest is breeding a new isolationism, a soullessness of spirit. The drive to work the system, to have more and to reach higher, is breaking down the essential restraints of community life. And the absence of a moral core in society has removed a sense of balance and perspective regarding the end results of human endeavour. The consequence is a growing neurosis, both at a personal and collective level, which has, if anything, widened the gulf for the middle class between success and fulfilment.

5

The Writing on the Wall

In mid-1991, the then Prime Minister, Narasimha Rao, ably guided by his erudite Finance Minister, Dr Manmohan Singh, announced a series of economic reforms which would help dismantle some of the inefficient State controls on the Indian economy and facilitate its greater integration with the world economy. This 'liberalization' package, tailored to make India a player in the 'globalized' economy, suddenly put the spotlight on the middle class for an entirely new reason: its ability to consume. If India was to open up to the world markets, it was essential to know how much it could buy. The segment with the largest concentration of purchasing power in India was the middle class. Its consumerist prowess had therefore to be accurately gauged.

This exercise was important not only for the Indian government, which wished to advertise the strength of the untapped Indian market to woo the economies of the developed world, but also for the latter, always sensitive to newer pastures for the sale of their goods and technologies. The logic of economic reform, therefore, dictated that the middle class now be analysed, not for its lack of ideological moorings, or its lack of commitment to anything but its own material well-being, or for its utter insensitivity to social and moral causes, but for its craving for and ability to buy what the developed countries could sell to it.

In this process the size of the Indian middle class became, for the first time, a matter of crucial importance. Several figures were bandied about, ranging from 200 million to 500 million. Overnight the consumerist thirst of the middle class became an asset, a sign of the dynamism of the Indian market. Learned proponents of the New Economic Policy (NEP) exulted in the revelation that 'urban India itself is the world's third largest country'.[1] Several systematic surveys were carried out to reinforce perception with facts. Of these, the most thorough was in 1994 by the National Council of Applied Economic Research (NCAER), appropriately titled 'The Consumer Classes'.[2] The survey revealed that the Very Rich comprise about six million people or a million households. Below them, the middle class consists of three segments: the Consuming Class accounting for thirty million households or 150 million people, the bulk of whom could be in the market for all kinds of consumer durables; the Climbers, consisting of fifty million households or 275 million people; and the Aspirants numbering another 275 million. The last two segments would 'need good reasons to, first, buy the product you make, and next, to choose your brand'.[3] The NCAER survey was based on identifying consumption patterns rather than income levels. It sought to break the myth of a monolithic middle class with similar or undifferentiated consumption abilities. 'With the mass market sliced into three segments rather than being one seamless entity', the survey was intended to 'enable marketeers to understand the real priority of their consumers' buying decisions rather than assuming direct correlations between income levels and demand for specific projects'.[4] Other organizations, such as the prestigious Confederation of Indian

Industry (CII), did their own spadework: CII concluded that there are 180 million people in India with an annual income exceeding $3197 or Rs 120,000.

The great Indian 'liberalized' economic machine was all set to roll with the middle class as its engine, but, unfortunately, many of these very surveys revealed that the power of the engine was hardly in conformity with the wishful thinking of the enthusiasts. According to the NCAER survey, households with incomes restricted to between Rs 12,500 and Rs 40,000 per year, accounted for as many as 331 million people. Only 4.1 per cent of the population, or 37 million people, had an income of over Rs 40,000 a year. And the rich, with an income of over five lakh rupees a year, did not number more than 1.4 million. Other indices were equally sobering. The number of cars in private possession was less than fourteen per 1000 households. In South Korea there were more than 400 cars per 1000 households. In Mexico the number was 112, and in Brazil eighty-five. The number of households with a telephone connection was about seven million, or less than four per cent of the total number of households in the country. Only 5.5 per cent of the total population owned a colour TV. Even with respect to all TV sets, including black-and-white ones, the comparison with South East Asia is instructive. Thailand and Malaysia had 11.4 and 14.8 sets per hundred people respectively, as against India's 3.2 sets per hundred people. The penetration of other consumer durables was as limited. Only 1.2 per cent of all households owned a video recorder or player; 1.8 per cent owned a washing machine; and 1.3 per cent had a storage or instant geyser. Only eighty-one per cent of middle-income households (sixteen per cent of the population) and fifty-nine per cent of lower middle households (thirty-three per cent of the population) owned even a fan. Figures for consumer goods in mass demand, such as bicycles and wrist watches, were also low. Only one out of five Indians possessed a wrist watch and only forty-eight per cent of households owned a bicycle. If India sold thirty watches per thousand people, China sold sixty, and the world average was 150. In a country of over 900 million people, with a middle class estimated in the scores of millions, there were only 1.6 million share holders and less twenty-five million graduates.

Such statistics did not indicate that the Indian middle class did not exist. It existed, but it was the middle class of a poor country. In pure numbers, the the Indian middle class has grown and so has its purchasing power, and even more strikingly, its consumerist ambitions. But it is still far removed from the fast-growing middle class of even a country like Poland, still struggling for economic recovery.

'People who wake up in the morning thinking that they have no history, no ancestors, are simply uncultured.'[5] This was a comment made by a leading Russian politician to *Newsweek* in March 1996, and should have been profoundly sobering for those in his country who thought that post-communist Russia could at one stroke forget the legacies of the past and, much in the nature of a quick-change artist, emerge totally at ease in the new attire presented to it by its Western benefactors. Some such perspective is perhaps of relevance in the Indian context as well. The NEP put a new focus on the middle class, primarily as a consumer, but the middle class was not suddenly conjured out of thin air the day the policies were announced. The middle class had 'ancestors', and a 'history' before policy makers began to carefully assess its buying capacity and size. Its origins and evolution, its behavioral traits, and the nature of its interaction with other elements in society, should have been as relevant to the architects of the liberalization policy as putting an accurate fix on its consumer choices or purchasing power. Such an approach would have made immediately clear that in a country where the destitute were numbered at over 200 million by the same surveys that mapped the predilections of the consuming classes, the middle class could not be expected to achieve an economic miracle in isolation; the Indian middle class could not be an entity unto itself, defined solely by its material desires, and autonomous to the economic realities of the country as a whole. The error, born out of historical myopia, was that it failed to take into account what the policies of liberalization would do to a class which was already morally rudderless, obsessively materialistic, and socially insensitive to the point of being unconcerned with anything but its own narrow self-interest.

As we shall discuss later, the intention here is not a simplistic critique of the policies of economic liberalization. Our critique is of the assumption that the wand of liberalization could cast its spell in a social vacuum, or succeed in magically separating the past from the present, so that the middle class, for instance, could suddenly be disassociated from all its other defining elements and be reborn only as the great consuming class, each of its members a sterilized statistic in an aggregate map of India's purchasing power. Economic policies deal with real people; real people do not exist in isolation but are the products of an evolutionary experience, with identifiable behavioral attributes, which in turn influences the impact and consequences of such economic policies in a manner quite distinct to the sanitized calculations of cause and effect drawn up in purely economic strategies.

Given the dominant traits of the Indian middle class in its evolution upto 1991, the impact of the policies of economic liberalization was to liberate it from even the pretence of any notion of restraint or reticence in the unchecked pursuit of its consumerist aspirations. For too long the professed bias of State policy was for the poor of India. The emphasis, however hypocritical, was on austerity, on restraining material pursuits in a country where the poor so greatly outnumbered the rich. No longer. Now it was state policy to 'open' the economy to the objects of desire. Consumerism was sanctified because the middle class' ability to consume was an index to progress. Material wants were suddenly severed from any notion of guilt. In a sense, it was the collective exorcism from the nation's psyche of the 'repressive and life-denying nature of Gandhi's idealism',[6] an exultant, exuberant escape from his emphasis on an austerity that could not be ignored but was inherently impossible to emulate. Liberalization provided the opportunity to make a break from the attitudes and thinking of the past, the moment to bring out into the open desires long held back, and to say: 'Now, at last, we can do what we had always wanted to do, without a sense of guilt, and, indeed, claim public approval for it.' Gandhi's 'love and praise of poverty and suffering and the ascetic life' had a critic in Nehru himself. 'Personally I dislike the praise of poverty and suffering,' Nehru wrote. 'I do not think they are at all desirable, and they ought to be abolished.'[7] But, however much Nehru railed against what he perceived as the obscurantisms in Gandhi's persona, he was acutely conscious of the moral imperative to orient State policy in favour of the poor. Nehru's socialism was the counterpart of Gandhi's emotional identification with the poor. If Gandhi was able, and willing, to live like the poor, Nehru was equally convinced about the vulgarity of flamboyant consumerism. Liberalization rendered the economic legacy of both these stalwarts redundant, specially for a middle class weary by now of the ineffectual socialist rhetoric of a host of previous governments. Indeed, the judgemental pendulum now swung to the other extreme: if the policies of 'protection' and 'self-reliance' and socialism were economically inefficient, the only answer was to forget the poor for a while and concentrate on the opportunities for greater material gratification for those who could benefit under the new economic dispensation.

Its economic prowess may have been limited, but there was no ceiling now on the middle class' aspiration to the good life. 'The lifestyle of the Indian elite is amazing,' commented Noam Chomsky during a visit to India in 1996. 'I've never seen such opulence even in America.'[8] It was this lifestyle, replete with expensive cars, the latest consumer gadgets, designer clothes and accessories, and five-star living, which became the role model for the middle class in the heady hedonism unleashed by the liberalization process. The urge to move up the consumption ladder, to somehow put an unbridgeable gap between the squalor of the poor and the plush material insularities of the rich, was always there. But now this urge had the stamp of 'official' acceptance, the justification of an ideology. 'We should all get this clear,' wrote an ideologue of the new school of thought on the editorial page of a national newspaper, 'that a country of the size and importance of India has no choice but *to clamber to its new tryst with destiny inside shiny buildings of chrome and glass at the free market. There is no mileage in looking wistfully at quaint mud huts rushing by the car windows because they, and their ilk, cannot meet our burgeoning needs, and if truth be told never have* [emphasis mine].'[9] The same rationale was argued with less euphoria but equal intensity by a new magazine whose glossy pages promised to provide an 'authoritative guide to good living': 'The economic liberalization that has been sweeping across the country for the last few years has altered the lives of a large section of India's burgeoning middle class. They have become far more international in their outlook and aspirations, more sophisticated and liberal in lifestyle and attitudes, and certainly more adventurous and demanding in terms of holiday and leisure activities. One of the psychological legacies of the Nehruvian socialistic era was that the more affluent sections of society were branded as being rather vulgar, and spending money to live well was considered an even greater sin. *Today, that stigma seems to have vanished for many* [emphasis mine]. With the new Manmohanomics, there are many more opportunities to make money and even more avenues to spend it.'[10]

The consumerist supports for such an outlook seemed to be well in place. Almost every consumer durable could now be had on installments. Enterprising firms opened up to offer exclusive services for helping with the right loan for the right product from the right source. The credit card industry mushroomed into a 1600-crore business. More than a million Indians gave up generations of financial conservatism, which stressed on the dangers of going into debt, to become credit card holders. In 1995 Master Card grew by 106 per cent in India, the highest growth in the Asia-Pacific region. Visa grew by an unprecedented ninety-four per cent, and American Express notched up a 102 per cent growth rate in 1994-95 and an even higher 135 per cent the next year. Consumer giants spent crores on advertising; according to a survey, the top ten of these spent close to a whopping 600 crores in 1995 to better target the consumer. The advertisement budget of India's biggest spender on advertising, Hindustan Lever, grew by twenty-two per cent in just one year. The advertisement expenditure of certain sectors such as consumer electronics, of special interest to the middle class, grew in 1995 by as much as seventy per cent as against a growth in sales of less than thirty per cent. The 'explosion' of satellite television brought the consumer message home in a manner that could hardly be conceived of but a few years ago. The 'revolution' commenced in 1991; by 1995 it was estimated that more than eighteen million homes were wired to cable or satellite. Suddenly, a great many middle-class people, long resigned to the monopoly of Doordarshan, had more than fifty channels to choose from, and each of these channels was essentially supported by advertising. Some people in the advertising business 'lamented the prostration of Indian advertising at the altar of Western ad idiom and grammar'. 'Delhi,' they felt, 'seemed to be drawing its sustenance from Dallas. The similarities are not merely in the superficial symbolism of advertising, but in the basic language and value system.'[11] The content of the hundreds of hours of programming reinforced the stereotypes of an entrenched elite or upper-middle-class world—cosmopolitan, well-off, and urban-centric. According to a monitoring effort in 1995 of as many as 200 episodes of the most popular serials on three major channels, it was found that over eighty per cent of female characters belonged to the upper stratum of society; for male characters the figure ranged between seventy and eighty per cent.

The impact of such depictions, in terms of the search for the desired lifestyle, cannot be overestimated. The Fifth National Readership Survey revealed that three-fifths of all urban homes had a TV set and that the reach of the medium shot up from nine per cent in 1990 to seventy-four per cent in 1995. Burgeoning aspirations wrapped themselves with commendable felicity around the most expensive goodies: Mercedes Benz cars; thirty-two-and even forty-six-inch television sets and state of the art refrigerators; Italian suiting, 'imported' brand-name shirts and Mont Blanc pens. Some of the messages in advertisements were also revealing for the mood they captured. 'The ultimate message was, like the grandmother in the hair oil ad observed: *Zamana badal gaya hai* (The times have changed). Or like Channel V put it: Keep up or be left out. It was quite simple. All one had to do was to *Wear Your Attitude*. *Meri Marzi* (My own sweet will) sang Govinda the Gambler. *It's My Life*, flashed a hoarding sponsored by Pepsi. I. Me. Enjoy. For this moment ENJOY. Nothing exists that can't be co-opted into this circle of consumption—not even bhujia, the Rajasthani snack that was traditionally made in small cottage industries in the state. The advertisements that use Hindi films to sell a multi-national bhujia have a killer for a last line, but it sums up the general mood: *Isme hai Mazaa Unlimited.*[12]

Children absorbed the general mood of consumerist buoyancy far more easily. 'The vision of the good life being drilled into viewers' minds is better internalized by children than the older generation', was the conclusion of researchers.[13] It was also established that children from middle-class homes watched TV the most; those from the upper-most class watched the least, for their options for recreation were more.[14] From among this new generation of TV children, seventy-five per cent said that they wanted to own the products advertised on television. A leading magazine which did a cover story on the 'Age of the Superbrats' concluded: 'In an upwardly mobile world, where grown-ups chase power, ambition and money, with money predominating, children are increasingly deciding how the cash is spent and on what . . . leading to a war whose only Hiroshima is a Toblerone, a Barbie or a Baskin Robbins.'[15]

Many adults—the 'discerning' ones—spoke eloquently about the new atmosphere of optimism generated by the economic reforms. 'New technologies, new ventures, new jobs are being introduced as never before. Foreign exchange coffers are filled as never before. Industry is booming as never before. Most of all, there is a palpable hope in the air. People are doing lucrative deals, getting well-paid jobs, travelling and vacationing, convinced that India is at last over the hump.'[16] Foreign newspapers and magazines were suddenly full of stories on India's impending economic turnaround. This was always a matter of special reassurance for the middle class. Observers noticed a new 'mindset' among Indians. 'There is confidence in the air, and people believe that their children will be better off than they were. It is particularly evident among business people and students, but you also find it among politicians, bureaucrats, trade-unionists and housewives. One feature of this mindset is that making money is an acceptable, legitimate route to success. Gone is our earlier hypocrisy towards money. There is a "can-do" attitude and all sorts of people are taking risks and starting new businesses . . . The business pages of newspapers have grown livelier. The circulation of the Economic Times which was under a lakh in 1990, crossed five lakhs in 1994, making it the second largest business paper in the world. The country abounds in rags-to-riches stories. There is the same heady sense of possibilities that existed in the early fifties.'[17]

Multinational corporations and their marketing strategists overestimated the 'heady possibilities' of the Indian market. The size of the middle class in terms of purchasing power for their goods was probably closer to 100 million, rather than the more euphoric estimates of 250 million. But on one aspect the MNCs were dead right, as the decade since the mid 1990s has proved: they knew that even if the middle class had limited money, there was little limitation to its wants; it was this collective 'mindset' of want that, the MNCs knew, would provide an enduring basis for their continued stay in India. Expectations could be scaled down in the short run, but it was the long term that mattered. 'Most (MNCs) have begun to look at the Indian market from a long-term perspective and, given the rupee-dollar exchange rate, can afford to pour in more investments and wait for a decade or more without feeling the pinch. Also, with Western markets saturated, India, warts and all, remains attractive. For, if the Indian consumer is cautious with his money, *he is also looking forward to excitement, the kind he hasn't experienced yet in his lifetime* [emphasis mine]. He hasn't forgotten the time when he would plead with every relative travelling abroad for a pair of Levi's ... Or when he haggled with the local smuggler over Head and Shoulders and Bangkok-made Lacoste T-shirts. He definitely wants to exercise his choice and feel pampered.'[18]

Typically, the middle class also implicitly believed that what was good for it was also good for the country as a whole. One unfortunate aspect of this general atmospherics of hope and optimism was that it pushed even more into the background some rather inconvenient messages about the real condition of the Indian economy. For those looking forward to 'well-paid jobs' and 'travelling and vacationing' as never before, it was not unnatural to forget that every day as many as 250 million Indians—at the very minimum—were still going hungry to bed at night. For those convinced that India was 'at last over the hump', it was easy to gloss over the fact that their country is home to the largest number of illiterates in the world. To those watching the glitzy ads on cable television it would seem improbable that every third human being in the world without safe and adequate water supply is an Indian, or that diarrhoea claims close to 1.5 million infants each year in this country—one every three minutes. For those who were supremely optimistic about their children being better off than themselves, it was quite in order to be ignorant of the fact that fifty-three per cent of all Indian children below the age of five are underweight and malnourished as against even Ethiopia's forty-eight per cent, or that the infant mortality rate in India is one of the highest in the world. For the upwardly mobile, suffused with a 'new confidence' in the opportunities to make money, it was of little consequence that rural female illiteracy in the country was close to seventy per cent, or that only fifteen per cent of scheduled caste women in UP and Bihar, the two most populous states in the country, were literate. For those celebrating the demise of the earlier stigma associated with the good life, it was possible to be unaware of or unconcerned about the fact that more than half of all Indians living in cities had no access to sanitation facilities, and that the absence of such a basic facility was as high as a staggering ninety-seven per cent for rural Indians.

Statistics tend to sanitize deprivation. When they represent a reality that is so appalling in its destitution, the sheer magnitude of numbers fails to make an impact, except as demographic data. In any case they pertain to the 'other' India, the one that lives in 'mud huts', and is an unnecessary distraction for those in a hurry to meet their 'tryst with destiny inside shiny buildings of chrome and glass at the free market'. Statistics can hardly convey the pulverizing, degrading poverty of the millions of Indians who, live below the poverty line (even by the government's own admission, they were 26 per cent of the the population in 2000). Especially when the far more visible message for close to two decades now has been the ubiquitous, persuasive and enticing possibility of imminent consumerist salvation. The debate then is not about the economic efficacy of the policy of liberalization. Few can deny the perilous straits the country had reached in pursuit of the moribund rhetoric of socialist transformation. The need for opening up the Indian economy was more than evident for some time before Dr Manmohan Singh introduced his new economic policies. There can be more than one opinion on the content and direction of these policies, not on their need. But for our purposes, the question of critical importance is the impact these policies had on most members of a class which for quite some time now had quite demonstrably surrendered all pretence of idealism or morality or social sensitivity on the twin altars of self-interest and material well-being. The policy of economic liberalization provided the Indian middle class an excuse to even more blatantly separate its 'world' from the vast masses of the destitute and deprived in India. It deadened even further any remaining sense of concern in it for the disadvantaged. It gave a flamboyant ideological justification for the creation of two Indias, one aspiring to be globalized, and the other hopelessly, despairingly marginalized. And, in terms of aspirations, it left most middle-class Indians, notwithstanding the modesty of their means, mesmerized by the lifestyle of the very rich; for it was this message of upper-class opulence and luxury that became inextricably linked, at least in popular perception, with the much proclaimed break with the ineffective socialistic restraints of the past.

The essential point then is that 'the current wave of liberalization has deepened the tendency which the wealthy Indian already had to ignore the sufferings of the poor . . . Once it becomes legitimate to ignore poverty, *the sense of community ceases to have a place in social life* [emphasis mine].'[19] It is this appraisal, of how a policy of economic reform, however well intentioned, affects the attitudes and behaviour of the more influential sections of society, that is as much the real issue as the often sterile and mechanically ideological debates with regard to the economic content of such a policy.

At the height of the euphoria about the dynamic new possibilities unleashed by the reform process, a leading weekly in the country carried a cover story on the Indians living on the brink of starvation in the poorest villages of India in Raigada, Orissa. The story had graphic pictures, including an enumeration of what the poorest of the poor eat during the year: no lunch, no dinner, twelve months of the year, and in some months only wild roots and seeds. The article concluded thus: 'The abiding memory (of one destitute family in Bursunda in Raigada) remains that of a group of children with swollen bellies—their bodies covered with sores and boils. Time for one last photograph of all of them together, and one thought flits through the mind: that there are family pictures and there are family pictures. All this in a country where "our culture", it is alleged, does not allow a fellow human being to starve? Where charity is supposedly ingrained in the collective consciousness of the masses? The all-pervading paralysis of thought and action is, in the deepest sense of the term, unacceptable.'[20] The readership of this popular weekly is largely from the middle class. What is unacceptable is that there was almost no reaction from this class to the report, no evidence of pause or introspection, no attempt at raising voluntary contributions to try and help, no outpouring of sympathy or expression of concern or anguish. Nothing. At best, the story invoked a sense of *deja vu*, a general reaction of: So what's new? There have always been starving Indians. Why make an issue of them, specially now when the country was trying to project its best image as a buoyant market and an attractive destination for foreign investment? This imperviousness to the travails of one's own countrymen, this inability to see beyond the neon lights advertising one more object of desire, this absolute conviction that there is little in common between the possibility of the good life and the state of deprivation of the vast majority, and finally this acceptance of poverty and destitution for one set of Indians, even as another, much smaller segment celebrates the 'heady possibilities' released by the reform process—it is this attitude which has become a pervasive aspect of middle class thinking. The malaise is serious enough to merit consideration beyond the ambit of partisan politics. For, the truth is that the social insensitivity of the educated and privileged Indian is writ large on the face of India, whether the professed goal of the country is socialism or capitalism. The new economic policies have accentuated this social insensitivity, and brought into sharp focus the psychological polarization between the worlds inhabited by the rich and the poor.

The seminal question for the middle class is: Can such a polarized world be sustained in perpetuity? Or has the time come for this class, in its own long-term interests, to move beyond the 'margins of elite vision'? A nation, in spite of its many particularities, is an indivisible whole. Unless all parts of it are part of a national consensus, unless all its people become part of a process of empowerment, and unless all its citizens feel they are part of a common destiny, no one class within it can sustain the illusion of progress for long. It is true that the illusion is difficult to give up. There are ideologies available that argue the hope that the uninhibited material pursuits of the privileged will automatically ensure the trickling down of benefits to the deprived. Perhaps such a scenario is possible in some societies. But the Indian middle and elite classes must necessarily ask themselves whether such a scenario is workable in their own country where as many as forty per cent of their people live in the most abject poverty and half the population cannot read or write. How many decades of this trickle-down process would lead to a transformation in the lives of the bulk of Indians? The other option is to ignore the other India and proceed unheedingly along the existing groove of consumerist satiation. But, alas, it is difficult if not impossible to structure a nation into watertight compartments, or draw a *cordon sanitaire* between one section's wants and another's needs, especially in a functioning democracy. An attempt to do so would lead to political stability and frightening social tensions which would, in the long term, militate against the very prosperity and material well-being which the middle class desires.

Is the middle class capable of pausing to think, of seeing what is good for its own enduring interests? Can it for a moment see beyond immediate self-interest, and think seriously about what the problem is and how best it can achieve on a more secure basis its goals for a better life, not just for tomorrow but for the next generation and the foreseeable future? Can middle-class Indians transcend the sound and fury of their myriad little worlds of desires and pursuits to forge a vision that is sustainable in the long run? Can they somehow escape the clutches of the illusion that their upwardly mobile aspirations can remain insulated from the basic deprivations that are the lot of most of their countrymen? The odds certainly appear to be stacked against their undertaking such a fundamental reappraisal. There is a total absence of any credible appeal to social commitment or a moral imperative that can counter the obsession with personal gain and promotion. The shrinking of the moral domain in national life cannot but destroy the resolve of even the most well intentioned. 'Moral losses are like radiation, colourless and odourless and the more terrifying for that.'[21] Greed—the desire to possess more and more irrespective of the means or the consequences—is a fertilizer that accelerates the growth of particularities; it can hardly be expected to produce a harvest of restraint or re-evaluation. The buoyant media messages of consumer nirvana crowd out the need for sobering introspection. The removal of any stigma associated with making money has ended hypocrisy but also the need to be concerned about anything else. 'When a long-suppressed desire becomes realizable, it drives the fortunate few unscrupulous.'[22] Unscrupulous in the single-minded pursuit of their own betterment to the exclusion of any other cause or concern. In such a milieu, the loss of one kind of restraint quickly leads to the unravelling of the whole system. A young fashion designer holds a 'loo' theme party at a disco in the countryside on the outskirts of Delhi. All the guests have to come dressed in apparel worn normally in the loo, and the decor is done up to resemble a loo. Is this great party idea just a frivolous, juvenile ripple of the affluent class? Or is there just the hint of the vulgar and the perverse? Not in moral terms at the choice of the theme, but in what the evening demonstrates: the unthinking acceptance of the enormous gulf that separates the tiny group of people living out, bang in the middle of a semi-rural setting, an idiom that fits in with the wild side of Manhattan from the thousands of people only a few yards away who still use the fields to defecate and walk a kilometre or more to obtain something as basic as drinking water. The comment is not on the event per se: that is of no consequence. The comment is on the sensibilities of a westernized affluent fringe, increasingly a role model for many in the middle class, that can find such ingenious and flamboyant ways to party, oblivious to the sense of revulsion such a lifestyle creates when juxtaposed to the backdrop for its shenanigans.

No, the imperative of stocktaking and introspection will not come easily to the middle class. But the effort, however stupendous, has to be made by it in its own long-term interests. The argument here is that even the prosperity and progress of the kind the middle class aspires to will be ensured better if the methodology to achieve this is more than merely the blind pursuit of what can be grabbed in the immediate. The argument also is that the perpetuation of a dual India— one which consumes or is exhorted to do so by a host of desirable brand names and the other, far more numerous, which struggles every day to even have one basic meal—is a very unstable and tenuous foundation for the good life. Self-interest, therefore, dictates that this inherently untenable state of affairs is remedied. Gandhiji's faith in the concern of the better endowed citizens for their poorer brethren was based on altruism. The rich, he said, should be but trustees of their wealth for the benefit of the poor. In the decades after him much has changed and we must accept that altruism will cut little ice. But, perhaps, self-interest will.

If self-interest, a sentiment with which the middle class is not unfamiliar, can jolt it to pause and reassess its strategies for its own benefit in the long run, then several convincing examples can be given to indicate to it what is the right track. The economies of East Asia are often held up by middle-class Indians (the recent setbacks notwithstanding) as examples of enviable material progress, in contrast to all that India could not achieve. However, it needs to be remembered that many of these economies 'successfully accomplished large-scale land reforms and built up rural infrastructure . . . Agriculture has played an important part in the "East Asian Miracle" . . . Agricultural growth stimulates non-agricultural growth. In Taiwan, for instance, agriculture, not exports, took the lead in generating domestic demand and employment.'[23] By contrast, in India, even among otherwise well-informed people, 'the entire debate about economic liberalization proceeds as if the agricultural sector or rural India does not exist or, if it exists, it does not matter. This is incredible in an economy where two-thirds of the work force is employed in agriculture and where three-fourths of the population lives in the rural sector. Even if their share of income in the economy is much smaller than their proportion in the population, it must be remembered that their share of votes in the polity is directly proportional. The electoral, if not political, compulsions of a democracy cannot be set aside for long.'[24] And, as we have argued before, political turmoil will militate directly against the middle-class dream of integrating with the affluent countries of the world economy.

It is also instructive to know that the investment in education has been 'crucial for the economic development of late industrializers, particularly the success stories of East Asia that are now perceived as role models'.[25] And yet, the euphoria, among many middle-class Indians, on account of economic liberalization, does not even take into account that roughly half of all Indians are illiterate. Middle-class Indians can be easily outraged by the banning of a book, or a 'cut' in a film, while remaining largely oblivious to the fact that illiteracy, specially of such a magnitude, 'is the most pervasive form of censorship.'[26]

In 1995 the World Competitiveness Report (WCR) ranked South Korea twenty-four among forty-eight countries. India ranked thirty-nine. Many middle-class Indians are rightfully proud that India has the second largest work force in the world with a wage structure much below that of the developed countries. It is also true that a part of this work force consists of highly skilled persons. Yet, the truth is that the bulk of India's manpower is dramatically below par in critical parameters such as productivity, quality and competency. 'Translated into worker's productivity, it means that the value added per worker in India's manufacturing sector is a tenth of that in Japan and a fourth of that in Singapore. In factors like "people" and "management", India is ranked forty-seven and thirty-nine respectively—in other words, both contribute little towards making the country competitive.'[27]

The writing on the wall is clear, and it is time that those who wish to approximate the prosperity of the East Asian economies or those of the developed world, begin to read it. 'Unless we invest enough in human beings, which will require substantial increases in resources required for education, productivity increases may not follow structural reform. And in the absence of sufficiently developed human resources *the benefits of integrating with the world economy will simply elude us* [emphasis mine].'[28] It is in this context that Galbraith's succinct inference that an educated populace is the first requirement for economic progress makes such luminescent sense: 'In this world there is no literate population that is poor, no illiterate population that is other than poor.'[29]

The tremendous poverty in India requires the better off citizens to be concerned about it. We have mentioned the fact that government reports of the year 2000 admit that twenty-six per cent of Indians live below the poverty line. The very calculation of the poverty line, for those not exposed to the grinding and stark destitution that it connotes, has become part of a 'measurement fetish', a remote statistical exercise that does not seem to be directly correlated to the world inhabited by the privileged. 'Privileged' is, of course, a relative term in the context of India, where even the averagely well-to-do are hardly affluent by the standards of the developed countries. But by the same yardstick of relativity even those who can have three square meals a day and send their children to school or have access to basic health care are 'privileged' in India. Because what is often forgotten or ignored is that apart from the vast number who live below the poverty line, another thirty to thirty-five per cent hover precariously above it and are poor by absolute standards. This means that the extent of poverty in the country 'prevents over three-fifths of our people from becoming full human beings endowed with literacy, numeracy and basic skills.'[30] This should be a matter of deep concern to middle-class Indians who are trying to create a sound basis for their material betterment, but it is not. Once again, the track record of the very countries which are looked up to by the middle class is significant. In Indonesia the percentage of people below the poverty line dropped from fifty-eight in 1972 to seventeen in 1982; in Malaysia it came down from thirty-seven in 1973 to fourteen in 1987; in Thailand from forty-nine in 1962 to twenty-six in 1986. It is true that the problems of these countries, and the strategies they adopted, were specific to themselves, and a comparison with India, even on an indicative basis, is not always relevant. But the essential point is that a reduction in poverty has obviously had a direct bearing on the ensuing prosperity of these countries. In India a major problem outside the realm of economic strategies is that the 'privileged' have progressively deluded themselves into believing that poverty does not exist, or that if it does, it need not influence their lifestyle choices. A great many middle-class Indians have consigned the poor to being a fixture on a landscape they do not wish to see. This insensitivity to poverty, especially among the influential, cannot but be an obstacle to the eradication of poverty, for unless a nation and a society produces citizens who care and not merely consumers who want, there cannot be a politically stable or economically resilient basis to prosperity.

Till such time as the existence of poverty of this magnitude motivates the privileged and the influential (and a great many of the latter belong to the middle class) to do something about it, there is no invisible hand or magic of the market that can remedy the inherently weak foundations of the soaring aspirations of these very elite. Policies, however apt or effective, do not operate in a social vacuum. People draft them and people implement them. If such people could understand that their own well-being is inextricably entwined with the amelioration of the conditions of the destitute, then there might emerge a social commitment that has as its basis enlightened self-interest and the good of the needy. In the presence of such a commitment, the debate, among many well-meaning members of the middle class, would not be simplistically restricted to the question of 'more' or 'less' government in mechanical imitation of the formulas and experience of other nations, but on how to give to government the right priorities and direction in conformity with India's basic needs and requirements. In the absence of such a commitment, the slogan of liberalization has only served to further erode an already weak sense of social concern in the bulk of the middle class.

The essential point needs to be reiterated without the slightest trace of ambivalence: unless the social virtues of care and concern inform the process of economic growth, the dangerous divide between unsustainable lifestyles and unacceptable poverty will remain. If 550 million people will become members of the middle class by the year 2025,[31] there will be, at a conservative estimate, still 750 million people below such an elevation, and a great many of these will still be absolutely poor by relative standards. And if the present degree of social insensitivity towards the poor is projected into the year 2025, we are likely to have a nation with a higher per capita income but a deeply fractured society and, given the existence of a functioning democracy, considerable political instability. The discrepancies of the Indian socio-economic fabric are such that there is a fundamental dichotomy of vision between those whom liberalization is empowering and those who need first to be empowered in order to be liberalized.

Any policy, be it of the left or the right, needs to bridge this dichotomy by changing the psychological perception of the 'haves' with regard to the 'have-nots'. The votaries of the current process of reform do disservice to the ultimate objective of any reform policy when, in the euphoria of greater consumerist choices, they show a total lack of concern about the fact that far more people have become poorer in the last five years than those who have benefitted by having a choice between Canada Dry and Coca-Cola. Once again the flaw is not in the policy per se but in the attitudes of those who see themselves as its immediate beneficiaries. 'Globalization' may be a valid buzz word, but there must be a value-based meeting ground between the economic imperatives espoused by the developed countries and the social predilections of the elite in a developing nation. Otherwise the largely urban 'liberalized' lot will begin to approximate the '*comprador*' species which flourished in the 'treaty ports' of China in the last century: 'They are half-caste in culture, bilingual in speech, and morally unstable. They are unscrupulous, pecuniary, individualistic . . . Treaty ports are ultra-urban. They are a land where the acquisition of wealth is the sole motive, devoid of tradition and culture. It is unfortunate that the East and the West should meet on such a ground.'[32]

M.S. Subbulakshmi, the legendary vocalist, when asked what makes her cry, had a simple answer: poverty. 'It is heart-rending,' she said, 'to see so many poor people.'[33] If the privileged Indian has even a fraction of this empathy for the poor, this feeling for their pain and deprivation, the chances are that any policy, whatever its ideological hue, will work. Fortunately, a sense of concern can very often be economically efficacious. For, 'a well-fed, healthy and educated population which does not have to trudge miles for drinking water provides the best guarantee for rapid economic growth as well.'[34] Once this realization dawns upon members of the middle class—who according to a 1996 survey, were eating '38000 tonnes of potato chips, spraying themselves with 15,100 tonnes of talcum powder, consuming 2880 million bottles of soft drinks, and flying ten million times a year'[35]—it is possible that the search for prosperity may acquire a new dimension.

It may come as a surprise to many educated Indians that the issue of social concern has been cropping up frequently and consistently in the last few years in the very Mecca of capitalism—USA. In deference to the new ethic of profitability before all else, American CEO's have been 'downsizing' their firms. Downsizing is another word for retrenchment of labour—both blue- and white-collar—on a fairly large scale. Corporate chiefs have argued that their only responsibility is to ensure profitability to their shareholders. In this process it is estimated that over three million workers have been laid off since the 1980s. The rich seem to have become richer, while the incomes of the bulk of the populace appear to have stagnated, if not depreciated. In the mid 1970s the income gap between the very rich and the very poor was at its narrowest: one per cent of the population controlled eighteen per cent of the wealth. By 1996 that one per cent was controlling forty per cent of the wealth. In the late 1990s, the ratio of the top twenty per cent of American incomes to the poorest twenty per cent was at its widest: nine to one. While workers were being unceremoniously retrenched, the salaries of chief executives of corporations went up from thirty-five times the average wage to compensation that was 187 times the average wage.

These are trends which have acquired visibility. America is certainly not on the brink of a revolution by the dispossessed and continues to be one of the most productive and buoyant economies of the world. The significant point is that even in a country where social inequities are not remotely as glaring as those in India, corporate restructuring has provoked an unprecedented outpouring of concern and introspection on such basic questions as the very meaning and purpose and end results of economic activity. The *New York Times* carried a series on the 'downsized', devoting more space to the issue than it gave even to the Pentagon Papers in the seventies. The series 'put human faces on those large, abstract figures of jobs eliminated at AT&T, Chase Manhattan and so many other companies. It has shown not just individual pain but the social consequences of the ruthless new economy: the loss of community, the rootless family, the fraying of hope.'[36] Columnists have lamented that 'the American social contract has been grievously damaged'. [37] They have drawn attention to the fact that 'in the past American commercialism was tempered by a religious puritanism with powerful traditions of civic service and public obligations . . . A code of public obligations was taught in American schools and universities.'[38] Influential journalists, politicians, government officials, academics and those in business have became part of an anguished debate on 'where American society is going in a world driven by market economics' and 'what social and economic policies might reduce the damage to individuals and communities'. Others have been more blunt: 'The current economic and business doctrine subordinating the interests of community and workforce to profit and market return must be challenged. The notion that business is responsible to society must be re-established in business education and corporate ethics.'[39] The interesting factor is that the focus on the plight of the downsized has led to the questioning—in the very womb where it was nurtured—of the role of the market. The *Washington Post* editorialized that the triumph of capitalism over socialism has not ended 'the two-centuries-old debate about *how to temper the efficiency and individualism of the free market with fairness and concern for community* [emphasis mine]. After a brief hiatus, that debate has resumed, impelled by the pressures of globalization in the developed world, the insecurity of transition in the formerly communist world and continuing misery in many developing countries.'[40]

If the relocation and disruption in the lives of a few fellow citizens can outrage the sensibilities of a great many influential Americans, and lead to the questioning of some of the most sacrosanct views underpinning that nation's economy, why is it that the disease and hunger and poverty of so many years of so many millions in India makes such little impact on the conscience and sensibility of the privileged Indian? The question needs to be squarely asked of those who project the immutable effectiveness of economic policies without taking into account the social milieu in which they are to be implemented. If the laudable intentions of socialism could be subverted by the entrenched class interests of the 'privilegentsia', what is there to prevent the anticipated benefits of the new economic policy from bypassing the poorest in favour of the already privileged? This is a prospect which is no longer the ranting of blind critics of the market mechanism. Klaus Schwab, the founder and president of the World Economic Forum at Davos, writes: 'It becomes apparent that the head-on mega-competition that is part and parcel of globalization leads to winner-take-all situations; those who come out on top win big, and the losers lose even bigger. The gap between those able to ride the wave of globalization, specially because they are knowledge and communication oriented, and those left behind is getting wider at the national, corporate and individual levels.'[41]

The middle and elite classes in India need to ponder over

this prognosis, and once again in their own long-term interests. Can it be honestly said that there is in this segment today a sense of civic obligation, or corporate ethics, or social responsibility, which could foster a vision encompassing the welfare of the community as a whole, and prevent the gap from widening between the winners and the losers? The laws that govern the impact of economic policies are not like the laws that operate in physics, bound by an unchanging truth of cause and effect. 'Economic behaviour is embedded in a social and political context whose complexity, and potentialities, are certainly subject to scientific analysis but not to comprehensive and scientifically objective conclusions.'[42] Many members of the middle class posit the inevitability of benefits from the opening up of the Indian economy, even for the poorest Indian, as conventional wisdom outside the purview of discussion. Such a faith, of course, is rather convenient. For, essentially, it means that there is no need for them to pause in their pursuit of the good life, or change their manifest insensitivity to the deprived; they need be concerned only with the better pursuit of profit and money, and, automatically, the poor and illiterate will go away. The faith is touching, but it is both selfish and, in terms of its intended rewards, illusory. An economically 'globalized' India will be prosperous only if there is a quantum increase in the social sensitivity of those who give its policies shape and direction. For, as a leading American columnist has put it in the context of his own country: 'One thing seems plain. We Americans cannot look to the magic of the market for solutions. *A culture provides the values of community and caring; if the society does not supply them, the market certainly will not* [emphasis mine]. If the society does, the market adjusts to them.'[43]

Does the Indian society of today provide the values of community and caring which could prevent the impact of economic policies from being restricted to only those in a position to benefit the most? The obvious answer to this question is no. The educated Indian seems to labour under the illusion that there is no link between his own lack of social responsibility and the prosperity of his class and that of the community as a whole. It is this illusion that is at the core of the socially deviant behaviour of large chunks of the middle class. Depending on the variables used, the strength of this class is anywhere between 150 and 250 million people. Of these, incredibly enough, only twelve million or so were tax assessees, and only four million tax payers. The successful Voluntary Disclosure of Income Scheme (VDIS) hardly changed this—the fact still remains that only about two per cent of urban India pays taxes. According to a newspaper report in 1996, seventy per cent of the top 1500 companies paid no taxes.[44] The situation hasn't changed much. Most of India's top fifty companies effectively avoid taxes by exploiting government loopholes (this when Indian companies spend as little as an average of 0.6 per cent of their revenue from sales in Research and Development; in advanced countries the figure stands between five and ten per cent).

The culture of evasion and dishonesty, based on the myopic assumption that short-term personal gain, even if illegitimate, does not affect long-term prosperity, pervades the thinking of the middle and elite classes. As always, there is an attempt to give an ideological justification for this willingness to avoid social obligations. It is argued that a simplified and lower tax rate structure is a better alternative to enhance tax revenues. The case for simplification is perhaps to the point, but the plea for lower taxation is often transparently an excuse to even further reduce the scope of a purely pecuniary instrumentality to ensure social responsibility. It is a trait of the middle class to be convinced about its disproportionate burden. Such an obsession only reinforces a world-view that sees material well-being, or the alleged lack of it, in isolation, divorced from the sea of poverty all around. There are many who could cogently argue that 'in a country as poor as India it is ridiculous that somebody with an annual income of Rs 60,000 will henceforth pay no more tax at all.'[45] It is also a moot point whether India is—as many in the middle class unquestioningly believe—a heavily taxed country. In 2001 central tax revenues constituted only 9.9 per cent of India's GDP, while the figure was 18 per cent in Malaysia, 14 per cent in Thailand, 17 per cent in South Korea, 36 per cent in the United Kingdom, and 42 per cent in France.[46]

The truth is that the collection of taxes—an almost universal mechanism in all countries to tap the incomes of the better off to do more for the needy—has in India less to do with tax planning and more with the malaise at the very core of things: the erosion of morality and the absence of any sense of social responsibility. It is more than likely that even if income taxes are reduced—a matter of great jubilation always for the middle class—the tax base will not significantly widen. For, 'the fact is that lower rates may reduce the tax burden, but evasion does away with it altogether.'[47] And if evasion is the acceptable pattern of behaviour for the influential, no enforcement machinery can really fully tackle the problem. This is all the more so because even the enforcement machinery must necessarily be a part of the same ethos. In the US, the infamous 1920s gangster, Al Capone, was finally nabbed not by the FBI but the IRS, the Internal Revenue System. The power and reach of the IRS is based not only on the punitive machinery backing it but on the conviction among most tax payees that evasion is wrong and a matter of social stigma.

In India the social stigma attached to socially illegitimate behaviour has largely vanished for the privileged. One of the reasons why much of the coarse grain meant for the urban and rural poor under the Public Distribution System never reaches them is because middle-class ration shop owners, many of whom are grain traders, divert the supply meant for their shops to their own godowns. This is not an unknown fact but the culprits have had no pangs of conscience, and, as if to vindicate their criminal insensitivity, there have been very few convictions. The over-invoicing of imports and the under-invoicing of exports is normal practice for many a respectable entrepreneur in the foreign trade sector. This is the most convenient route to move significant amounts of capital from the country. The annual flight of capital from the country through this mechanism has been estimated to be anywhere between one to three billion dollars every year. According to a World Bank estimate at the beginning of the nineties, the unaccounted money of Indians in various tax havens abroad was of the magnitude of $100 billion, more than the total external debt of India at that time. And within the country, black money, which can yield as much as Rs 1.6 lakh crore of direct taxes, is estimated to be thirty-five per cent of the country's GDP.

The figures can vary. Economists are often notorious about the number of ways they can find to differ about the obvious. In India, the obvious fact is that the long-term prospect of economic growth is increasingly being held to ransom by the unbridled greed and unscrupulousness of the empowered. Foreign loans cannot be the sole answer to the State's chronic shortage of resources. Where then is the government to find the resources to tackle the problems of hunger and education and disease, and undertake developmental work, including the building of infrastructure so necessary to the reform process itself? These problems cannot be ignored, nor is it—

as we have sought to emphasize—in the ultimate interests of the middle and elite classes to ignore them.

A young bureaucrat hit the nail on the head with regard to the real problem in India. 'How to rescue society from the clutches of its own better endowed citizens,' he writes, 'is a central issue of governability.'[48] In matters of economic policy the better endowed citizens have a simple agenda: the freer import of consumer durables, lower taxation, and continuity in rise of income. Their support for economic liberalization is in large measure due to their perception that this is precisely what it will deliver. There is thus a serious dysfunction between elite expectations and what any economic policy in India must actually set out to achieve. Even the World Bank in its report 'India: Achievements and Challenges in Reducing Poverty', released in 1997, came around to grasping the real priorities. 'India has not achieved the momentum to lift the great majority of its poor into the country's economic mainstream,' the report says. 'For India, the lessons for the future are clear—promote growth and invest more in making people healthier and better educated and spend more on the physical infrastructure which underpins a country's growth at the local and national level.'

For the Indian middle class, therefore, the moment has come for some very critical decisions. Either it must pause, in its own interest, and take a hard look at what needs to be done to ensure its well-being in the long run, or persist with its current short-sighted obsession only with what can be had, by any and all means, in the here and now. Either it must curb its frenetic preoccupation with immediate material gain, or contribute to enduring material progress by preoccupying itself a little more with the good of the nation as a whole. Either it must seek to inculcate in itself a greater social sensitivity, or accept the fact that all that it is seeking to acquire can be set aside insensitively by forces beyond its control. India may not see, for a variety of reasons, a violent revolution by the dispossessed. But if their needs are not addressed in a more concerned and interventionist manner by those who are in a better position to do so, there is likely to be great political instability, which could be as inimical to economic growth and prosperity as violent upheaval. A functioning democracy—and there is no reason to assume that India will not remain one—renders illusory the prospect of the secession of the successful. The time has come to definitively bury that illusion.

≈

Can the Indian middle class take the right fork in this historic crossroad before it? Of course, a qualitative change in the established patterns of thinking and behaviour will not be easy. The polity is devoid of an ideology that can inspire a larger vision, or a leadership that can invoke a credible alternative to the existing state of affairs. An utter lack of morality has become a feature of society. A call for greater social responsibility can effortlessly be swamped by the imminent consumer seductions of a newly liberalized economy. But, whatever the odds, enlightened self-interest demands some very serious soul searching and introspection that can facilitate a break from the past.

The first step in this process is to link self-interest to long-term goals rather than only immediate benefit. The experience of India has shown that it is not the efficacy or inefficacy of policies, but the proclivity of the better off segments to use such policies only for their own benefit which has subverted professed policy goals. The need for social concern has thus as much to do with idealism as it has to do with the ultimate fulfilment of the aspiration for the good life. Klaus Schwab sums up the proposition cogently: 'Moral considerations aside, there can be no sustainable growth without the public at large seeing itself as the major stakeholder in the successful functioning of the economy.'[49]

How can a middle class and its elite role models, long immune to anything but their own interests, develop this much needed virtue of social concern? Apart from the transparency of class interests and the absence of a leadership that could credibly convey the importance of the community over self, an identifiable trend, directly contributing to the entrenchment of social insensitivities, is the growing 'physical' distance between the poor and the privileged in India. The poverty and deprivation in the country is so great that those who have moved up the income ladder seek to 'barricade' themselves from its pervasive presence. The years of 'socialist' rhetoric have also bred the notion that it is the government alone which is responsible for dealing with such things. Somewhere, in this growing duality between the two Indias and this artificial divide between the government and the individual, the concerned citizen has completely given way to the self-obsessed aspirant. What can be done to resurrect the citizen who cares? Clearly, and most emphatically, coercion is not the answer. Nor can exhortation cut much ice, since the one thing Indian public life has achieved is to take for granted the insincerity of the preacher. The answer appears to be a conscious and quantum increase in voluntary activities outside government, particularly in the areas of education, poverty eradication and health.

The first reaction of many in the middle class will be to dismiss such an idea as idealistic fantasizing. But the proposal is not as unrealistic as it may sound. The elite in the country have always had considerable influence on middle-class aspirations, lifestyle choices and behavioral trends. Within this elite there are quite a few of the very moneyed and professionally successful; and there is evidence that at least some of them, still a great minority, have pioneered an involvement in projects that demonstrate a much required sense of social purpose.

Some years ago the Tata Iron and Steel Company (TISCO), the country's premier steel making company in the private sector, set up a separate body called Tata Steel Rural Development Society for community service in thirty-two clusters of villages around Jamshedpur. Today, the Society operates in 600 villages in eight districts in Bihar, Orissa and Madhya Pradesh, and is making a difference in such areas as developing sources of water both for irrigation and domestic use, helping farmers to adopt improved methods of cultivation and animal care, construction of school buildings, promotion of rural industry and entrepreneurship, adult literacy, empowerment of women, rural sanitation and other health care facilities.

Ranbaxy, the pharmaceutical giant, set up the Ranbaxy Community Health Care Society in 1980, with a view to taking health care to the villages close to each of the company's plant locations. The Society operates five mobile health care units from Delhi, Dewas in Madhya Pradesh, Paonta Sahib in Himachal Pradesh and Mohali and Beas in Punjab. Each unit is manned by a doctor, health visitors and a pharmacist. In the last decade, the health centres have treated over a million patients, immunized more than a million and a half children, covered over 20,000 couples under the family welfare programme, and administered vitamin A prophylaxis as an anti-blindness measure to as many as 40,000 children. The Society is now planning to set up family welfare centres for slums in cities.

Bajaj Auto Limited, the country's largest scooter making firm, undertook near Pune, its corporate headquarters, an integrated project to raise awareness of the need for clean water, provide solutions for water supply problems, and educate people on how to implement these solutions. The company has also set up pilot projects in which it provides expertise for construction of community toilets. It's community work also includes watershed development, agricultural improvement, tree planting, providing potable drinking water and irrigation facilities, and construction of low-cost houses.

The Indal Aluminium Company Limited (INDAL) set aside rupees one crore for literacy promotion programmes and another two and a half crores for a vocational education trust to support elementary and adult education programmes. The conglomerate ICI India Limited adopted thirty-five villages and spent over five crores in benefitting over 85,000 families through activities in the educational, environmental and health fields. And Asea Brown Boveri (ABB) is engaged in community development work at ten factory locations across India. In Baroda, its projects focus on adult education, health care and family welfare, targetting employees' wives and villagers.[50]

More recently, corporates have started projects to transform the way we have traditionally looked at helping citizens. For instance, ITC started 'e-Choupal', a unique web based initiative that offers farmers all the information, products and services they need to enhance farm productivity, improve farm-gate price realization and cut transaction costs. Farmers access latest local and global information on weather, scientific farming practicises as well as market prices at the village itself through the web portal and in regional languages. Launched in June 2000, 'e-Choupal', has already become the largest initiative among all Internet-based interventions in rural India. 'e-Choupal' services today reach out to more than

3.5 million farmers growing a range of crops—soyabean, coffee, wheat, rice, pulses, and even shrimp—in over 31,000 villages through 5200 kiosks across six states (Madhya Pradesh, Karnataka, Andhra Pradesh, Uttar Pradesh, Maharashtra and Rajasthan).

Then there is the example of Narayana Hrudayalaya in Bangalore. In collaboration with the state government in Karnataka this premier cardiac hospital spearheaded a health insurance scheme for 25 lakh farmers and their families. *Yeshasvini*, as the scheme was called, was launched in 2002 for farmers belonging to various state cooperatives. For Rs. 5 a month, cardholders had access to free treatment at 150 hospitals in 29 districts of the state for any medical procedure costing upto Rs 1 lakh. Under this scheme in the frst year alone 9000 farmers underwent operations and 35,000 received outpatient treatment across the state. [51]

If such examples of social concern by the corporate elite can be expanded manifold and replicated across the country—and the government through appropriate policy incentives should actively encourage the effort—it will send a powerful message of social activism to the millions of upwardly mobile middle-class Indians who are particularly porous to variations of behaviour in the elite segments of the country. The intention is not to glorify corporate philanthropy as the panacea for the ills in the country, but to highlight the few yet encouraging examples of social sensitivity which can play a catalytic role in changing the attitudes of the many whose sole motivation is to approximate the material well-being of the rich. It is true that the priority of social welfare may have dawned on these corporate giants only after the acquisition of wealth. It is also true that they could, relative to their profits, be doing much more, or that the reason for their display of social commitment could be nothing more than the advice of their chartered accountants. It is also possible that the overly sensitive may discern in such activities little more than the condescension of the rich towards the poor, a few crumbs given in charity and a few undeserving consciences assuaged.

It does not matter. For something in the right direction is better than nothing. The country is replete with thousands of corporate success stories where a display of social concern does not even constitute a footnote in the annual balance sheets. In most cases, commercial success has only to do with more conspicuous consumption, and it is this insulation from any other concern which is internalized by the middle class as the dominant and valid bias of society. In any case, remedies have to be weighed against existing options. An appeal by the government is unlikely to incline the average middle-class Indian towards voluntary work for the disadvantaged. But there is a possibility that he may pause to consider his own inclinations if such activity is a visibly identifiable trend in the lives of those whom he holds in esteem or seeks to emulate. Voluntary social work by corporate firms on as large a scale as possible can be an important influencing factor. Similarly, others who constitute the pinnacle of the average middle-class person's social aspirations, such as fashion models and designers and film and television personalities, can also set an effective example. If leading fashion designers, many of whom dominate the gossip columns of magazines and newspapers, were to visit a village not to hold a theme party on the loo but to 'adopt' the local primary school, their example may send a signal on what is socially desirable behaviour to at least some, specially in the younger generation, for whom they have become symbols of the desired lifestyle.

The project here is the arousal of social concern in the long-term interests of both the elite and the middle class.

The instrumentalities to achieve this are very limited. If the elite can help in this process, it is a responsibility they can forego at the cost of very considerable social and political turmoil in the future. In a reversal of conventional ideology, the privileged in India will begin to notice the poor only if the more privileged begin to do so: demonstrably, frequently, and with as much media projection as is possible. A process has to begin. The elite must set an example, not at the cost of profit or commercial pursuits, but as a strategy to better preserve these very interests in the long run.

If such a process could begin, there are elements within the middle class, that could perhaps carry the process farther. The obsession with the material, and the pervasive absence of moral values, has created in at least some members of the middle class a subconscious predisposition to give a wider, more meaningful dimension to their lives. There are examples in other countries where an overweening preoccupation with only material pursuits has fostered an idealism that only a few years ago would have seemed unthinkable. In Spain, the young, tired of the 'me first' attitude of the boom years upto 1994, staged a hunger strike for the government to donate 0.7 per cent of the country's economic output to developing countries![52]

In India such a predisposition is as yet distressingly weak and directionless and easily overwhelmed by the strength of the valueless milieu. But there are examples of socially purposeful activity, fledgling yet tenacious, which could perhaps form an expanding nucleus to channelize such a trend. The Self Employed Women's Association (SEWA), a non-government organization (NGO), has over the years done creditable work in the field of credit and banking facilities for women from poorer backgrounds. Another NGO, the Deccan Development Society, run by the Society for Promotion of Area Resources Centre, is doing excellent work in enabling scheduled caste women's collectives in over sixty villages of Medak district of Andhra Pradesh to have access to land and land-based resources. The Social Work and Research Centre, Tilonia, is working in the most neglected and backward parts of Rajasthan, and elsewhere, to ensure that developmental resources reach the intended beneficiary. Housewives, school students, and the retired have joined as volunteers to assist in educating the over one million illiterates in Delhi. Social agencies, such as Casplan and Deepalaya, who have opened schools in slums, and other NGOs like the Shramik Vidyapeeth and the Community Education and Development Foundation, are helping in the campaign, with support from the Rotary and Lion's Clubs and the Parent Teacher's Association. Other NGOs such as the Comprehensive Rural Health Project (CRHP) in Jamkhed in Maharashtra and Streehitkarani in Bombay have won international recognition for delivering, at lower cost, basic services to the poor.

Relative to the size of the population, NGO activity in India is one of the lowest in the world. But the existence and success of such organizations sustains the hope that others can be formed and gain momentum, should a concerted movement begin to revive the dormant instincts of social responsibility among the privileged. At least one effort, the *Swadhyaya* movement, is seeking to bridge the gap between the haves and the have-nots by going back to the teachings of Hinduism. Taking the Gita as the guide, the founder of the movement (Pandurang Shastri Athavale) advises its adherents to pursue the three prescribed paths of *Bhakti*, *Karma* and *Gyana*, exercising critical reason in all they do and dedicating their endeavours to the divine Yogeshwar . . . Swadhyaya's principal method of work designed to establish mutuality between people is *bhaktipheri* (which) initiates human contact which is not exploitative, restores conditions for a living active community . . . (and) generates a sentiment of fellowship which is so lacking in society.'[53] Swadhyaya is not in politics, nor does it encourage religious fundamentalism. By overarching the soulless and mechanical misinterpretation of secularism, it has gone back to religion and established a link between such concepts as dharma, sewa and bhakti, and constructive social work for the needy. The success of its endeavours shows how certain universal values in all religions can be harnessed to motivate people to work for the welfare of the community. Not all aspects of religion are communal. This is a truth of considerable importance, and presents both an opportunity and a challenge, given the renewed and persistent appeal of religion for an increasing number of middle-class people.

There are other enabling mechanisms that could be utilized in trying to build a 'coalition of the concerned'. Middle-class urban life is dotted with 'welfare' associations. Apartment blocks have one, colonies have their own; there are service associations, 'community' groupings and 'societies', and all kinds of recreational clubs, apart from such pan-Indian organizations such as the Rotary and Lions' Clubs. Currently, most of such groupings have been conceived as forums to strengthen negotiating abilities with a view to 'gaining' from the system. Their welfare activities are largely confined to their own welfare. This is a legitimate pursuit. But some of them could also be motivated to involve their members in some concrete work of social significance, such as the financing of text books for children who cannot afford them, or assistance to a 'government' school near a slum where classes are held only occasionally and that too out in the open because the roof has not yet been built, or the provision of a sanitary facility where defecation in the open is creating the threat of disease, or the provision of potable water in a village near by where diarrhoea is taking a toll because of contaminated water, then the very nature of this involvement will perhaps make them concerned citizens as well.

The impact of such a hands-on involvement in activity which is outside the normal ken of preoccupations cannot be overestimated. For instance, a volunteer who has once made an illiterate person read and write can never again be completely oblivious to the realities that exists on the fringes of the good life. The very nature of such a venture is a transforming one. Illiterate people don't live in affluent residential areas. In reaching out to such an individual, a person comes directly in touch with the textures of the 'other' India. It is a learning process where the dry statistics of deprivation suddenly acquire a body and a background. There is also a pride of achievement which is related to the larger good and unrelated to the narrow priorities of routine pursuits and ambitions. Similarly, a residents' association that has once involved itself in ensuring basic health care to even one village will have definitively transcended, at least for some of its members, a vision of the world restricted to the glitzy ads on television.

There is an important point which needs clarification: the intention here is not a denigration of the aspiration for the good life, but of the absorption in such a pursuit without the slightest sense of identification with the many, all around, whose destitution hardly allows them to have any aspirations in the foreseeable future. The idea is not to make the average middle-class Indian into a Mahatma Gandhi. Realism must intervene, however laudable the aims of visionaries may be. But between the unachievable social activism of the Mahatma and the supreme social indifference of the present generation of the privileged, there must be a halfway house, a modus vivendi, which does not jettison all that he stood for merely because what he did is so difficult to do. There must be some sane via media between the hypocrisy of ritual obeisance to his memory and the total amnesia as regards his legacy in real life. Every society sustains a degree of variance between ideals and reality. The problem with Indian society is that the ideal was so high that the variance could not but be dramatic. When failure is abject, it takes away the incentive to try. When a goal is too high, the inability to succeed is justified. When societies do not concede the gap between the desirable and the feasible, there is always the possibility that both will be forgotten. There is, thus, the need to reduce the pitch of idealism to levels where it can still be heard and not ignored out of fear that it may demand unacceptable sacrifices. If the definition of rectitude is too austere, most people will accept the fact that they are, in smaller or bigger measure, crooks, and act accordingly. India needs a pragmatic revolution, which can stabilize the pendulum of social involvement somewhere between doing something as significant as Gandhi and not doing anything at all.

If the middle and the elite classes can be convinced that a small display of social concern will not seriously jeopardize their preferred lifestyles, and that, in fact, such a display will enhance the chances of better sustaining them in the long run, then it may be possible for a middle path to emerge that allows both social concern and self-interest to coexist. In a scenario so singularly devoid of idealism, small beginnings that can gradually create space for the more concerned citizen to emerge are the need of the hour. There is evidence that when something of such a nature is attempted, either in the form of the NGO initiatives we have referred to earlier or through the personal example of sincerity and commitment of a motivated individual, the results are not always disappointing. In Delhi, H.D. Shourie started the organization Common Cause in 1980. At that time Shourie was seventy, retired, and had the option to gracefully fade away as so many of his friends and contemporaries were resigned to doing. But Shourie was concerned at the degree of apathy in educated middle-class people about causes which should be concerning them: the helpless interface of the individual with inefficient, arbitrary and corrupt government departments, and other issues of public probity and accountability where the ordinary citizen had little chance to express himself in an organized or effective manner. Common Cause started as a one-man crusade, and remains even today a largely one-person show, but Shourie's civic activism quickly caught the imagination of the people and he was overwhelmed by offers of voluntary support from people not only in Delhi but other cities in the country. More recently, in 1997, a young businessmen in the capital, Satya Sheel, and his IIM Ahmedabad educated brother, Saurabh, took the initiative to start a public awareness campaign against Delhi's killing pollution. The focus of the movement was to involve the young in the campaign, to make school-going children not only aware of the quality of the air they breathed, but motivate them to become hands-on participants in checking polluting vehicles. In but a few months the Students Against Pollution movement was able to enrol 184 schools in the city and count close to three hundred thousand enthusiastic children as effective foot soldiers in a voluntary campaign outside the purview of governmental efforts.

Such instances sustain the hope that the largely smothered notion of individuals making a difference can be revived. In Surat a young government official, S.R. Rao, through personal effort and example, motivated an entire city to clean up its filth and garbage. In a remarkable turn around, Surat, the city from where the plague epidemic surfaced in 1994, has become one of the cleanest cities in western India. There is no dearth of the bright and talented in the middle and elite classes of India. The problem is that too few of them consider it either necessary or desirable to be like Rao. In the premier management institutes in the country as many as twenty-five per cent of the entrants are graduates from the elite Indian Institutes of Technology. Most of the others are from the top of the class of the best colleges in the country. Yet their only aspiration is to insulate themselves from the realities of their own country through lucrative placements in multinational corporations, particularly in the low-risk and much sought after service sectors. Once again, the critique here is not of the desire to do well in terms of material perquisites. But there has to be something wrong in a country if its brightest products are content to remain 'superior' and socially insensitive, with little or no touch with the engulfing deprivations of the bulk of their countrymen and preoccupied with only such resentments as the higher salaries paid to foreigners in their sanitized corporate offices. There has to be something very wrong if several middle-class aspirants to government service have little hesitation in openly citing their preference for the Customs and Income Tax services because of the possibility of extra 'earnings' that they promise.

In Discovery of India Nehru had made an unusually prophetic statement: 'Classes that have ceased to play a vital part in society are particularly lacking in wisdom.'[54] A key component in the emergence of a prosperous India is to somehow involve the influential middle class in the vital project of civic engagement. It is only such an engagement that can perhaps help it transcend its obsession with short-term gain at the expense of the long-term good of the nation and its own enduring well-being. It is only such an engagement that can, hopefully, give birth to a social concern that will give primacy to the real priorities for a resurgent India. And it is only such an engagement that can give a content and direction to the new economic policies so as to harmonize the 'globalizing' aspirations of the few with the immediate and basic needs of the many.

The key issue that will determine the emergence of India in the twenty-first century as a united, democratic, stable and prosperous country—in conformity with the 'great power' vision of its middle and elite classes—will be the ability of middle-class Indians to forge a national consensus, a strategy of progress and development that involves all Indians. Unless this consensus develops, and subsumes the narrow, short-sighted agenda of the privileged as it exists today, no policy of economic renewal will succeed within a sustainable time frame. A nation is not a hot-house plant that can be made to grow on the fevered fantasies of its better endowed citizens. A nation to grow must derive its sap from the fertile soil of care and concern that nurtures all its citizens, specially the poor and the vulnerable. No society can survive if it is only an aggregation of personal wants. That is also why a country cannot be only a market. Profit, if sought to be pursued in exclusion, destroys the very basis for it to multiply. Self-interest, if unchecked, corrodes the very foundations for its fulfilment. There can be no intervening miracle of technology, or revolution in productivity, that will be able to bridge the widening and self-defeating gap between the two Indias— the upwardly mobile and the pathetically deprived. The only factor that can make a difference is a change in the attitude, in their own interests, of the privileged themselves.

Will the great Indian middle class be able to read the writing on the wall? If it does, there is still hope. If it does not, the India of today will be the envy of the amoral, cynical, economically lacklustre and debilitatingly divided nation that can emerge tomorrow, the harvest of an opportunity lost, a heritage wasted.

Notes

INTRODUCTION
1. Malini Bhupta, The Job, India Today, May 7, 2007, pg 39.
2. Diana Farrell and Eric Beinhocker, How India's rising and unique middle class will reshape global consumer markets, Newsweek, May 28, 2007, pg 32.

CHAPTER ONE
1. Prof. Ravinder Kumar's article in The Times of India, April 24, 1991, 'Contemporary Hinduism, Existential or Instrumental Religion'.
2. Ravinder Kumar, The Making of a Nation : Essays in Indian History and Politics (New Delhi, 1989), p.84.
3. Quoted in Ashis Nandy, At the Edge of Psychology—Essays in Politics and Culture (New Delhi, 1980), p.60
4. John Plamenatz, 'Two Types of Nationalism' in Eugene Kamenka, ed., Nationalism : The Nature and Evolution of an Idea (London, 1976), p.31
5. Jawaharlal Nehru, An Autobiography (Reprinted, New Delhi, 1980), p.23
6. Ibid., pp 3, 5, 24
7. Ibid., p. 48
8. Ibid., p. 27
9. Ibid., p. 29
10. Ravinder Kumar, in his Introduction to Myth and Reality: The Struggle for Freedom in India, 1945-47, ed., A.K. Gupta (New Delhi, 1987)

11. Ibid.
12. Shahid Amin, 'Gandhi as Mahatma' in Subaltern Studies, Vol III, Writings on South Asian History and Society, ed. Ranajit Guha (New Delhi, 1985), p.4
13. Ibid., pp. 4-5
14. Nehru, op. cit., p. 515
15. Ibid., p. 416
16. Ibid., p. 416
17. Ibid., p. 557
18. Ibid., p. 138
19. Ibid., p. 32
20. Ravinder Kumar, Introduction to Myth and Reality, op. cit.
21. Ibid.
22. Constituent Assembly Debates, Official Debates Vol. 1 (New Delhi, 1985), p. 5
23. Quoted in Bhabani Sen Gupta, India : Problem of Governance (New Delhi, 1996).
24. Achin Vanaik, The Painful Transitions (London, 1990), p. 72
25. Nehru, An Autobiography, op. cit., p. 446
26. Ibid., p. 455
27. Quoted in Rajmohan Gandhi, The Good Boatman (New Delhi, 1995), p. 352
28. Ibid., pp. 389-90
29. Partha Chatterjee, Nationalist Thought and the Colonial World (New Delhi, 1986), p. 169

CHAPTER TWO
1. Yogendra Singh, Social Change in India—Crisis and Resilience (New Delhi, 1993), p. 46
2. D.L. Sheth, 'The Great Language Debate', Crisis and Change in Contemporary India, eds. Upendra Baxi and Bhikhu Parekh (New Delhi, 1995), p. 192
3. Ibid., p. 199
4. Ibid., p. 199
5. Nehru, An Autobiography, op. cit., p.429
6. Ibid., p.431
7. Ibid., p.431
8. Gunnar Myrdal, An Inquiry into the Poverty of Nations, Vol 1,

(London, 1968), p.61

9. Jawaharlal Nehru, The Discovery of India (London, 1956), p.522
10. D.K. Rangnekar, Poverty and Capital Development in India (London, 1958), p.81
11. Nehru, The Discovery of India, op. cit., p.343
12. Gunnar Myrdal, op. cit., p.119
13. Upendra Baxi, 'Emancipation and Justice : Babasaheb Ambedkar's Legacy and Vision', Crisis and Change in Contemporary India, op. cit., p. 130
14. Quoted in V.S. Naipaul, India : A Wounded Civilization (London, 1979), p.156
15. Indian & Foreign Review, June 15, 1964, p.4
16. Yogendra Singh, Social Change in India, op. cit, p. 85
17. Constituent Assembly Debates, op cit., pp. 269-70
18. Ibid.
19. Pranab Bardhan, The Political Economy of Development in India, Fourth Impression (New Delhi, 1994), p.38
20. Atul Kohli, 'Democracy and Discontent', India's Growing Crisis of Governability, Indian Edition (Princeton, 1992), p.31
21. Barrington Moore Jr., Social Origins of Dictatorship and Democracy (London, 1966/91), p.390
22. Paul R. Brass, The Politics of India Since Independence (Cambridge, 1994), pp. 278-79
23. Barrington Moore Jr., op. cit., p.394
24. Nehru, quoted in Frank Moraes, Jawaharlal Nehru (New York, 1956), p.428
25. Paul R. Brass, op. cit., p.289
26. Ibid., p.292
27. An expression coined by C. Rajagopalachari in the late 1950s.
28. Pranab Bardhan, op. cit., p.58
29. Paul R. Brass, op. cit., p.301
30. Jayashree P. Mehta, in a overview of the health scenario in India (See Crisis & Change in Contemporary India, op. cit.), has forcefully brought out the 'heavy reliance on Western, urban, elitist models of specialized health care'. Such policies, in evidence since 1947, have created, in spite of some important achievements, disparities with regard to the health conditions of infants, children and mothers, between the urban

and rural population.
31. Amartya Sen, in Indian Development, Selected Regional Perspectives, eds. Jean Dreze and Amartya Sen (New Delhi, 1997), p.14.
32. Ibid., p.IX
33. Pranab Bardhan, op. cit., p.52
34. Gunnar Myrdal, Vol III, op. cit., pp.1645-46
35. Constituent Assembly Debates, op. cit.
36. Constructive Programme, Navjivan Press (Ahemdabad, 1944), p.16
37. Nehru, The Discovery of India, op. cit., pp.413-414
38. D.L. Sheth, in Crisis and Charge in Contemporary India, op. cit., p.200
39. Krishna Kumar, Learning from Conflict (New Delhi, 1996), from a review of the book in The Pioneer, February 1, 1997.
40. Nehru, An Autobiography, op.cit., p.422
41. Antonio Gramsci, Selections from the Prison Notebooks, quoted in Partha Chatterjee, op. cit., p.30

CHAPTER THREE
1. V.S. Naipaul, India: A Wounded Civilisation (London, 1979), p.137
2. Inder Malhotra, Indira Gandhi (London, 1989), p.87
3. Ibid., p.125
4. Ibid., p.117
5. Dom Moraes, Indira Gandhi (USA, 1980), p.135
6. Barrington Moore Jr., Social Origins of Dictatorship, op. cit., pp.395, 407
7. Inder Malhotra, op. cit., p.151
8. Quoted by Umesh Anand, in The Times of India, March 7, 1996.
9. GOI, Ministry of Home Affairs, Report of the Committee on Prevention of Corruption (New Delhi, 1964), pp.12, 13, 101
10. Inder Malhotra, op. cit., p.146
11. Quoted in R.K. Karanjia, The Mind of Mr Nehru (London, 1960), p.61
12. Quoted in Ashis Nandy, At the Edge of Psychology—Essays in Politics and Culture (New Delhi, 1980).

13. Achin Vanaik, The Painful Transition (London, 1990), p.29
14. Ibid.
15. Pranab Bardhan, The Political Economy of Development in India (New Delhi, 1984), p.43
16. Achin Vanaik, op. cit., p.36
17. Ibid., p.29
18. Lloyd and Susan Rudolph, In Pursuit of Lakshmi (Chicago, 1987), p.324
19. V.S. Naipaul, op. cit., p.93
20. Inder Malhotra, op. cit., pp.158–59
21. Dom Moraes, op. cit., p.207
22. Ibid., p.226
23. Pranab Bardhan, op. cit., p.61
24. Quoted in Sonia Gandhi, Rajiv. (New Delhi, 1992), p.88
25. Yogendra Singh, Social Change in India—Crisis and Resilience (New Delhi, 1993), p.75
26. Ibid.
27. Quoted by Anirudh Deshpande, The Hindustan Times, September 9, 1996.
28. The Times of India, August 1, 1995. See also M.N. Srinivas, Caste: Its Twentieth Century Avatar (New Delhi, 1996).

CHAPTER FOUR
1. Gunnar Myrdal, Asian Drama, op. cit., Vol II, p.767
2. M. Rosenthal, 'The Future in Retrospect: "Mother India" Thirty Years After', Foreign Affairs Vol 35, No 4, July 1957, p.623
3. An observation made by Arthur Koestler in The Lotus and the Robot (New York, 1961), p.280
4. Gunnar Myrdal, op. cit., Vol II, pp 896-97
5. V.S. Naipaul, India: A Wounded Civilisation, op. cit., p.45
6. A.D. Moddie in The Statesman, March 14, 1996.
7. Arvind N. Das in The Indian Express, May 17, 1996.
8. Raghu Dayal in The Times of India, September 10, 1995.
9. Pankaj Mishra, Butter Chicken in Ludhiana (New Delhi, 1995), pp. 8-9
10. P. Puryakastha, in The Times of India, August 6, 1996.
11. Iqbal Malik, in The Indian Express, June 5, 1996.
12. Rajiv Shah, in The Times of India, July 2, 1997.

13. Thorstein Veblen, 'The Theory of the Leisure Class' in Class, Status & Power, eds. Richard Bendix, Seymour Maitin Lipset. (London, 1963).

14. Eric Hobsbawm, Age of Extremes—The Short Twentieth Century (1914-1991) (London, 1995), p.337

15. Achin Vanaik, op. cit., p.161

16. Sudhir Kakar, The Colours of Violence (New Delhi, 1995), p.187

17. Lloyd and Susan Rudolph, op. cit., p.9

18. Pankaj Mishra, op. cit., p.11

19. Eric Hobsbawm, op. cit., p.369

20. The Indian Express, January 10, 1996.

21. Rajdeep Sardesai in Sunday, March 25-April 1.

22. O.V. Vijayan in The Indian Express, June 17, 1996.

23. Jawaharlal Nehru, An Autobiography, op. cit., p.591

24. India Today—ICSSR-CSDS Survey, August 31, 1996.

25. Paul R. Brass, The Politics of India Since Independence op. cit., p.362

26. Information Service of India, Stockholm, Nehru in Scandinavia, 1958, p. 19

27. M.R. Masani, Afro-Asian Attitudes (New Delhi, 1961), p.71

28. V.S. Naipaul, India: A Million Mutinies Now (London, 1990), p.420

29. Sudhir Kakar, quoted in V.S. Naipaul, India: A Wounded Civilisation, op. cit., p.102

30. Ashis Nandy, At the Edge of Psychology—Essays in Politics & Culture, op. cit., p.108

31. Ibid., p.105

32. Anirudh Deshpande in The Pioneer, January 24, 1996.

33. Jawaharlal Nehru, An Autobiography, op. cit., p.596

34. Letter to Krishna Menon in 1937. Quoted in Bhikhu Parekh, 'Jawaharlal Nehru and the Crisis of Modernisation', Crisis and Change in Contemporary India, eds. Upendra Baxi, Bhikhu Parekh, op. cit., p.42

35. S. Gopal ed., Selected Works, Volume 6, p.282

36. Bhikhu Parekh, op. cit., p.42

37. Dinesh Mohan, 'Modern Technological Revolution and Social Development' in Muchkund Dubey, ed., Indian Society Today,

Challenges of Equality, Integration and Empowerment (New Delhi, 1995), p.254

38. Sandeep in The Hindustan Times, August 20, 1996.
39. See Gautam Bhatia, Punjabi Baroque and Other Memories of Architecture (Penguin Books India, New Delhi, 1994).
40. Krishna Kumar in The Times of India, August 3, 1996. Barbie is a $2 billion industry. It is sold in 140 countries at the rate of two dolls per second.
41. For an instructive and detailed study on British perception of Hindu religion, society and culture, see Suhash Chakravarty's The Raj Syndrome (New Delhi, 1991).
42. Pavan K. Varma, Krishna, The Playful Divine, (New Delhi, 1995), p.137
43. Quoted in Sudhir Kakkar, Intimate Relations: Exploring Indian Sexuality (New Delhi, 1989), p.95
44. See Pavan K. Varma, op. cit., p.138
45. Nirad C. Choudhary, Three Horsemen of the New Apocalypse (London, 1997), from extracts in India Today, July 28, 1997.
46. Reported in The Indian Express, November 24, 1996.
47. Ibid.
48. Rajender Kumar in The Times of India, May 18, 1996.
49. Outlook, June 19, 1996.
50. Madhu Jain, India Today, April 15, 1996.

CHAPTER FIVE
1. Jairam Ramesh, in The Hindustan Times, March 14, 1996.
2. Indian Market Demographics, The Consumer Classes, National Council of Applied Economic Research, 1996.
3. 'The New Marketplace', a summary of The NCAER Report, published by Business Today, Vol 5 No 4, 1996.
4. Ibid.
5. Gennady Zhyuganov, Communist Party chief in Russia, quoted in Newsweek, March 11, 1996.
6. Ashok Celly, in The Times of India, 26 May, 1996.
7. Jawaharlal Nehru, An Autobiography, op. cit., p.510.
8. India Today, February 15, 1996.
9. Gautam Mukherjee in The Pioneer, February 26, 1996.
10. Aroon Purie in Inaugural Issue of India Today Plus, First Quarter,

1996.
11. S.H. Venkatramani in The Pioneer, March, 30, 1996.
12. The Indian Express, Dec 31, 1995.
13. Namita Unnikrishnan, quoted in Outlook, August 28, 1996.
14. Namita Unnikrishnan, in The Hindustan Times, April 27, 1996
15. Outlook, August 28, 1996.
16. Rajiv Desai, in The Times of India, April 21, 1996
17. Gurcharan Das, in The Times of India, March 11, 1996.
18. Ibid.
19. Krishna Kumar, in The Times of India, August 3, 1996.
20. Ishan Joshi, in Outlook, February 14, 1996.
21. Alexander Terekhov, a Russian writer, in the Moscow Tribune, February 7, 1996.
22. Hsiao Tung Fei, in The American Journal of Sociology (1946).
23. R. Sudarshan, in The Hindu, June 22, 1996.
24. Amit Bhaduri and Deepak Nayyar, The Intelligent Person's Guide to Liberalisation (New Delhi, 1996), pp 107-8.
25. Ibid., p.117
26. Subhash Agarwal in Outlook, April 10, 1996.
27. Shefali Rakhi in India Today, November 15, 1995.
28. Amit Bhaduri and Deepak Nayyar, op. cit., p.117.
29. J.K. Galbraith, 'World Economy, The Larger Perspective', Lecture delivered at the Rajiv Gandhi Institute for Contemporary Studies, 1992.
30. Praful Bidwai, in The Times of India, August 2, 1996.
31. Gurcharan Das in The Times of India, August 22, 1997.
32. Hsiao Tung Fei, op. cit.
33. Interview with India Today, September 30, 1996.
34. Siddhartha Varadarajan, in The Times of India, December 7, 1996.
35. Survey, reported by UNI, in The Pioneer, February 15, 1996.
36. Anthony Lewis, in International Herald Tribune, March 9-10, 1996.
37. William Pfoff, in International Herald Tribune, March 16-17, 1996.
38. William Pfoff, International Herald Tribune, August 8, 1996.
39. Ibid.
40. The Washington Post, June 12, 1996.

41. Klaus Schwab and Claude Smadja, in International Herald Tribune, February 1, 1996.
42. William Pfoff, International Herald Tribune, February 3-4, 1996.
43. Anthony Lewis, op. cit.
44. The Pioneer, July 19, 1996.
45. K.S. Krishnaswamy, in The Economic & Political Weekly, July 27, 1996.
46. United Nations Online Network in Public Administration and Finance (UNPAN) Virtual Library: http://unpan1.un.org/intradoc/groups/public/documents/UN/UNPAN014046.pdf
47. Editorial in The Pioneer, January, 14, 1997.
48. Srivatsa Krishna, in Outlook, April, 1996.
49. Klaus Schwab, op. cit.
50. For reportage on the social responsibility initiatives of Indian corporate giants, see The Pioneer, August 3, 1996.
51. Andrew Selshy, in The Times of India, November 26, 1996.
52. Tarun Khanna, Kasturi Rangan and Merlina Manocaran, Harvard Business School Case Study on Narayana Hrudayalaya, June 14, 2004
53. Gopal Krishna, in the Times of India, April 4, 1996.
54. Jawaharlal Nehru, the Discovery of India, op. cit.

Index